Treatise on Critical Reason

# HANS ALBERT

# Treatise on Critical Reason

TRANSLATED
BY MARY VARNEY RORTY

Princeton University Press
Princeton, New Jersey

Published by Princeton University Press, 41 William Street,
Princeton, New Jersey 08540
In the United Kingdom: Princeton University Press,
Guildford, Surrey

Library of Congress Cataloging in Publication Data will
be found on the last printed page of this book

ISBN 0-691-07295-7

Publication of this book has been aided by a grant from The
Whitney Darrow Fund of Princeton University Press

This book has been composed in Linotron Sabon type

Clothbound editions of Princeton Unversity Press books
are printed on acid-free paper, and binding materials are
chosen for strength and durability

Printed in the United States of America by Princeton
University Press, Princeton, New Jersey

*To Karl Popper*

# Contents

CONTENTS

# Foreword

HANS ALBERT is, in my opinion, by far the most important contemporary German social philosopher. He is equally important as a student of epistemology, especially the epistemology of the social sciences. I say "in my opinion" because, first, I do not of course know all German books and papers published in the field and, secondly, because my judgment, though well considered, may be biased. It is not, however, biased by the fact that he agrees with most (though not all) I have written, or that he claims to have learned much from me: there are others who claim the same and who agree with even more of my writings, but who do not, in my opinion, have the originality of Hans Albert, or the depth and the width of his knowledge of the field—a knowledge that far surpasses mine and, in fact, leaves me gasping.

The present book, *A Treatise on Critical Reason*, is the first of a set of two which so far are the most important ones published by Hans Albert. It is compulsory reading for everybody who is interested in philosophy or social science, and especially for those interested in German philosophy or German social science. For all others it will be a great pleasure.

Penn, Buckinghamshire                                         Karl Popper
25 September 1983

# Preface to the American Edition

THIS book was written in 1967 and went unchanged through the first two German editions of 1968 and 1970. The third edition (1975) was supplemented by an epilogue, "Der Kritizismus und seine Kritiker," in which I replied to objections of critics, and to the fourth German edition (1980) I added some corrections and supplements. The epilogue is not included in this American edition because it would have been extremely difficult for the American reader unfamiliar with the German background to understand the points I made in response to the objections I had received. The book itself arose out of a particular problem situation which to this day has been portrayed only one-sidedly in America; the further discussions to which it led are virtually unknown there. It may be useful, then, to acquaint the American reader with this problem situation and to familiarize him with some of the discussions to which it led.

An important motivation for writing this book was the so-called "positivist dispute" in German sociology, which by then had gone on for some years in Germany and later spread to other European countries and to other parts of the world. The American reader has been made familiar with this dispute almost exclusively through the eyes of one of the contending parties, that is, through the translations of the works of Jürgen Habermas and Karl Otto Apel, not to mention the meager information found in *The Positivist Dispute in German Sociology* by Theodor W. Adorno et al. (London, 1976), which contains a detailed and sympathetic introduction by David Frisby. The controversy began at the conference of the German Sociological Society in October 1961 at Tübingen, where Karl

Popper presented a paper on the logic of the social sciences, to which Theodor W. Adorno replied. Popper argued for methodological individualism and the application of normal scientific method in the social sciences, as he had already done in his book, *The Poverty of Historicism* (London, 1957). Adorno commented on Popper's theses, tried to show limitations, and developed views that were characteristic for the so-called Frankfurt School and that on essential points, especially with respect to methodology, have implications incompatible with Popper's views. The discussion following the two papers was, as Dahrendorf pointed out afterwards, unsatisfactory for all participants: the essential contrasts between the two views defended did not emerge clearly.

Jürgen Habermas took up the discussion in the Adorno Festschrift, *Zeugnisse* (Frankfurt, 1963), with an attack on Popper's views regarding the problems of the role of values, of theories, and of experience in science, as he understood them. In a volume of essays published in the same year with the title *Theorie und Praxis*, he further attacked the conception of rationality in critical rationalism as allegedly "positivistically limited" and confronted it with the claims of dialectical reason, which, he purported, could overcome these limitations. In April 1964, at the fifteenth conference of the German Sociological Society in Heidelberg, which was dedicated to Max Weber and the relevance of his work for the present day, a further confrontation with the views of the Frankfurt School occurred, for, concerning the logic of the social sciences, Max Weber could be seen as one of the most important predecessors of critical rationalism. One of the main papers at this conference was read by Herbert Marcuse, whose interpretation of Weber's thinking contained many misunderstandings, because he failed to take account of the main methodological writings of Weber that were published after 1900. Marcuse's paper was inspired by a Marxist critique of ideology, which had also been the background of the Popper critique by Adorno and Habermas. It is my impression that all three had great difficulties in understanding the views they attempted to criticize.

The attacks on critical rationalism by Habermas stimulated me to write an essay against his theses and objections. He had labeled Popper and me "positivists," and his criticism involved blatant misunderstandings connected with this misguided labeling. Since I had revised my former positivistic views myself under the influence of Popper's thinking, I had good reason to clear up Habermas's misinterpretations. Habermas answered in the same year and continued to call me a positivist. But his way of handling my questions and objections seemed to me completely inadequate, and so I felt that I had to answer his criticism a second time.

The misunderstandings and contrasting opinions that emerged in this controversy as well as in other discussions stimulated me to present my philosophical views in the whole, as done in this book. The book was devised to present critical rationalism as an alternative to the philosophical views characteristic of the German situation: the conception of the Frankfurt School; hermeneutic thinking as represented by Hans Georg Gadamer, a former student of Martin Heidegger; analytic philosophy, which—foremost under the influence of the posthumous writings of Ludwig Wittgenstein—began to gain a foothold here; and logical empiricism, which had then influenced philosophy of science through the writings of Wolfgang Stegmüller. I had had the idea of a book of this kind for a long time and had done some preparatory work, so that I could begin writing in the summer of 1967 and finish in January 1968.

The views I defend in this book are not only opposed to the philosophical trends that were prevalent in the German-speaking countries at the time, but they are also directed against some of my own earlier views. In 1952 I had written a thesis on "Rationalität und Existenz," in which I had analyzed, in turn, the problems of technology, ethics, economics, and politics. Proceeding from the conceptions of the philosopher and anthropologist Arnold Gehlen and the philosopher of science Hugo Dingler, both of whom represented some kind of pragmatism, I had interpreted human knowledge exclusively from the viewpoint of practice, conceiving of the interest in adequate action as being decisive for all the sciences. It strikes me as ironic that in this respect my earlier view was quite similar to the views developed by Jürgen Habermas and Karl Otto Apel ten years later. They claimed the existence of three forms of knowledge that are guided by different practical interests. Their doctrine involved a reinterpretation of a scheme constructed by the German phenomenologist Max Scheler in the twenties, as anyone acquainted with Scheler's writings could see immediately. Max Scheler, as later Arnold Gehlen, had been influenced by American pragmatists.

In my thesis, knowledge was considered only as an analysis of possibilities in the service of action; that was the rational aspect of practice. On the other side I held that there were decisions that had existential character—in the sense of existentialism—and therefore could not be rendered rational. This in turn led me to criticize sharply neoclassical economics, which, according to my view, had made such an attempt to rationalize decisions by its solution of the value problem. All attempts to justify political decisions and to solve the problem of an adequate social order, which were based on this doctrine, had to be refuted, in my opinion, as completely ideological. In my view there could be no bridge between knowledge and decision. In this respect my conception without doubt contrasted sharply with the later doctrine of Habermas and Apel, who tried to bridge the gap with dialectical reason. Unfortunately, they have not been able to elucidate its functioning in a way plausible to people who do not claim to be in command of such a faculty.

In the meantime, in the fifties, I had discovered the teachings of the Vienna Circle, of logical empiricism, and of analytical philosophy in general, and in connection with that, modern logic. I had accepted the existing criticism of the views of Hugo Dingler—for example, that by Viktor Kraft—and finally came across Karl Popper's critical rationalism, which convinced me in its essential points. Popper's views seemed to supply the means to overcome the dichotomy between knowledge and decision which I had defended for a long time, and thereby also the limitation of rationality to the sphere of knowledge. The change in my views also influenced my approach to social, economic, and political problems. Thus this book contains a criticism of views I have myself defended in former times, but which I had long since abandoned through the influence of Popper's thought by the time members of the Frankfurt School were attacking critical rationalism as a kind of positivism.

In this book the dichotomy of knowledge and decision is replaced by the thesis that cognition is itself a part of human practice and that the cognitive practice of science is interspersed with norms, valuations, and decisions—a fact quite compatible with the principle of value neutrality defended by the great sociologist Max Weber. The problem of rationality is a general problem of human practice and is therefore not limited to the sphere of knowledge or of cognitive practice. Human reason is competent in all realms of problem-solving behavior. At the same time, reason is also fallible in these realms, from logic and mathematics—where some people are inclined to see a province of certainty—to all other sciences, and of course also to philosophy, to law and politics, and to religion, where some people would like to make an exception. Instead of foundationalism, which has been connected with the classical solution of the problem of rationality since the time of Plato and Aristotle, I defend a consistent fallibilism, as Karl Popper has done for a long time. The policy of rejecting procedures of immunization—for example, of rejecting conventionalist stratagems to protect theories against criticism, analyzed and criticized by Popper in his *Logik der Forschung* (Vienna, 1935)—can, therefore, be defended for any problem area. Dogmatization—that is, immunization against criticism—is a possibility of human practice in general, not only of religious faith or even of cognitive practice, and it is useful nowhere if one likes to solve problems in the best possible way. But at the same time there is no reason to abandon critical realism, which is so closely connected with classical philosophy and with the practice of science. There is no need to give up the idea of truth and of the possibility of approaching truth by the method of science. Neither skepticism nor any kind of relativism should have a claim on us. Those who abandon the fusion of truth and certainty that is usual in classical thinking have no reason to surrender to skeptical or relativistic views, as they are fashionable today even in analytic philosophy. By no means do we need to choose between a consistent empiricism with relativistic and skeptical consequences on the one hand and a transcendentalist dogmatism on the other, as Leszek Kolakowski has tried to show in his analysis of Husserl's philosophy in his book, *Husserl and the Search for Certitude* (London, 1975).

Now I would like to add some remarks about the discussions and arguments in which I was entangled after the publication of the German edition of this book. Many people tried to show that the Münchhausen trilemma which I formulate early in the book is inconsistent, untenable, or of limited validity. Sometimes they thought of resurrecting classical rationalism in this way. The first to be mentioned in this connection is Karl Otto Apel who, together with Jürgen Habermas, developed the trichotomous conception of knowledge mentioned above, defends a consensus theory of truth, and wants to maintain the classical idea of an absolute foundation—the idea of "Letztbegründung"—for philosophical reflection. He objected to consistent fallibilism and to other views of mine, partly in accordance with the criticism voiced by Jürgen Habermas. I have replied to Apel's objections and criticized his general conception in an article "Hermeneutik und Realwissenschaft" (1971), and in a small book entitled *Transzendentale Träumereien* (Hamburg, 1975). I have rejected another attack on my views based on Apel's "Transzendentalpragmatik" in "Münchhausen oder der Zauber der Reflexion"—a chapter in my book, *Die Wissenschaft und die Fehlbarkeit der Vernunft* (Tübingen, 1982). Some points of my criticism apply to the views of Jürgen Habermas as well, though he has, as far as I can see, recently abandoned the idea of an absolute justification.

As to the transcendental question—the problem of the conditions of the possibility of knowledge that has been taken up by Habermas, Apel, and other contemporary German philosophers—it should be mentioned that Oswald Külpe, the founder of the Würzburg School of the psychology of thinking and a follower of Kant, has tried to give a realistic interpretation to it, which, as I have shown in "Transzendentaler Realismus und rationale Heuristik"—a chapter in my last-mentioned book—can be reformulated on the basis of Popper's philosophy.

There is another group of philosophers in Germany, who are also influential in some of the sciences, whose members still defend the idea of an ultimate foundation in continuing the ideas of Hugo Dingler, whom I have mentioned above as one of the thinkers whose ideas I took up in my thesis. This group is the so-called Erlangen School, which was founded by Paul Lorenzen. I have responded in the above-mentioned epilogue to the objections of representatives of this school—Jürgen Mittelstrass, Friedrich Kambartel, and Peter Janich. I have tried to show that these authors, who would like to achieve an absolute justification based on certain kinds of action, are not able to carry through their program because they are forced to make concessions to fallibilism. Some of them have abandoned Dingler's demand for certainty in their later writings, a demand which in the beginning was the main motive for their special approach to philosophical problems. But it seems to me that this renunciation makes the Erlangen approach as a whole implausible.

The Berlin psychologist Klaus Holzkamp, who has strongly influenced the methodological discussion in German psychology, has also used elements of Dingler's thought in his conception. When in the seventies he sharply criticized so-called "bourgeois" psychology and its methodology, he had supplemented his views with elements of Marxism. He defended an antirealist position—abandoning the pursuit of truth as pointless in psychology—and obviously intended to subject science to an ideological steering under Marxist viewpoints. I have criticized his attempt to overcome the idea of truth on the basis of critical realism where this idea plays the role of a regulative idea for cognitive practice. In addition I attacked his idea of ideological control, which in any case could only be defended from an instrumentalist position, which I reject. In his answer he withdrew his objections against the idea of truth but he maintained his criticism of my position in spite of this, so that I published a further reply. My articles on this matter, together with other criticisms of his position, have been published in Albert and Keuth (eds.), *Kritik der kritischen Psychologie* (Hamburg, 1973).

Another quarrel concerns the hermeneutical currents in German philosophy. My attacks in the present book obviously induced the misunderstanding that hermeneutical problems, in my opinion, are illegitimate or insignificant. But any impartial reader can see that my statements hardly give any indications for this opinion. Yet Hans Georg Gadamer, the nestor of hermeneutical thinking in Germany, claimed—in his epilogue to the third edition of his influential book, *Wahrheit und Methode* (Tübingen, 1972)—that those people who declare "critical rationality" as an absolute measuring rod for truth would be forced to view hermeneutical reflection as theological obscurantism. Now I certainly have sharply criticized the overstretching of the hermeneutic viewpoint to the so-called "universal hermeneutics" inspired by Martin Heidegger, a mode of thinking that made the model of the interpretation of texts the paradigm of knowledge and hermeneutical reflection the dominant philosophical method. In this, hermeneutics is analogous to that kind of analytic philosophy inspired by Ludwig Wittgenstein, where the same was claimed for language analysis. In addition, my judgment about the relationship of this kind of hermeneutics to theological thinking has been, in my opinion, essentially correct. Here, too, an analogy in analytical thinking seems to exist.

On the other side I have emphasized that I want neither to judge as unimportant nor to neglect the problems of understanding and of interpretation of texts. Quite on the contrary, it can even be shown that the program of the older hermeneutical school can be continued within the framework of critical rationalism by taking into account the linguistic work of Karl Bühler. I have tried to elucidate this thesis in the abovementioned article, "Hermeneutik und Realwissenschaft." If one considers hermeneutics as an art or technology of understanding, then it is not necessarily connected with the views that are currently peddled off under this name. On the contrary, strong objections arise against these views if one properly analyzes the problems of understanding. Moreover, such an analysis shows that methodological historism, so prominent in Germany since the last century in the humanities and the social sciences, is untenable, because it involves theses that are incompatible with each other. I tried to show this in "Geschichte und Gesetz," my contribution to the Festschrift for Ernst Topitsch, *Sozialphilosophie als Aufklärung*, edited by K. Salamun (Tübingen, 1979).

Because of my attack on the Protestant theology of the Bultmann School, which was connected with the philosophy of Martin Heidegger, the discussion about hermeneutics was continued under the influence of theologians. The editors of the *Zeitschrift für Theologie und Kirche* invited me in February 1972 to a discussion in the castle of Sindelfingen near Tübingen. I took this opportunity to correct some misunderstandings about my epistemological views and to discuss some theological questions with them. The spokesman for the theologians was Gerhard Ebeling. I thought that I had correctly identified his misunderstandings and sufficiently criticized his theses in detail, but he nevertheless presented them again in his book, *Kritischer Rationalismus?* (Tübingen, 1973). My answer came in the same year in a small book, *Theologische Holzwege* (Tübingen, 1973), where I corrected his mistakes a second time and criticized his method of interpretation. I also explained once more why I am not able to accept the assumption of the existence of God. Here, as sometimes later, I made the interesting discovery that a criticism of theological practices of argumentation is often understood by their defenders as a disparagement of religion as such or as a symptom of an anti-theological resentment.

In the same year a book about philosophy of science and theology was published by another well-known Protestant theologian, namely, Wolfhart Pannenberg's *Wissenschaftstheorie und Theologie* (Frankfurt, 1973). He partly accepted my philosophical views in this book, but with some characteristic modifications and limitations. Among other things Pannenberg declared that he is prepared to treat the assumption that there is a God as a hypothesis that can be evaluated with respect to its corroboration. But if one looks closely at his analysis of the problem of corroboration with respect to this hypothesis, then one can see without difficulty that he obviously did not intend to undertake a genuine critical examination of it. Indeed, he arranged the conditions of adequacy of his test in such a way that there is no danger that the hypothesis might be refuted.

A few years later the Catholic theologian Hans Küng, who was in conflict with his church and who had gained great publicity in Germany and all over the world, attempted a "rationally responsible" solution of the problem of the existence of God in his book, *Existiert Gott?* (Munich, 1978). In epistemological matters, Küng chose critical rationalism as the main target of his criticism. He claimed that my views could be overcome and that one could arrive then at a "genuine critical rationality." His book is full of misunderstandings and mistakes of all kinds, but it was translated into many languages within a very short time and distributed the world over—obviously because it satisfied a very strong need, the need to reconcile reason and faith. I answered with a book, *Das Elend der Theologie* (Hamburg, 1979), in which I showed in detail the deficiencies of Küng's argumentation and the untenability of the whole enterprise. I came to conclusions similar to those of J. L. Mackie in his book, *The Miracle of Theism* (Oxford, 1982). Further attacks by theologians induced me to take up these problems once more and also to analyze the views of Pannenberg and other critics in "Theologie und Weltauffassung"—a chapter of the above-mentioned book of 1982.

I shall end this short report by turning to political thought. Karl Popper had already investigated the implications of critical rationalism for political thought in his book, *The Open Society and its Enemies* (London, 1944). I have dedicated the last chapter of this book to this question, though it gives only a very rough outline of my views. Some objections to my theses have been answered in the epilogue to the third and fourth German editions. But I finally published a separate book, *Traktat über rationale Praxis* (Tübingen, 1978), in which I tackled this problem in detail. Here I tried to show that the problems of social control and political order can be solved on the basis of the idea of methodical practice, which critical rationalism defends. In this context I have given a criticism of usual conceptions of jurisprudence, and I have developed in contrast to them the idea of a rational jurisprudence on a realistic basis, which can be treated as a kind of social technology. Moreover, I have maintained that welfare economics is the result of a fallacious development in neoclassical economics, and I have tried to show that a consistent fallibilism in political thinking must lead to revisionism. While revisionism as a political methodology today is in general only repudiated by thinkers inspired by Marxism, the consistent application of the critical method and the refusal of attempts of dogmatization in the domain of moral questions is rejected—as it was to be expected—above all by social philosophers with a Catholic background. Thus in Germany, apart from representatives of hermeneutic and dialectical thinking, Catholic theologians and philosophers have taken the lead in making objections to the epistemology and the social philosophy of critical rationalism.

Gadamer's hermeneutic thinking has spread to America, as has the thinking of the Frankfurt School and Küng's theology.

But when I tried to discuss these views with people outside of Germany, I found that many know nothing at all about the criticisms that are available in Germany. The American reader, especially, might be totally misguided, for instance, by the careless report about my views by Rüdiger Bubner, a student of Gadamer, in his book, *Modern German Philosophy* (Cambridge, 1981). Bubner has managed to distort some of my views to the point where they are incompatible with my oft-stated arguments. Moreover, he ignores the fact that in my answers to critics I usually reconstruct very carefully every step in their argumentation. Reading his text has confirmed my experience that hermeneutic confessions are frequently connected with a remarkable inability to understand people who think differently.

On the whole one can say that critical rationalism in German-speaking countries is considered not only as a contribution to the philosophy of science but also, and above all, as a general philosophical outlook that continues the Enlightenment in contrast to the dominant philosophical currents and the various kinds of theological thinking. As a social philosophy it has even influenced the discussion within political parties, and as a philosophy of science it has been influential mainly in the humanities and the social sciences.

This book has been in translation for more than ten years, during which time I have become indebted to several people. In the first place, I must give thanks to the late Walter Kaufmann for the encouragement he gave this project from the outset. His initiative sent this venture on its way, and though he unfortunately did not live to see it come to fruition, I would undoubtedly not have persevered without his constant support and prodding. I also thank the following: Mary Rorty and Michael Sukale, for bringing the project to an end at a time when I feared I would never see a finished English manuscript; Tanja de Launay, John Wettersten, and Robert Wachbroit, who read the translation and proposed corrections; and Erika Eck, who typed the manuscript once and xeroxed several versions several times.

# PREFACE

The German editions of this book were dedicated to Karl Popper, the philosopher who had the most decisive influence on my thinking, and who kindly wrote a preface for this edition. I dedicate the American edition to him as well, with gratitude.

Heidelberg, March 1984                                    Hans Albert

# Translator's Note

I wish to acknowledge my debt to Professor John Bednall, whose translation of the first three chapters of this book provided the foundation for my own version; and for the suggestions of Michael Sukale and his colleagues. I owe a particular debt to Professor Sukale, whose advice and encouragement at every stage of the translation inspired my efforts and enriched my understanding of the text.

Mary Varney Rorty

Treatise on Critical Reason

# Rationality and Commitment

SHORTLY after the Second World War there was a temptation for competent observers of the philosophical scene to speak of three spheres of philosophical thought, each relatively closed and geographically easily definable. There was scarcely any discussion between them because dominant trends were from the beginning so very different that mutual understanding seemed almost impossible.[1] In the Anglo-Saxon sphere the analytical trend in philosophy appeared finally to have prevailed and whoever was disinclined to make the effort of constructing a more differentiated picture tended to speak of the dominance of positivism. On the Western European continent and in areas influenced by it, hermeneutic tendencies, of which existentialism appeared representative, retained the upper hand. And in the Soviet sphere of influence, that type of dialectical thought customarily described as orthodox Marxism had remained victorious. That this situation should have arisen was so much attributable to political developments that many have seen it as evidence for the thesis that thought is a product of the existential situation. Of course, on closer inspection one could see that in reality the situation could not be adequately described by simple reference to the three apparently typical conceptions of positivism, existentialism, and Marxism; but the existence of three spheres relatively isolated and with exclusively internal discussions, which, at least in terms of their basic tendency, could be so described, could hardly be denied. Even the fundamental conception of the possibilities and tasks of philosophy was obviously basically

[1] Cf. José Ferrater Mora, "Die drei Philosophien," in *Der Monat* (1957), p. 105.

different in the three spheres. A philosophy claiming neutrality and objectivity and employing predominantly analytical techniques confronted, on the one hand, a committed subjectivism using hermeneutic procedures, and on the other a consciously partisan and political type of thought which proclaimed itself able to master all essential problems by use of the dialectical method.

Since then, however, the hitherto prevailing isolation has been shattered, and thought has been once more set in motion. It has been discovered that discussions which range across previous boundaries are not only possible but in some circumstances may even be of great interest. One recognizes that some trends customarily attributed to different orientations show common features which would not, at first, have been expected, and that some habitual classifications are highly questionable. Positions hitherto labeled "positivism" and declared basically irrelevant by the proponents of views long entrenched in the German-speaking countries now prove to encompass such a widely differentiated spectrum of ideas that one is forced to abandon the customary global classification and draw more subtle distinctions. Thus the late philosophy of Wittgenstein, which is extraordinarily influential in the Anglo-Saxon world, reveals in some respects surprising parallels with hermeneutic thought, as influenced by Heidegger; and both modes of thought show positivist tendencies that clearly distinguish them from the critical rationalism of Karl Popper, which is still pigeonholed in Germany under "positivism" for polemical reasons. Some types of Marxism, furthermore, which in Germany—and not only in East Germany—are sometimes dismissed as "revisionist" and which dissociate themselves from Anglo-Saxon thought—as, for instance, the ideas of Leszek Kolakowski—reveal very interesting points of agreement with not only critical rationalism, but also with hermeneutic thought.

Although people have become aware of similarities such as these, and despite a growing willingness to regard other ideas as at least worthy of discussion, in Germany there still, in the main, prevails what could be called the contemporary "Ger-

man ideology": a line of thought determined above all by
Hegel and Heidegger, which takes hardly any account of ideas
which may not be grasped in terms of these two points of
view. Yet we have every reason to view in a somewhat different light the exaggerated claims associated with the notion,
still very popular in Germany, of a decisive turning point
brought about by Heidegger, when we are forced to realize
that the predominance of this type of philosophizing is in no
small way responsible for the fact that we missed the development of modern epistemology, and for the fact that German
moves in this direction, which there certainly were in the
twenties and early thirties, have fallen into oblivion. The return to Hegel, which after the Second World War presented
itself partly as the means of overcoming Heidegger, may perhaps facilitate dialogue with Eastern Europe; but, in any case,
it is not going to make good this loss and carry us any further.
To absorb the thought of Wittgenstein simply because his
posthumous works and those of his pupils at Oxford and
elsewhere seem to reveal a way of thinking related to our own
established hermeneutic form, leads to a reinforcement of what
should be questionable to us rather than to a self-examination
which would at last enable us to challenge that claim to pro-
fundity associated in our country with every sufficiently opaque
train of thought expressed in esoteric jargon, whether it be
that of "authenticity," "reification," or "alienation"—to challenge it, that is, as long as jargon is a substitute for rational
argumentation.

As for the late philosophy of Wittgenstein, which is now
gradually becoming respectable in Germany, and the philosophical orientation deriving from it, it seems to me that one
thing to which we have so far paid little heed is of first importance. This orientation, which restricts philosophy to linguistic analysis, represents a philosophical descriptivism similar to that of Heidegger with its phenomenological cast. It
totally rejects explanation and criticism, and involves a thesis
of neutrality which turns philosophy into an esoteric activity
completely devoid of consequences for other fields of thought

and for society. If one allows oneself to be unduly influenced by the emphasis that existentialism seems to place on decision and personal commitment, it is difficult to understand how many proponents of hermeneutic thought, who feel indebted to Heidegger, can let themselves at the same time be so fascinated by Wittgenstein. It has, however, been rightly stressed for a long time that the emptiness of existence, and the consequent indeterminacy of the content of that commitment, which in this philosophy is, even if only descriptively, emphasized as essential, are de facto such as to leave eternally open the question of which particular stance to adopt.[2] As a result, this philosophy of commitment is really not so remote from analytic neutrality. Further, this neutrality, which already in analytical thought has in part decidedly conservative features, in the "passive reason" (*vernehmende Vernunft*) of the hermeneutic thinkers—who on occasion consciously and expressly disavow an attitude of critical distance toward tradition—appears to degenerate into a kind of quasi-theological thought which is attuned to revelations of meaning, and frequently pays open homage to the dogmatic and apologetic claims of theology. In both cases the critical impulse of thought disappears under the influence of a theory of nonintervention, which from a philosophical point of view is curious indeed. Science and morality, religion and politics are left to themselves and may claim an autonomy which could never be conceded to them by a mode of thought committed to enlightenment. Nevertheless, this philosophical self-limitation, as has been fairly pointed out, has certain practical consequences, above all because, even when it retains rational thought in its own sphere, it provides scope for the development of irrationalism in other areas. But if the consequences of neutrality are of such a nature, one will undoubtedly have to ask whether, in view of this situation, one should not prefer a philosophy which does not flinch from a commitment which

[2] Cf. Ernst Topitsch, "Soziologie des Existenzialismus," *Merkur* 7 (1953), pp. 501 ff.

6

is explicit and determinate in content—which in certain circumstances may well mean a politically structured content—such as is to be found, for example, in Marxist thought. But this at once gives rise to a second question which touches on the relationship between knowledge and decision: whether and how rationality and commitment are at all consistent with one another.

With the rise of the two philosophical spheres of influence lying outside the Marxist sphere described above, the impression has also arisen in Western thought (perhaps seldom fully brought to consciousness, but apparently still very influential) that rationality and commitment are irreconcilable and that knowledge and decision belong to separate spheres with no essential overlap. Existential problems, it is often assumed, are incapable of rational treatment because they require genuine decisions which calculative reason cannot provide. On the other hand, rational analysis certainly seems to apply in the sphere of knowledge, but in this sphere there are neither decision nor commitments, and the problems solvable in this manner are apparently ipso facto devoid of existential significance. While the advocates of analytical and hermeneutic reason frequently formulate conceptions which come close to such theories, the proponents of dialectical reason are often so convinced of the compatibility of knowledge and commitment that in their thought the political attitude on occasion arises directly—one might even say, surprisingly undialectically—from the philosophical orientation.

Now there are, no doubt, connections between knowledge and commitment, between rational thought and existential decision, between philosophy and politics; but they are not so simple as committed thinkers often imagine them to be. For certain types of commitment corrupt thought, and in consequence can make no sensible contribution to the solution of problems, whether these be cognitive or ethical, social or political, or even religious in nature. There is a *total commitment* which prevents or at least impedes the unbiased pursuit of truth and critical-rational thought, and as its final

7

result—no matter whether it speaks in the name of faith and a divine power, in the name of history, or in that of reason— has led again and again to *totalitarian consequences*. Not all those who hold such a commitment to be right and proper seem aware of this, but there are many who are in a position to know it, because they know history. I have no sympathy for contemporary definitions of totalitarianism which treat secular political religions and the institutional structures which bear their stamp as forms of decadence to be sharply marked off from the political-religious traditions of the Christian West; for hisory is full of totalitarian excesses committed in the name of Christianity, right up until the most recent times. Rather, the important thing is that seen from certain structural view- points, Catholicism, Calvinism, communism, and fascism be- long together, not because all these historically very complex phenomena are in every respect the same in nature or even in value, but because in all of them the extreme opposite of the neutrality posited by analytical thought was or is at work; blind partisanship, obedient faith, incorrigible commitment. Thus there are common structural features here that in no way can be dismissed as superficial—features which are not merely psychologically or sociologically interesting, but are of epistemological, ethical, and sociophilosophical interest as well. It is necessary to recognize these characteristics, regard- less of the varying degrees of sympathy one may feel for the systems in which they appear.

Many who must have seen through these common features and relationships frequently neglect to point them out, some- times for readily understandable "existential" reasons, and frequently also because they would like to set off their own type of total commitment as completely different from the other variants. Perhaps the utopian component of their thought sometimes misleads them and others into the illusion that their own commitment, when translated into collective actions, must have consequences fundamentally different from those we know from history. But such thought is romantic and illusory, even when preached from chairs of philosophy or theology and gladly adopted by malcontents who imagine that with its aid they can articulate their present situation without the exertion required by objective rational analysis, and also without considering the social costs of the actions for which they make their propaganda. Enthusiasm for a holy cause leads, as we know, not infrequently to fanaticism and intolerance, to diabolizing one's opponents, and finally to terror and violence. Total commitment, even when it supports its claims and demands by invoking the name of dialectical or critical reason, can, therefore, in no way save us from the irrationalism to which both analytical thought—demanding neutrality—and heremeneutic thought—putting us at the mercy of traditions of whatever kind—give free play. For such commitment is itself merely one form of this irrationalism.

There is, however, no necessity to choose between complete neutrality and total commitment if one is prepared to envision another possibility which allows for the combination of rationality and commitment: a critical rationalism such as that found, above all, in the philosophy of Karl Popper and in philosophical positions related to it. That new critical philosophy overcomes the neutrality of analytical thought; it opposes the total commitment of theological and quasi-theological modes of thought and their anti-liberal implications, and favors a critical commitment to rational thought and to the unprejudiced search for truth and open-ended solutions to problems—solutions which are always subject to revision in the light of fresh insights. It links up with an ancient tradition that may be traced back to Greek antiquity, which again rose to importance during the formative period of modern science; in the age of Enlightenment it determined, for a time, the general consciousness, but since the beginning of the nineteenth century it has been subjected to pressure from the outbreak of new types of irrationalism.

The present book is an investigation elucidating the problems of our present situation from the standpoint of this critical philosophy, seeking to show what consequences emerge from it for the solution of cognitive, moral, and political problems. This is the reason for the book's dual approach, and for its polemical tone which, as will be seen, I do not try to conceal in any way. It is directed against philosophy which would like to protect itself from open commitment by restricting itself to the analysis of the "given," any brand of "pure" philosophy—linguistic or existential analysis—which exhausts itself with the description of phenomena and concedes at best a very limited significance to critical thought. The polemic is, however, also directed against any philosophy which abandons itself to total commitment and claims the certain possession of truth, thus bearing within itself a tendency to turn into a system of thought of a radical friend-or-foe kind, whose political consequences again and again have shown themselves to be catastrophic.

A critical rationalism of this kind cannot limit rationality to the sphere of science, nor to those technical and economic fields for which its usefulness is customarily conceded. It cannot consent to halt at boundaries of any kind—neither at those of scientific disciplines, nor at those of any social sphere that appears to be immunized against rational criticism by virtue of custom or tradition or conscious protective screening. Against all tendencies, whether neutral-analytic, conservative-hermeneutic, dogmatic-apologetic, or utopian-eschatological, found in present-day philosophical and theological thinking—and in scientific thought as well—critical rationalism advocates a critical model of rationality which may, in a quite special sense, be termed dialectical, although not in the sense of those philosophers who under the influence of Hegelian thought continually assure us that "the subject matter itself" moves in their reflections, while other people merely propound opinions.

I have attempted, from the point of view described above, to reveal a connection between the general problem of knowledge (Chapters One and Two), the moral problem (Chapter Three), the problem of ideology (Chapter Four), the problems posed by modern theology (Chapter Five), the problem of meaning accentuated by hermeneutics and analysis (Chapter

Six), and the problems of politics (Chapter Seven), for which certain results also emerge from critical philosophy. It is by no means the case, as is often maintained in German-speaking countries by critics of this philosophical view, that this approach is subject to limitations which render it incapable of handling certain types of problems. Rather, anyone who argues in this fashion will have to show from his own point of view what alternatives to the one proposed here are possible. For critical philosophy, too, the critique of knowledge and ideology, and of morality, religion, and society are closely connected; in what manner they are connected will become apparent in the following investigation.

# ONE

## The Problem of Foundation

### 1. THE SEARCH FOR FIRM BASES

WHOEVER seeks to grasp the nature of knowledge or to distinguish genuine knowledge and true understanding from mere opinions, assumptions, or subjective views, will very quickly come up against a problem which is normally regarded as a central—if not *the* central—problem of epistemology: *the problem of foundation*. This problem appears to be of particular importance for the sciences, for they are considered by virtue of their procedures and their results to be a model for all of human knowledge. They generate knowledge purported to be more systematic than everyday knowledge, more methodologically secure and especially solid in its foundation, which must, therefore, be preferred to everyday knowledge. Anyone who agrees with such assertions would find it tempting to inquire after the basis of our knowledge as such and thereby to pose the problem of foundation in a form which initially appears very plausible.

In order to understand this problem—the question of how our knowledge is grounded—one might take as a starting-point a situation which may be characterized as follows: when we strive for knowledge we obviously want to find out the *truth* about the nature of some real relationship; we wish to form for ourselves true convictions concerning definite areas, sections, or parts of *reality*. In doing this it seems quite natural that we strive for *certitude* as to whether what we find is also true; and such a certitude seems attainable only if we possess a *basis* for our knowledge, i.e., if we can establish this knowledge so securely that it is beyond all doubt. It seems, then, as if truth and certitude are closely connected in human knowledge. The search for truth, for true conceptions, convictions,

12

or statements—and thus also for true theories—seems to be inseparably bound up with the search for secure grounds, for an absolute foundation, and hence a justification for our convictions—for an *Archimedean point* appropriate to the sphere of knowledge.[1]

The idea of an absolute foundation presupposed by this search for an Archimedean point of knowledge obviously links together the recognizability of reality and the determinability of truth. That is to say, the *attainability* and the *decidability* of truth are linked together in a manner which suggests a particular kind of solution for methodological problems. In order to characterize this kind it may be useful to refer back to the so-called *principle of sufficient reason (principium rationis sufficientis)*, which one often finds stated in old books of logic as a first principle of thought, an axiom of logic.[2] As

---

[1] Cf. René Descartes, *Meditations on First Philosophy* (1641): "And I shall ever follow in this road until I have met with something which is certain, or at least, if I can do nothing else, until I have learned for certain that there is nothing in the world that is certain. Archimedes, in order that he might draw the terrestrial globe out of its place, and transport it elsewhere, demanded that only one point should be fixed and immovable; in the same way I shall have the right to conceive high hopes if I am happy enough to discover one thing only which is certain and indubitable" (2d Meditation). *The Philosophical Works of Descartes*, vol. 1, trans. Haldane and Ross (Cambridge, Eng., 1931), p. 149. In other philosophers, too, this striving for certainty, for a certain foundation, finds clear expression; cf., e.g., Johann Gottlieb Fichte, *Grundlage der gesamten Wissenschaftslehre* (1794), Meiner edition (Hamburg, 1954), pp. 11 ff., or the work of Hugo Dingler.

[2] It is well known that this principle plays an essential role in the thought of Leibniz, *Monadology* (1714), where (in §31 and §32) the principle of contradiction and the principle of sufficient reason are depicted as the two great principles on which the use of reason is based: "... the principle of contradiction in virtue of which we judge false that which involves a contradiction, and true that which is opposed or contradictory to what is false ..." and "... the principle of sufficient reason, in virtue of which we hold that there can be no fact real or existing, no statement true, unless there be a sufficient reason why it should be so and not otherwise, although these reasons usually cannot be known to us." (Latta translation of Monadology [Oxford, 1898]) One sees that two assertions are combined here, one relating to facts, the other to statements. It was Arthur Schopenhauer who indicated

an axiom it has disappeared from textbooks of logic. More-over, it is hard to see how it could nowadays be accommo-dated in them or how it could be reformulated in such a way as to make its inclusion appropriate. It would at the very least have no function and might even be disruptive. If, however, we formulate it as a methodological principle, we have gained something which we may with some justice regard as a general *postulate of the classical methodology of rational thought*, as the fundamental principle of that model of rationality that appears to dominate in classical epistemology. This principle states: always seek an adequate foundation—a sufficient jus-tification—for all your convictions.[3] One sees at once that this principle of adequate foundation or sufficient justification may be extended without further ado from theoretical to moral and political convictions—and indeed, to assertions of all kinds, if only one is ready to make a *decision* not to restrict arbitrarily the application of this model of rationality to a single sphere. Whoever strives for certainty will assume the self-evidence of this demand that all convictions should be based upon cer-tainties—and that means not only convictions involving cog-nitive claims, but also others, such as those possessing a nor-mative character—as long, that is, as he has not come up against the difficulties that follow from this principle. So he will be ready to admit that only sufficiently justified statements

most clearly the significance of this distinction, cf. his dissertation, "*Über die vierfache Wurzel des Satzes vom zureichenden Grunde*," translated into Eng-lish by E.F.J. Payne (La Salle, Ill., 1974) as "*On the Fourfold Root of the Principle of Sufficient Reason*" (1813); on its importance as the "foundation of all science," see the first section. He maintains that there are grounds for distinguishing at least between real cause and reason, and thus between the causal principle and the principle of sufficient reason in the narrower sense. The latter is what interests us here, since it concerns the foundation of our knowledge.

[3] In his book, *Abriss der Logik* (Berlin, 1958), Kasimierz Ajdukiewicz points out (in part 2, chapter 1, "Über die Arten und die Notwendigkeit der Begründung von Sätzen," §11: "Der Staz des zureichenden Grundes," pp. 72 ff.) that the principle may be formulated as a postulate. It is then identical with the demand of critical thought, which is opposed to any kind of dog-matism. We shall see that this thesis is problematic.

in the above-mentioned sense can lay claim to general recognition. Only a recourse to the Archimedean point of thought presupposed by this demand can provide the certainty necessary for an adequate foundation. Of course, at this point the question at once arises as to whether and in what manner the Archimedean problem may be solved in the sphere of thought, for the application of the principle of sufficient justification presupposes that this problem has been solved.

If this methodological idea can be made a reality in the sphere of knowledge or in one of its subdivisions, then clearly one can know of that sphere that the search for truth has been successful, that one has attained true convictions. Anything, however, which does not harmonize with the true view must be not only unfounded, but also false. Thus the process of the acquisition of knowledge seems, for the particular sphere concerned, to have come to an end. The problems have been solved; their solutions may be learned, passed on, and applied without any need to subject them to further questioning. From this a further methodological principle of rational thought seems to emerge: the demand that at any given time the sole true view, the correct theory for the sphere in question, should be sought, and accordingly *all possible alternatives rejected*; for alternatives to the truth must obviously be false. In fact, any kind of thinking in alternatives appears incompatible with the idea of truth. Thus the postulate of sufficient justification is apparently closely connected with a further principle: the *postulate of theoretical monism*. The one true theory relevant to the field of thought in question or the sector of reality to be analyzed must be extracted and adequately grounded so that one may be certain of its truth. Classical epistemology seems to be inspired by this conception of rational thought; but not it alone. For one cannot possibly maintain that foundationalism of this type has been overcome in all fields of thought. On the contrary, even today it is more or less the basis of many methodological approaches in philosophy, the sciences, and in social practice without ever being clearly stated. These approaches often differ in many details, above all in their answer to the question of what an adequate foundation looks like in individual cases; but they all concur in their basic principle: in the demand for such a justification, for a foundation for knowledge and action.

## 2. THE PRINCIPLE OF SUFFICIENT JUSTIFICATION AND THE MÜNCHHAUSEN TRILEMMA

The question of what a sufficient justification might be seems necessarily to point toward that science which is primarily involved when the validity of arguments is to be judged: the science of *logic*. We may assume that logical inferences play an essential role in the justification of views of all kinds. We may regard the problem of logical inference as the central theme of formal logic.[4] It provides us with information as to what a valid deductive argument looks like and what such an argument can do. It may be advisable at this point to consider the matter very briefly.

A valid deductive argument—a logical inference—is a sequence of statements, of premises and conclusions, between which definite logical relationships exist; a conclusion, namely, is deducible from the premises in question with the aid of the rules of logic. "Premise" and "conclusion" are to be understood as deduction-relative concepts; they refer to the logical role of the statements in question in a particular inferential context, not to the statements per se. For our purposes—in the context of our foundation problem—a few simple relationships, familiar from formal logic, are of interest:

1. Logical inference can never achieve an increase of content.[5] The logical range of the propositions involved may in-

[4] Cf. Karl R. Popper, "New Foundations for Logic," *Mind*, vol. 56, NS (1947), pp. 193 ff.

[5] Cf., e.g., Rudolf Carnap, *Introduction to Symbolic Logic and its Application*, trans. William Meyer and John Wilkinson (New York, 1958), p. 20 and passim. The importance of the content of statements for the structure of our scientific knowledge was elaborated by Karl R. Popper in his book, *Logik der Forschung* (Vienna, 1935); 2d enlarged ed., Tübingen, 1966); translated as *Logic of Scientific Discovery* (London, 1959).

crease as the deduction proceeds or it may remain the same; the information content may decrease in this process or it may remain the same. From a set of propositions one may, as it were, derive by a deductive process only the information already contained in it. Such a process serves to "milk" a set of statements, not to generate fresh information. This means among other things that no propositions with content may be deduced from analytical statements. Conversely, however, analytical propositions are deducible from statements with content, for they are deducible from any statement whatever. That a proposition may be logically deducible from informative statements thus says nothing about its own logical content. On the other hand any kind of proposition may be deduced from contradictory statements.[6]

2. The validity of a deductive argument says nothing about the truth of its components. More precisely: in such an argument all the components may be false, the premises may be all or partly false and the conclusions may be either true or false; only one case is impossible: false conclusions cannot follow from entirely true premises. If, then, all the premises are true, the conclusions derived from them are also true. To put it another way: the validity of a deductive argument only guarantees

  a. the *transfer* of the *positive* truth value—the *truth*—from the set of premises to the conclusion; and thus
  b. the *transfer* of the *negative* truth value—the *falseness*—from the conclusion back to the set of premises.

3. An invalid deductive argument produces a wrong inference that affords no such guarantee. In this case, therefore, no combination of positive or negative truth values of the components of the argument is excluded. This concludes our excursus into logic.

Now, back to the problem of foundation. What role can logical inference play here? In accordance with the principle

---

[6] Cf. Rudolf Carnap, *The Logical Syntax of Language* (London, 1937), p. 184, theorems 52.7 and 52.8.

formulated above, we may assume that the goal of the foundation procedure must consist in securing the truth of the views involved, and thus of the statements in which they are formulated. The truth—the positive truth value—is, however, transferable by logical inference. This gives rise to the idea that it may be possible to found a conviction—and thus a set or system of statements—by referring it back to secure and indubitable grounds by logical means, i.e., with the help of logical inferences; and that in such a way that all components of the set of propositions involved are produced from this foundation by logical inference.

If, however, our principle is to be taken seriously, the following problem arises at once: if one demands a justification for *everything*, one must also demand a justification for the knowledge to which one has referred back the views initially requiring foundation. This leads to a situation with three alternatives, all of which appear unacceptable: in other words, to a trilemma which, in view of the analogy existing between our problem and one which that celebrated and mendacious baron once had to solve, I should like to call the *Münchhausen trilemma*. For, obviously, one must choose here between

1. an *infinite regress*, which seems to arise from the necessity to go further and further back in the search for foundations, and which, since it is in practice impossible, affords no secure basis;
2. a *logical circle* in the deduction, which arises because, in the process of justification, statements are used which were characterized before as in need of foundation, so that they can provide no secure basis; and, finally,
3. the *breaking-off of the process* at a particular point, which, admittedly, can always be done in principle, but involves an arbitrary suspension of the principle of sufficient justification.

Since both an infinite regress and a circular argument seem clearly unacceptable, one is inclined to accept the third possibility, for the simple reason that no other way out of the situation is thought to be possible.[7] Of statements where one is prepared to break off the foundation process, it is customary to use words such as "self-evident," "self-authenticating," "based upon *immediate* knowledge"—upon intuition or experience—or in some other way to render palatable the fact that one is prepared to break off the foundation regress at some particular point and suspend the foundation postulate with respect to this point, declaring it to be an Archimedean point of knowledge. The procedure is analogous to the suspending of the causal principle by the introduction of a *causa sui*. But what are we to make of a statement that cannot itself be justified, but must assist in justifying everything else; that is represented as certain, despite the fact that one can really doubt everything—including the statement—on principle; that is an *assertion*, the *truth* of which is *certain* and therefore *not in need of foundation*? If such a conviction or statement is called a *dogma*, then our third possibility is revealed as something one would have least expected in a solution to the foundation problem: justification by *recourse to a dogma*. It looks as if the search for the Archimedean point of knowledge must end in dogmatism; for at some point the foundation postulate of classical methodology needs to be suspended.[8] A recourse

---

[7] In this connection Hugo Dingler's treatment of the problem of the validity of logical principles should be pointed out; cf. his *Philosophie der Logik und Arithmetik* (Munich, 1931), pp. 21 ff. In connection with the criterion of truth, he constructs a situation that completely corresponds to the Münchhausen trilemma in its structure. Dingler has grasped the structure of the situation very clearly and found a solution, to which we shall return. Incidentally, even earlier the question of the justification of knowledge had produced analyses in which the trilemma emerged in a more or less clear form; cf. Richard H. Popkin, *The History of Scepticism from Erasmus to Descartes* (rev. ed., Assen, 1964), pp. 3, 52, 137, and passim. The total *crise pyrrhonienne* brought about by the Reformation, the Renaissance, and the rise of the new natural sciences—a crisis that simultaneously rendered faith and knowledge problematical—was overcome philosophically by the answers of classical rationalism, which themselves later turned out to be questionable. On this problem see also Gerard Radnitzky, "Über empfehlenswerte und verwerfliche Spielarten der Skepsis," *Ratio*, vol. 7 (1965), pp. 109 ff.

[8] Blaise Pascal saw this very clearly in his day; see his short work "De

to extralinguistic authorities of whatever kind affords no assistance in this respect, as is easily seen.[9] Quite apart from the particular problems that can arise where such authorities are concerned, there is always the possibility that a demand for justification may be made of them as well. All claims of self-justification made for ultimate authorities of this kind must, like similar claims made for particular statements, be regarded as a masquerade disguising a decision to waive the principle in this particular instance. It then looks as if such a decision is unavoidable, so that the dogmatism connected with it seems a necessary evil—or even totally harmless.

Incidentally, the situation is not essentially altered if inferential processes other than those of deductive logic are introduced in order to bring about the foundation regress. Neither the use of inductive procedures of any kind nor recourse to some transcendental deduction can help to remedy the situation; nor is it basically altered if one shifts the problem from the horizontal plane—that is, from the analysis of contexts of statements on the same linguistic level—to the vertical, on which one seeks adequate justification of one's criteria for

---

l'esprit géometrique et de l'art de persuader" (1658), in which the "true method" of demonstration, which consists in "defining all concepts and proving all assertions," is reduced *ad absurdum*, because it would involve an infinite regress (Pascal, *Oeuvres complètes*, ed. Louis Lafuma [Paris, 1963], p. 348). On this problem see also William Warren Bartley III, *The Retreat to Commitment* (New York, 1962), especially chapters 4 and 5.

[9] Such a procedure was proposed and elucidated in detail by the Fries-Nelson school of Kantianism. What is involved is a recourse to so-called *immediate* knowledge, which in itself is *certain*—pure and sensual intuition or rational cognition whose content is expressed in mediated knowledge, that is, in true judgments. Leonard Nelson has applied this doctrine also in the sphere of practical reason; see his book, *Kritik der praktischen Vernunft* (Leipzig, 1917). This doctrine was subjected to a thorough analysis and criticism in the twenties, which are in the main still valid; cf. Walter Dubislav, *Die Friessche Lehre von der Begründung. Darstellung und Kritik* (Dömitz, 1926). Fries's principle of the self-confidence of reason in the truth of its immediate knowledge, which claims that freedom from error is guaranteed with respect to certain assertions, is merely the expression of a psychologistic form of dogmatism.

workable inferential procedures and for ultimate linguistic or extralinguistic authorities which may be used as a basis for inference. Here, too, the trilemma must necessarily arise: infinite regress, circularity, or that kind of dogmatism that is seen as a necessary evil—a solution one can resign oneself to accepting in view of the obvious unserviceability of both the other alternatives.

Anyone who is unwilling to rest content with the dogmatizing of statements, criteria, or other authorities of whatever kind will be obliged to ask himself whether the whole situation, which inevitably leads to the Münchhausen trilemma, may not be avoided. It is perfectly possible that the search for the Archimedean point of knowledge that dominates the thought of classical methodology arises through formulating the problem situation in a way that could not withstand criticism. One must not overlook the possibility that formulations of problems, too, can contain presuppositions that may be false and consequently misleading. The problem of the Archimedean point of knowledge may be one of the wrongly formulated problems. But before we turn to this question, let us review the various versions of classical epistemology.

### 3. THE REVELATION MODEL IN EPISTEMOLOGY

Classical epistemology, which developed parallel to modern science, arose out of controversy with a tradition bearing the stamp of scholastic thought, which it sought to overcome. Nevertheless, it shares with this tradition a general way of thinking which one could call a *revelation model of knowledge*. Karl Popper[10] has pointed out that the core of optimistic epistemology, which inspired the birth of modern science, consists of the doctrine that *truth is manifest*, that it lies open to view, and that one need merely open one's eyes to see it.

---

[10] Cf. Popper's article, "On the Sources of Knowledge and Ignorance" (1960), reprinted in his volume of essays, *Conjectures and Refutations. The Growth of Scientific Knowledge* (London, 1963).

It may be veiled, and on occasion it may not be easy to draw aside the veil; but "as soon as the naked truth stands revealed before our eyes, we have the power to see it, to distinguish it from falsehood, and to know that it *is* truth." This epistemology, found as well in thinkers of classical antiquity, was bound up, as Popper demonstrates, with an ideological theory of error: the view that error is in need of explanation, while the perception of truth is a matter of course, and that the causes of error are to be sought in the sphere of the will, of personal interest and of prejudice. Bad will disturbs, as it were, the pure process of knowledge: the seeing of truth. Personal interest and prejudice intervene and falsify the result, impair the revelation.

One can speak here with some justice of a pseudomorphosis of the methodology of critical thought, of its development in a guise determined by traditional theological modes of thought; a garb which renders intelligible the manner of coming to terms with the foundation problem outlined above. For if rational thought can link up with ultimate "givens" mediated by some kind of revelation, then a recourse to secure foundations as demanded by the above-mentioned postulate of sufficient justification seems to succeed without invoking arbitrary human choices. In cognition possessing the character of revelation, the sector of reality in question enters immediately and unmistakably into the field of vision of the knowing subject, who is, one may suppose, a passive receiver, so that there can be no question of doubt. Admittedly, the knower must acknowledge not merely the content but also the revelatory character of such cognitions: he must *identify them as* revelations. But should doubts once arise, the discussion about adequate criteria starts, and the interrupted foundation regress seems in principle to be capable of continuation. The illusion of an Archimedean point has disappeared.

The various versions of the revelation model are distinguished from one another primarily by the *source of knowledge* specified in each case, but also by the manner in which *access* to this source is regulated. It is especially in this last

22

point that the sociological character of the epistemology concerned tends to show itself, as does the fact that these doctrines by no means manifest that philosophical purity and freedom from all empirical relations that philosophers are inclined to attribute to them. A unique supernatural revelation, historically limited to a particular circle of human beings, to which the rest of mankind, including later generations, has access only via a tradition partly written: this is a pattern for the mediation of truth that is widespread in the theology of the major religions. A revelation of this kind can take on widely varying social expressions. The intent of this model is to found a once-revealed and unchangeable truth and place it once and for all beyond the reach of all possible criticism. But, as is well known, such a fixation by no means excludes all modifications. Rather, the real problem is by this means shifted to the *identification and interpretation of this revelation*; that is to say, it becomes a matter of determining which of the utterances contained in the particular tradition possess a canonical character and can therefore be regarded as revelatory in content, and how they should be interpreted so that this content may emerge pure and free from distortion.[11] At decisive points the analysis of factual questions, untrammeled by dogma, is replaced by exegesis, the interpretation of preestablished texts. This interpretation is of course always selective in a certain direction and, in addition, is constructive and can consequently lead to widely differing conceptions, although

[11] The method employed by the Jesuit François Veron at the beginning of the seventeenth century to combat Calvinism was based on the fact that the answers to both these questions must not as a matter of principle be regarded as a foregone conclusion; cf. Popkin, *History of Scepticism*, pp. 70 ff. What happened then, of course, was that his Calvinist opponents discovered the usefulness of this method for the corresponding counterargument. In modern theology, too, both questions are examined; cf. Willi Marxsen, *Das Neue Testament als Buch der Kirche* (Stuttgart, 1966), pp. 16 ff. and passim, a book which makes clear the extent to which the modern-day overemphasis on hermeneutical problems has forced the fundamental epistemological problems into the background. We shall return to this later.

the fact is not always readily admitted.[12] Thus factual problems of various sorts may be authoritatively resolved by being clothed in a hermeneutic garb by a person called to that task; and this may be done in a manner which secures such solutions as far as is possible against doubt and objections.

In such societies the institutional question regularly crops up as to which persons are qualified to provide valid interpretations. On occasion a relatively closed and hierarchically structured group, a bureaucracy of religious or ideological experts, succeeds in setting up a *monopoly of interpretation*. When this happens, the promulgation of particular beliefs based on revelation[13] is combined with a claim to obedience by those occupying certain social positions—men qualified to interpret revelation who, in establishing their claims and promulgating their own forms of belief, have at their disposal sanctions of many and varied kinds, ranging from the imposition of transcendental punishments to the employment of physical force. One may regard a social and intellectual development of this kind as reaching its apogee when certain officials acquire a *claim to infallibility* for their interpretations, which claim becomes dogmatically fixed. This is a process that expresses the authoritarian and dogmatic character of such an epistemology in a particularly salient manner, and at the same time clearly shows that in this case epistemology and social theory are inseparably linked.

Extreme versions of the revelation model of knowledge, with their monopoly of interpretation, claim to obedience, obligatory belief and persecutions of the heterodox, serve to demonstrate most clearly the connection between epistemological problems of justification and problems involving social

[12] On the interpretative techniques in use in the Christian world, see above all the critical analysis, so far insufficiently noticed by theologians, in Walter Kaufmann's *Critique of Religion and Philosophy* (New York, 1958), chapter 6, as well as chapters 5 to 10 of his *The Faith of a Heretic* (New York, 1960). See also Bartley's *Retreat to Commitment*.

[13] It is hardly necessary to mention that revelation claims arise also in connection with nonreligious convictions.

structure, morality, and politics. But such a connection is present not only in these extreme authoritarian cases but also in less dramatic ones. It would be wrong to regard epistemologies associated with religio-theological or secular-ideological positions as being "impure" special cases that could be left to ideology critique, while regarding the epistemology of the natural sciences, for example, as a "pure" doctrine free from any empirical admixture and social or political implications, imagining, perhaps, that such an epistemology can be constructed in a purely formal, semantic, or analytical manner and constituted as an autonomous discipline unconnected with any philosophy of life, as a pure theory of science. I do not wish to deny that one can proceed thus in certain circumstances; nor is it disputed that such a procedure may nowadays expect to meet with applause. But that an epistemology of this kind can then be relevant to the solution of important problems may legitimately be doubted.[14] On the contrary, it must here be stated right away, first, that epistemology and critique of ideology are closely connected, that neither can be "neutral"— any more than can moral philosophy—without becoming irrelevant to its own peculiar problems;[15] and second, that over and above this they have a connection with sociopolitical problems that cannot be set aside without reducing their significance. This is also true of solutions that employ the revelation model in a less drastic manner, or that even operate with a genuine alternative to this model in which the principle of sufficient justification no longer plays a part. Let us leave this point for the time being and concentrate for the present

[14] In his essay, "The Nature of Philosophical Problems and Their Roots in Science" (1952), reprinted in *Conjectures and Refutations*, pp. 66 ff., Karl Popper has emphasized that the "purification" of philosophy and its detachment from the cosmological, mathematical, political, social, and religious problems in which it is rooted is a sign of degeneracy, which has the effect of causing interesting problems simply to disappear altogether.

[15] Cf. my essay, "Ethik und Meta-Ethik. Das Dilemma der analytischen Moralphilosophie," *Archiv für Philosophie*, vol. 11 (1961), reprinted in my collection of essays, *Konstruktion und Kritik* (Hamburg, 1975).

on the fact that the relevation model affords, in the first instance, an apparently plausible solution to the problem of the Archimedean point of knowledge, a solution that varies according to the source of knowledge preferred in the relevant epistemologies and then develops into various conceptions of rationality.

Modern philosophy has certainly not emancipated itself from this theological model, which to a considerable extent has focused the process of knowing upon the interpretation of given statements endowed with authority, a process in which error comes close to sin, while knowledge assumes the character of grace. Classical epistemology, which developed alongside modern science, also operated with a revelation theory of truth; a theory in which revelation was naturalized and democratized, i.e., divested of its supernatural and at the same time of its historical character and transposed to individual intuition or individual perception. This was paralleled by the Reformation emphasis on individual conscience with regard to certain moral and political decisions, an emphasis typical of the Protestant tradition then in the process of formation. In this way the epistemological privileges hitherto granted in Christian doctrine to the holders of certain social positions, at least where important problems were involved, were fundamentally questioned, and a doctrine of knowledge was created which had to come into collision with the official teaching of the Catholic church, as it in fact has again and again up to the present day. In the Protestant sphere the removal of the central authority and its monopoly of interpretation, and the attachment of faith to the Bible, led to a multiplicity of competing interpretations and to attempts to adapt theology to the modern sciences, which appeared to render the core of Christian belief at least partially immune to critical objections from that source. The hermeneutic philosophy which then developed in this sphere has produced a style of thought that not only approaches that of the theologians, but in addition has made it possible to render epistemological assistance to theological thought, as we shall see later.

With respect to the widespread view that the Protestant emphasis on the Bible and the individual conscience has had a direct liberating effect upon society, it is necessary nowadays to have serious misgivings. The Reformation and the Counter-Reformation led, in the first instance, to an interruption of the development toward freedom of thought and toleration initiated by the Renaissance; to the suppression of the Erasmian tendencies that had been spreading vigorously until then; and to a fanaticizing of the masses. As a result, more liberal ideas could only reassert themselves after a long intervening period filled with religious struggles, witch trials, and heretic hunting.[16] The ideas of the Enlightenment met with resistance not only from Catholic but also from Protestant orthodoxy. The conscience, formed by the influence of the cultural milieu existing at any given time, can function, as has been seen, in a thoroughly authoritarian and dogmatic fashion;[17] and the Bible can be read in a way that confirms this, even when the Catholic monopoly of interpretation has been broken.[18] But

[16] Cf. H. R. Trevor-Roper, "Religion, the Reformation and Social Change," in his volume of the same name (London/Melbourne/Toronto, 1967), which is primarily concerned with subjecting to criticism the Weber-Tawney thesis of the connection between Calvinism and capitalism; see also his essay, "The Religious Origins of the Enlightenment," in the same volume, in which the thesis of the positive influence of Calvinism on science and philosophy is corrected; and finally, his thorough analysis of the witch craze that increased at the time of the Reformation and Counter-Reformation, "The European Witch-Craze of the Sixteenth and Seventeenth Centuries," also in the same volume.

[17] Incidentally, freedom of conscience was kept within very narrow limits especially in the Lutheran world; moreover, politically speaking, it was combined with an authoritarian mode of thought with extraordinarily important consequences; cf., e.g., Karl Kupisch, "Protestantismus und Zeitverständnis. Politische Aspekte der Reformation," *Blätter für deutsche und internationale Politik*, vol. 12, no. 4 (1967), pp. 355 ff.

[18] Cf. the criticism of the Protestant theory of knowledge in Paul K. Feyerabend's contribution, "On the Improvement of the Sciences and the Arts, and the Possible Identity of the Two," in *Boston Studies in the Philosophy of Science*, vol. 3, ed. Robert S. Cohen and Marx W. Wartofsky (Dordrecht, 1967), pp. 391 ff.

let us turn our attention once more to the philosophy of knowledge, which is not immediately tied to the theological doctrines of the churches.

The naturalizing and democratizing of the idea of revelation in classical epistemology detached knowledge from its traditional connections and made it into a revelation of *nature* by means of *reason* or the *senses*. Within the realm for which this doctrine claimed to be valid, it was no longer possible to legitimize cognitions by appealing to texts invested with authority; instead, one had recourse to intellectual intuition or sense perceptions. That means, however, only that one authority had been replaced by others of similar dogmatic function, while the authoritarian scheme of justification was still, in the end, retained: knowledge is justified through recourse to some absolutely certain authority.[19] Truth was now accessible to anyone who used his reason or his senses in the correct manner; but at the same time the idea of a guarantee of truth, the image of a certain knowledge, initially still often based upon theological considerations, was retained.

### 4. CLASSICAL EPISTEMOLOGY: INTELLECTUALISM AND EMPIRICISM

In the classical phase of modern philosophy we find two versions of the revelation model of rationality:

a. classical intellectualism which took as its starting point the sovereignty of reason, of intellectual intuition, and the primacy of theoretical knowledge, and

b. classical empiricism, which emphasized the sovereignty of observation, of sense perception, and the primacy of facts.

We find classical intellectualism clearly expressed in Descartes, who was willing to concede as valid for the unmediated

[19] Cf. Popper's above-mentioned essay, "On the Sources of Knowledge and Ignorance."

knowledge of objects only clear and evident intuition, and by this, as he clearly states, he means,

> not the manifold and changing testimony of the senses or the deceptive judgment that bases itself upon the confused images of sensual perception, . . . , but the simple and distinctive apprehension of the pure and attentive spirit, so that no further doubt remains about what has been perceived, or, what amounts to the same thing, the apprehension, superior to all doubt, of a pure and attentive spirit, springing solely from the light of reason.[20]

He goes on to speak of the self-evidence and certainty of intuition, and then moves to the procedure he acknowledges as a method for attaining to mediate knowledge, namely, deduction, by the aid of which all those things may be affirmed "which may be necessarily deduced from other particular things known with certainty." According to his view, deduction must be introduced "because after all, one has certain knowledge of most things, even if they are not evident by themselves, provided they are deduced from true and clearly recognized principles by means of a continuous, uninterrupted movement of thought intuitively producing each single stage of the process." Thus, through intuition we have immediate access to the truth and, in particular, we have immediate access to general truths, to those principles from which we may deduce further knowledge. Thus the intuitive apprehension of particular "givens" is supplemented by deduction as a procedure of derivation. Basically, all truth is attainable through the joint action of self-evident intuition and necessary deduction. For Descartes there is no other way to the certain cognition of truth. Moreover, clarity and distinctness are assumed very early to be criteria of truth.[21] For him, the goal of the scientific process consists in making true and well-founded judgments and thus

---

[20] René Descartes, *Regeln zur Leitung des Geistes*, Meiner-Ausgabe (Hamburg, 1962), pp. 10 ff.; author's translation.

[21] Cf. René Descartes, *Discourse on Method*, trans. Haldane and Ross (Cambridge, 1931).

penetrating to secure and certain knowledge. The connection very quickly becomes obvious between the idea of sufficient justification, which leads him to propose the combining of the two procedures of intuition and deduction, and the demand for certainty, which dominates his search for truth.[22] His methodical doubt aims exclusively at cleansing the intellect from all prejudice in order to advance to a secure basis for knowledge, to an Archimedean point from which will be generated the first and fundamental certainty for the whole process of knowing.

We encounter classical empiricism in Bacon, although in a form less significant for the actual development of the scientific method than for the ideology of science. In his view, it is only through sense perception that one has direct access to reality and thus to truth—that is, access to the concrete facts from which, if one wishes to proceed with assurance, one can climb higher only gradually and by stages, attaining to the most general principles only at the very end.[23] The inadequacies of sense perception are perfectly plain to him, but he believes he can satisfactorily compensate for them by means of instruments and experiments.[24] Sense perception that is improved in this way can serve as a basis for all further cognitive operations. To be sure, in order to achieve certainty with the aid of sense perception, one must first of all purge the intellect of all prejudices.[25] This demand subordinates all theoretical

[22] Wolfgang Röd, *Descartes. Die innere Genesis des cartesianischen Systems. Die Genese des cartesianischen Rationalismus* (1964; rev. 2d ed., Munich, 1982), in which the significance of the postulate of certainty for Cartesian philosophy is elaborated.

[23] Cf. Francis Bacon, *Novum organon* (1620), book 1, section 19, *Works of Francis Bacon*, vol. 1, ed. Ellis Spedding (London, 1905), p. 159.

[24] Ibid., sections 50, 69.

[25] Ibid., section 68: "So much concerning the several classes of idols, and their equipage; all of which must be renounced and put away with a fixed and solemn determination, and the understanding thoroughly freed and cleansed; the entrance into the kingdom of man, founded on the sciences, being not much other than the entrance into the kingdom of heaven, where into none may enter except as a little child."

anticipations of the results of later investigations to the verdict of an empiricism oriented toward immediately apprehensible facts. All such anticipations on the part of the intellect are to be dispensed with in favor of an interpretation of nature that does not rest content with assumptions and probabilities, but demands the security of certain knowledge. Bacon postulated induction as the process by which indirect knowledge might be gained; by its aid one could, starting from the results of observation, climb up "a correct, steadily rising ladder first of all to the lowest principles, then to the middle ones and only at the very end to the most general."[26] Induction is thus added to the observation of the particular data as an inferential procedure.[27] Through the cooperation of certain observation, attained under some circumstances by experimental methods, and of step-by-step (and therefore certain) induction, all truth would finally be attainable. The goal, as in Descartes, consists in making true and well-founded judgments and thus achieving secure and certain knowledge. In Bacon, too, one can observe a connection between the idea of sufficient justification, which doubtless lies behind his proposed combination of observation and induction, and the longing for certainty, which characterizes his epistemological ideal.

It has been rightly pointed out that there are basic similarities between the Cartesian and the Baconian method, similarities above all in the fact that in both cases the intellect must be purged of prejudices in order to attain to evident truth, to a certain basis for knowledge—be it rational intuitions or sense perceptions—from which everything else may

[26] Ibid., book 1, section 104. Bacon's ladder of induction has a certain similarity to the deductive chain of which Descartes speaks on occasion. In both cases, importance is attached to the greatest possible continuity of movement.

[27] In contrast to Aristotle, Bacon develops a theory of induction that seeks to take account of the importance of negative cases and provides for a method of elimination.

be inferred by deductive or inductive procedures.[28] According to this view, Bacon and Descartes were unable to keep their epistemologies free from authoritarian traits, since they only succeeded in replacing existing authorities with new ones, those of the senses or the intellect. Both versions of classical epistemology have in common the idea of an immediate access to truth through self-evident intellectual insight or careful observation. Truths of some sort are "given" to knowledge and must therefore be accepted. Obviously, in this conception a view of the sources of cognition is linked with a criterion of validity so that the problems of origin and justification are solved at one and the same time. Derivation from reason or perception is regarded as decisive for the legitimation of knowledge. Such a derivation appears to provide knowledge with a guarantee of truth and thus to give it the requisite certainty; for one must be able to have recourse to some secure basis, some unshakable foundation, in order to justify everything. In the *origins* of knowledge, truth and certainty hang together and both are transmitted by the preferred inferential process to all other knowledge. Thus, as one may see, the Münchhausen trilemma outlined above is resolved by the third alternative: breaking-off of the foundation regress at a particular point by recourse to convictions that bear the stamp of truth and must therefore be believed—beliefs that are untouchable because they are legitimized by the new authorities. Since it is always possible to have recourse to self-evident "givens" revealed to the percipient through reason or sense perception, error can only be rendered comprehensible by attribution to some active intervention.

Descartes and Bacon are not the only representatives of classical epistemology who can be subjected to critical investigation. Both the intellectualist and the empiricist alternatives were developed further, and during the course of this devel-

---

[28] Cf. Popper, "On the Sources of Knowledge and Ignorance," p. 53. This kind of epistemology is in his view basically a religious doctrine in which the source of all knowledge is divine authority.

opment the various difficulties inherent in these positions emerged and prompted remedial efforts. The conventionalism of Pierre Duhem and other theorists of science could be regarded as a modern version of intellectualism, and the positivism of Ernst Mach and the members of the Vienna Circle as a modern version of empiricism. It can hardly be doubted that the teachings of the early as well as of the later representatives of classical epistemology made many advances, and it is impossible to do full justice to these advances in a short space. But on the basis of the foregoing sketch of the Baconian and Cartesian positions, one can discuss the essential problems that must arise in epistemologies of this kind—those, that is to say, that are unwilling to sacrifice the principle of sufficient justification and consequently retreat to a revelation model in order to render comprehensible the certainty of the ultimate "givens" that provide the basis of knowledge.

The intellectualist version of classical epistemology overestimates speculation, as is revealed above all by the fact that it seeks to emancipate itself in large measure from the supervisory control of experience. It seeks certainty through pure rational insight; but derivation from reason hardly suffices as a guarantee of truth. Many an intuitive insight has, in the course of scientific development, later turned out to be false, although it previously appeared self-evident. This is always possible where theoretical assertions are concerned because one may succeed in deriving from them contradictory statements, or else conclusions that prove untenable when subjected to the test of empirical procedures. Intuitive certainty turns out to be valueless in such a case. And when this has once proved to be the case, it is advisable to abandon its use as a criterion, for such a situation may recur at any time. Psychologically speaking, there appears to be a close connection between intuition and habit. Intuitive insights bear the stamp of certainty above all because they tend to correspond with our habits of thought.[29] But our habits of thought are,

[29] Cf. Russell's criticism of intuition as an epistemological authority in

as we know, by no means sacrosanct; in any case, we should not treat them as such, for they are frequently resistant to fruitful theoretical innovations. The hypotheses that bring about scientific progress frequently have a *counterintuitive* character.[30] One need only recall the obstacles that, on various occasions in the history of the modern sciences, have impeded the acceptance of revolutionary theories—of theories, that is, which forced people to revise deeply rooted habits of thought. One of the latest examples of this is Einstein's theory of relativity. If one wishes to protect one's convictions against risks of this kind, this may certainly be done, but it is mostly at the cost of their content and explanatory force, consequences that not everyone is prepared to accept. We certainly tend intuitively to maintain our old prejudices against innovations of all kinds. It is not necessary to encourage such an attitude by according it the status of a theory of science.[31]

Deduction, the procedure of inference preferred by classical intellectualism, is relatively unproblematical; but one thing we know about it is that it only allows logical transformations in which the information content of the respective statements is not increased,[32] so that, for example, from principles that are relatively lacking in content—possibly even analytical—

Bertrand Russell, "Mysticism and Logic" (1914), in *Mysticism and Logic and Other Essays* (Penguin Books, 1953), pp. 9 ff. especially pp. 18 ff., where intuition is characterized as an aspect and development of instinct that can go grievously astray in unfamiliar situations. Russell at that time seems to have attached no importance to the distinction between instinct and habit. See also Herbert Feigl, "Validation and Vindication: An Analysis of the Nature and Limits of Ethical Arguments," in *Readings in Ethical Theory*, ed. W. Sellars and J. Hospers (New York, 1952), p. 673; and also Mario Bunge, *Intuition and Science* (Englewood Cliffs, N.J., 1962).

[30] See, for instance, the investigations of Alexander Koyré in *Galilean Studies* (Sussex, 1975), and the same author's *Newtonian Studies* (London, 1965), passim. See also Charles Coulston Gillispie, *The Edge of Objectivity: An Essay in the History of Scientific Ideas* (Princeton, 1960).

[31] Cf. Nelson Goodman, *Fact, Fiction, and Forecast* (London, 1954), pp. 94 ff., where a methodology is developed involving the favoring of deeply rooted predicates.

[32] Cf. section 2 above.

no conclusions possessing high information content may be inferred. Truths of reason, the negations of which are contradictory, and insights into essences that take the form of definitions are not able to lead to conclusions that are useful for the explanation of real relationships. Incidentally, for logic itself, for the discipline, that is to say, in which the deductive procedures employed in cognition are codified, it is of course also possible to raise the problem of foundation,[33] although the fact that logic makes no claim for material knowledge appears to make the solution of the problem easier.

The theories that are of interest for the interpretation of reality are, contrary to what the classical doctrine suggests, not revelations of reason but rather inventions, constructions—in other words, products of the imagination, no matter whether they are collections of true or false statements, or whether they possess greater or lesser truth content. Theory formation is a creative activity, not a passive contemplation mirroring "givens." But for that very reason, constant criticism and checks are necessary in order to eliminate errors of theoretical thought. Revelations may suggest their own certainty; constructs, on the other hand, make no claim to be final or unrevisable.

The empiricist version of classical epistemology underestimates speculation. This is particularly evident in the way in which it tends fundamentally to replace speculation with inductive inferences from the results of accurate observation. Only through sense perception, the empiricist claims, is immediate access to reality, and thus to certainty, possible.

Theories are considered valueless if not based upon sense perception, inductively derived from perceptual data. But, as Hume recognized long ago, this process of inference—induc-

---

[33] Cf. Herbert Feigl, "Validation and Vindication," pp. 672 ff., and Imre Lakatos, "Infinite Regress and Foundation of Mathematics," in *Proceedings of the Aristotelian Society*, Supplementary Volume 36 (London, 1962), in which on pp. 168 ff. the role of *logical intuition* in foundationalism is analyzed.

tion—is a fiction.[34] Let us assume for the moment that the experiential basis of induction is present and unproblematical and that we have at our disposal a set of serviceable singular propositions expressing the results of empirical observation. To move from this starting point to general laws by an inductive process would require a principle of induction to permit such inferences, for deductive logic, as is well known, can do no such thing. Since such a principle cannot be analytic and cannot emerge in the form of a rule from an analytical statement, it must have a synthetic character; but if one demands an inductive foundation for every synthetic statement, this leads to an insoluble problem.[35] At this point in the process of grounding the principle of induction, we fall into the previously outlined Münchhausen trilemma, so that the only practicable possibility is to break off the process at a particular point. But that involves an a priori attitude incompatible with the empiricist position; and it makes no difference whether one is disposed to fall back on deductive or inductive methods in order to justify the principle. One cannot base theories upon observation without a principle of induction because such theories always go beyond existing observations, in that they exclude certain states of affairs for all possible spatio-temporal areas;[36] and they do this in such a way as to involve counterfactual conditionals. Thus they transcend all immediate experiences and their linguistic correlates. For that very reason they are able to explain observable facts and even lead to the prediction of hitherto unknown facts. Indeed, successful theory building can even have a *counterinductive* character; that is to say, it can lead to theoretical statements that call into question prior observations,[37] reveal them as mistakes, or show their formulation to be the result of misinterpretation.

---

[34] Cf. David Hume, *A Treatise on Human Nature* (1738), vol. 1, book 1, part 3, section 6, "Of the Inference from the Impression to the Idea."

[35] Karl Popper has demonstrated in chapter 1 of his *Logic of Scientific Discovery* that this problem leads to a dilemma between an infinite regress and apriorism.

[36] Cf. *Logic of Scientific Discovery*, chapters 3 and 4, and appendix 10.

[37] Cf. Karl R. Popper, "Die Zielsetzung der Erfahrungswissenschaft," in

Thus, we come to the so-called factual basis of induction, the alleged certainty of which is supposed to show its suitability to be the basis for the justification of theories. That derivation from sense perception can afford no guarantee of truth is demonstrated by the fact that theories based upon such perceptions have again and again proved false. Occasionally it is even possible to demonstrate contradictions between observation statements made by one and the same person,[38] and it is well known that different observers can come to differing conclusions. Furthermore, perceptions themselves tend to a great degree to be theory-determined and theory-directed.[39] This means, among other things, that under the influence of prevailing theories, observational habits and predispositions can be formed that favor the production of observational results that support those theories—a possibility to which we shall return.[40] Moreover, it is by no means necessary for this effect that the theoretical elements involved should be dominant in our consciousness.[41] It is precisely the

---

*Theorie und Realität*, ed. Hans Albert (Tübingen, 1964), pp. 79 ff.; Paul K. Feyerabend, "Problems of Empiricism," in *Beyond the Edge of Certainty*, ed. Robert G. Colodny (Englewood Cliffs, N.J., 1965), pp. 152 ff. and passim; Joseph Agassi, "Sensationalism," *Mind*, vol. 75 (1966), p. 10 and passim.

[38] Cf. the reference to experiments by Tranekjaer-Rasmussen in Paul K. Feyerabend, "Das Problem der Existenz theoretischer Entitäten," in *Probleme der Wissenschaftstheorie. Festschrift für Viktor Kraft*, ed. Ernst Topitsch (Vienna, 1960), p. 55, and his analysis of those experiments.

[39] We know today from psychological research that perception *depends on its context* and that *cognitive factors* are also part of the context—factors that are customarily referred to as "set," "expectancy," "hypotheses," etc. Cf., e.g., William N. Dember, *The Psychology of Perception* (New York/Chicago/San Francisco/Toronto/London, 1960), pp. 271 ff. and passim. The familiar Whorf hypothesis about the influence of the linguistic framework may be regarded, as Dember states, as a special case of the more general thesis concerning the relationship of set and perception; see pp. 290 ff. For an analysis of the epistemological significance of such facts, see Alfred Bohnen, "Zur Kritik des modernen Empirismus. Beobachtungssprache, Beobachtungstatsachen und Theorien," *Ratio*, vol. 11 (1969), reprinted in the 2d ed. of Hans Albert (ed.), *Theorie und Realität* (Tübingen, 1972).

[40] Cf., int. al., Thomas S. Kuhn, *The Structure of Scientific Revolution* (Chicago, 1962), passim.

[41] The fact that in our perception we always operate implicitly with "as-

person who is at pains, in the manner of classical inductivism, to construct a theory-free basis of observation in order to later inductively formulate theories who will not infrequently make observations confirming his implicit prejudices.[42] Observations and the statements resulting from them are not merely invariably selective: they contain as well an interpretation corresponding to more or less explicit theoretical points of view. Such points of view must be developed and elaborated if one wishes to assess the relevance of the observations, to devise interesting experiments, or to produce observations that run counter to theory. Observation, measurement, and experiment are without doubt important elements of the scientific process, but not as a means of providing a firm basis for the inductive acquisition and founding of theories, as sources of guaranteed truth. Rather, they are means for criticizing and thus running a check on theoretical conceptions.

---

sumptions" is shown very clearly when we look at pictures that are constructed so that the assumptions mobilized by their components contradict one another; cf. E. H. Gombrich, "Illusion and Visual Deadlock," in his volume of essays, *Meditations on a Hobby Horse and Other Essays on the Theory of Art* (London, 1963); see also idem, *Art and Illusion: A Study in the Psychology of Pictorial Representation*, 2d ed. (New York, 1961), in which a theory of art is developed that takes account of modern psychology of perception and has interesting consequences for art history.

[42] It is well known that at the same time that the modern natural sciences were being constructed, a systematic *demonology* developed that had an inductive foundation and was in fact widely regarded as a genuine science; cf. Trevor-Roper, "The European Witch-Craze," in which he shows that this "theory" played a part in the manufacture of the proof supporting it, with the result that an effective refutation appears extraordinarily difficult; see also Paul K. Feyerabend, *Knowledge without Foundations* (Oberlin, Ohio, 1961), pp. 20 ff.

# TWO

## The Idea of Criticism

### 5. OVERCOMING DOGMATISM: THE PRINCIPLE OF CRITICAL EXAMINATION

CLASSICAL methodology, as expressed in the epistemology of classical rationalism in both its intellectualist and empiricist variants, as we have seen, was based upon a methodological version of the principle of sufficient reason—on the idea, that is, that every view, every conviction, every belief must be justified through reference to positive, certain grounds, to an unshakable foundation. In order to avoid circularity or infinite regress, however, it was necessary to fall back upon some kind of ultimate and indubitable "givens," the certainty of which can best be made plausible by invoking their revelatory character. The process of justification must find its dogmatic conclusion in something indubitable. There the difficulty immediately arises that precisely this fundamental methodological postulate of the classical theory justifies calling into question any hitherto-attained Archimedean point, and with it the basis of the whole procedure.[1] It does not help to refer to the revelatory character of certain insights; for the investigator must in the end simply decide whether he is prepared to acknowledge certain presumed insights as revelations. Whether it concerns divine, supernatural evidence, or natural revelations

---

[1] See William Warren Bartley III's *The Retreat to Commitment*, which analyzes the problem of the foundation regress. See also Franz Kröner, *Die Anarchie der philosophischen Systeme* (Leipzig, 1929), which I did not see until after completing the manuscript for the present book. In his book Kröner carries out a systematological investigation concerning the problems of philosophical pluralism, the incompleteness of philosophical systems, and the foundation of such systems. In so doing he reduces *ad absurdum* the fiction of a secure basis and the claim to completeness found in many philosophical conceptions.

through reason or sense, such an acknowledgment is always a judgment that incorporates the relevant insights into a wider context, and thus suspends their function as first principles. Within the bounds of a foundationalist methodology, it is simply impossible to consider the interruption of the procedure at a certain point as anything but arbitrary.

The dogmatic character of the classical model of rationality is not as harmless as one might have thought. In our discussion of the two versions of classical epistemology we have already determined that the dogmatizing of intuitive insights and direct sense perceptions which occurs in these views tends to fix knowledge at whatever stage it has attained, thus defending it against fundamentally new insights. That means, among other things, the inhibition of scientific advances, which frequently are established in counterintuitive and counterinductive ways—that is, through radical alteration of our usual modes of thought and perception. Orientation toward the classical foundationalist postulate therefore leads de facto to a preference for conservative strategies. If we now draw a conclusion from our earlier discussions, we can proceed from a proposition that may sound fairly radical but nonetheless concisely summarizes the essential criticism of the classical model of rationality and its underlying quest for certainty: the proposition that *all certainties in knowledge are self-made, and thus worthless for comprehending reality*. In other words, through *dogmatization* we can at any point achieve certainty, by *immunizing* any particular component of our convictions *against every possible criticism*, thus *securing it from the risk of failure*. Such an immunity is of course not a necessary characteristic of certain components of convictions, as is suggested by the application of the model of revelation to epistemological problems. Rather, it is attainable at any point, if one is prepared to apply the appropriate procedures, and we may thus proceed at any time. That which is postulated as necessary by classical methodology—though with respect to different components of knowledge— and by the various theological epistemologies is thus revealed de facto as a general possibility of thought, the realization of which is subject to our free choice. The very fact that classical intellectualism believed it unnecessary to acknowledge the certainty of sense perception, while classical empiricism considered it possible to reject the certainty of intuitive insights of reason as irrelevant to knowledge, illustrates this freedom. Such freedom constitutes an embarrassment for any system of thought oriented toward the idea of justification.

Above all others, Hugo Dingler saw that the certainty of the ultimate foundation required by the regress of justification can and must be established essentially through our own decision, and he took this into consideration in his philosophy, which remained within the framework of the classical conception of rationality[2] but renounced the model of revelation. In his theory the role of the indubitable final "given" was explicitly replaced by the will as legislator: "If one *wishes* ultimate certainty," he said "then the only possibility is to wrest it from the *will*."[3] This position incorporates the important insight that all certainty in cognition is self-made. Dingler attempted to base logic on the desire for unambiguous

[2] Dingler expressly proclaims the problem of certainty as the central problem of thought; cf., e.g., his book *Grundriss der methodischen Philosophie. Die Lösungen der philosophischen Hauptprobleme* (Füssen, 1949), p. 8. In his book *Der Zusammenbruch der Wissenschaft und der Primat der Philosophie* (Munich, 1926), pp. 18 ff., he has dealt as follows with the foundation chain: "Under these circumstances, of course, as soon as the idea of such a foundation chain had been grasped, the following questions had to arise: (1) Where does this chain of foundations end? (2) How is the last (or better, the next to last) of these foundations itself founded in its certainty? (Or, ultimately the first, on which all else depends?) The second question, which actually includes the first, is *the central question of philosophy*." Or certainly, of all philosophy that acknowledges the postulate of adequate foundation. In Dingler's *Philosophie der Logik und Arithmetik* (Munich, 1931), we find, as has already been mentioned, our Münchhausen trilemma; but he has *not recognized* it as a *trilemma*. Dingler, too, mentions the breaking-off of the process at a particular point as the only practicable possibility, but he describes this resolution as an act of will, instead of considering it the acknowledgment of a self-revealing ultimate "given."

[3] Dingler, *Philosophie der Logik und Arithmetik*, p. 23.

41

concept formation by replacing the fundamental laws of logic with a demand for unequivocal meaning.[4] He wished thereby to construct "a completely closed system of rational mastery and manipulation of being,"[5] which proceeded from unambiguous directives for action, and onto which all systematic sciences would eventually be grafted. In this system only "the free, self-legitimizing will" could be considered as the final validating ground, not only for concept formation, but also for the necessary activities of realization.[6] Through the procedure he called "exhaustion"[7] it could be brought about that the "laws" of this system need never be revised. Through "realization"—that is, production by planned activities—they would be incorporated into reality, fixed and wrung out—"exhausted"—so that eventually the result of experiments appropriate to them could be logically inferred from conditions producible at any time. The absolute certainty of such laws of nature derives from their analytic character;[8] their usefulness, from the replicability of the relevant experimental conditions. They do not speak to the character of reality as such.

Thus the foundationalism of the classical model of rationality, which originally aimed at making knowledge secure by linking truth and certainty, leads in the last analysis to this: that in order to achieve absolute certainty, one must sacrifice

[4] Ibid., pp. 21 ff. and p. 24. The basic laws of logic are to be taken here in the sense of traditional logic, meaning principles of identity, contradiction, and excluded middle. These three principles represent a genuine basic science to him, "insofar as they are taken as practical directives for action in generating clear concepts" (p. 62).

[5] Cf. Hugo Dingler, *Das System. Das philosophisch-rationale Grundproblem und die exakte Methode der Philosophie* (Munich, 1930), pp. 16 ff. and passim.

[6] For an attempt to generate geometry from "the point of view of construction," see Hugo Dingler, *Die Grundlagen der Geometrie. Ihre Bedeutung für Philosophie, Mathematik, Physik und Technik* (Stuttgart, 1932).

[7] Cf. Hugo Dingler, *Die Grundlagen der Physik. Synthetische Prinzipien der mathematischen Naturphilosophie*, 2d ed. (Berlin and Leipzig, 1923), pp. 133 ff.

[8] Cf. Dingler, *Grundriss der methodischen Philosophie*, p. 50, where this is expressly dealt with.

realism, and with it the idea of informative truth; for analytic sentences are indeed, as is well known, "necessarily" true, but they do not describe reality. Radical application of the principle of sufficient—and hence certain—justification thus leads to the *substitution of decision for knowledge*. "All production of science and so-called knowledge," said Dingler, "consists, according to nature, . . . of actions. Thus all sciences must have their ultimate basis in the theory of action, and thereby in ethics."[9] Even if one does not accept Dinglerian a priorism—which could, with some justification, be termed an epistemological "decisionism"; he himself called it "decernism" to distinguish it from other forms of conventionalism—one could admit that Dingler carries the development of the classical conception of rationality to a consistent conclusion. Precisely through the dominance of decision in this doctrine the crucial problem of the role of decision in the knowing process is accentuated. The influence of the revelation model had hitherto obscured the considerable role played by decision at many stages of this process.

The radicalization of the foundationalist position in Dingler's doctrine calls into question the entire classical conception of rationality. At the same time, it makes us aware that a fundamental decision in favor of the methodological postulate of sufficient justification is at stake, determining the whole construction of science, its ideal, and its program, and that this decision can in principle be made otherwise. In the face of so important a choice it might be well to consider anew the problematic which lies at its root. In order to do so, let us assume for the moment that the Dinglerian process of exhaustion can be generally carried out.[10] Then the question

[9] Dingler, *Die Philosophie der Logik und Arithmetik*, p. 32. It should be noted that he is speaking expressly here about *so-called* knowledge, and rightly so, when one considers that he restricts science to pragmatically justified analytical statements.

[10] See also Popper, *Logic of Scientific Discovery*, p. 12 and pp. 47 ff., where he concedes that Dingler's program is capable of being carried out, but nevertheless objects to it substantially. Viktor Kraft, in his critique of con-

arises of what considerations can be adduced for or against
a decision in the Dinglerian sense, and what alternatives are
available. An important consideration here might well be this:
that a method whose objective is to save the constructs of
human thought at all costs offers no opportunity for the reality
to which these constructs refer to have a decisive influence.
So a substantive alternative to the Dinglerian view might consist in finding suitable methodological principles for the possible overthrow of our theoretical constructions when confronted with reality.[11] If we provide an occasion for our
convictions—and with them the theoretical constructs in which
they are embodied—to confront the resistance of the real world,
then it becomes possible to check their truth content, and to
come closer to the truth by correcting our errors. To do that
we must sacrifice the drive for certainty which lies at the root
of the classical doctrine, and accept the price of permanent
uncertainty about whether our theories will continue to be
confirmed, and thus maintained, in the future.

The development of the classical view has made perfectly
clear that the drive for certainty and the search for truth are
in the end mutually exclusive unless one is content with empty
truth. Through its radicalization of foundationalism, Dingler's
position, which develops out of this view, shows the basically

ventionalism—cf. his book *Mathematik, Logik und Erfahrung* (Vienna, 1947),
pp. 79 ff.—expressed misgivings about the general practicability of this method;
but if one wishes to adhere to it, one can always point out, of course, that
the discovery of appropriate ad hoc assumptions to explain deviations can
easily go wrong on occasion, without thereby making it necessary to reject
the whole procedure, for the use of other procedures in science does not
always immediately lead to success, either. Thomas S. Kuhn, in his book,
*The Structure of Scientific Revolutions*, supports the view that a science
normally—i.e., in a normal phase—remains within the framework of a paradigm, and his description of the investigators' avoidance of questioning the
dominant theory—the relevant paradigm—amounts to nothing more or less
than the application of an exhaustion method in Dingler's sense.

[11] It is probably not necessary to emphasize that here I am now speaking
of the methodology developed by Popper in *The Logic of Scientific Discovery*
in debate with other views, and expanded in later works.

*pragmatic character of all dogmatization*, and the fact that in classical rationalism the desire for certainty overpowers the will to knowledge. Moreover, behind the dogmatizing of components of our convictions there frequently lurks a determination to maintain our theories, regardless of what objections might be raised against them, and regardless, too, of what reality might be. In general, we do not admit—and often, indeed, do not even see—that immunity to criticism of a system or statement is not an advantage so far as knowledge is concerned. On the contrary, it is a considerable disadvantage, no matter what one thinks of the pragmatic value of certainty. The realization that all certainty in knowledge is self-made and thus radically subjective and without value for the comprehension of reality—that one can produce certainty at will, should one decide to immunize the relevant conviction against all possible objections—this realization undermines the cognitive value of every dogma, and the methodological value of every strategy of dogmatization. This, as we will see, has very wide-ranging consequences, not only for science, but for all other areas of societal life.

Let us review again the situation that arises once one questions the acceptability of the fundamental decision in favor of the classical principle of justification. One might say that so-called *ultimate presuppositions* or *highest principles* are at stake, so that rational discussion is in this case completely preluded; one must simply decide for or against the principle in question. Only after this decision can a rational discussion be conducted about the problems of the further stages, for what is initially at stake is accepting or rejecting a fundamental conception of rationality; in other words: *de principiis non disputandum*. Now, it is certainly possible to decide to accept a certain statement or demand as a first presupposition and thus remove it from discussion. So one could, without hindrance, treat the classical principle of sufficient justification this way. Because of the obviously fundamental nature of the principle, this might seem a particularly plausible move in this case. On the other hand, one might equally well hold the view that precisely those principles that are basic and important need rational discussion the most. But since we know that one can dogmatize practically any thesis, that one can *make* any point in our belief-space into an Archimedean point, it is probably worthwhile to inquire next whether this procedure is either necessary or appropriate here.

That it is necessary to proceed thus can be refuted in the easiest possible way—that is, by in fact proceeding quite otherwise. Thus in the present discussion we may suspend the principle of sufficient justification as the highest principle, seeking other alternatives and keeping an eye out for superordinate viewpoints from which to judge the relevant principle. We can accomplish all that, in fact, without difficulty. That dogmatization of the principle, at least in this context, is not appropriate is seen from the fact that we decided to evaluate it and hence not to treat it for the moment as an ultimate presupposition. Considerations relevant to this evaluation have already emerged from our analysis up to this point. We have seen that the consistent application of the idea of foundations—the idea of positive justification—eventuates in difficulties, mainly because in order to attain certainty, one must be prepared to renounce to that degree an approach to truth. But if foundationalism is replaced with the *idea of critical examination*, of critical discussion of all statements that come in question with the help of rational argument, then indeed we will have to give up self-produced certainties; but we gain the prospect of ever more closely approximating truth—though without ever attaining certainty—through trial and error, through tentative construction of testable theories and critical discussion of them in the light of relevant points of view. We may assume that defenders of foundationalism generally began with the assumption that one can combine the search for truth and the desire for certainty. For them, consequently, the principle of justification was relatively unproblematic. But in the course of development of the classical conception of rationality, difficulties arose that render this view problematic, and thereby radically alter the epistemological problem situation. In such a case, the Popperian postulate of critical examination and the methodology based upon it offer an alternative which, from the point of view of knowledge, ought to be preferred.

This solution to the problem has the further advantage that the above-mentioned Münchhausen trilemma does not arise, for this trilemma stems solely from the search for an Archimedean point. The method of critical examination, which supplants that of sufficient justification, can come to terms with the fact that there is no such Archimedean point save one that is self-produced. And then it is worthless. Thus the trilemma is overcome by proceeding from a different conception of the whole problem situation. The new solution avoids the difficulties that were unsurmountable for those earlier foundationalist attempts. The solution lies in demoting the principle of justification from its status as a dogma—or, if you prefer, as self-evident—to a *hypothesis* to be examined,[12] and then confronting it with an alternative hypothesis, the principle of examination.

The new concept of rationality embodied in the principle of critical examination differs from the classical doctrine principally in that it does not necessitate recourse to any dogma whatsoever, and does not allow the dogmatization of answers of any sort—of metaphysical or scientific theories, of ethical systems, historical theses, or practical and thus also political proposals. Simultaneously all claims for the *infallibility* of any court of appeal are rejected in favor of a thoroughgoing *fallibilism*. Anyone who attributes infallibility to any particular court of appeal—to reason, intuition, or experience; to consciousness; to will or feeling; to a person, a group, or class of persons, such as particular officeholders—claims that this authority could never err in the relevant respects.[13] That claim goes considerably further than the thesis that this authority

---

[12] It goes without saying that the word "hypothesis" is used here in a wider sense than is customary.

[13] Cf. Richard Robinson, *An Atheist's Values* (Oxford, 1964), pp. 207 ff.

de facto, in a particular case and with greater or less certainty, expressed the truth, and thus in the case actually did not err. The thesis of infallibility, accordingly, is meaningful only when applied to a general class of cases. It affirms the impossibility of error for a specific authority under specified circumstances and thus goes much further than the dogmatizing of certain statements, demands, or decisions, for it implies the dogmatizing of *all* members of a specific class of statements. Every *infallibilism* is thus a heightened form of *dogmatism*. A thoroughgoing *criticism*, on the other hand, which allows no dogmas, necessarily involves a fallibilism with respect to every possible authority. Classical rationalism elevated certain courts of appeal—reason, or the senses—to epistemological authorities, trying thereby to make them infallible and thus immune to criticism, since otherwise the goal of certain foundations seemed unattainable. But critical rationalism cannot allow infallibility for any authority, nor the right of dogmatization of any particular problem solutions. There is no conclusion, no authority appropriate to the solution of particular problems, which must from the outset be protected from criticism. One might even go so far as to suggest that authorities to which such an immunity to criticism is attributed are often honored in this way because their answers have little prospect of withstanding criticism, should it be allowed. The more strongly such a demand is emphasized, the more the suspicion seems justified that behind it stands fear of the exposure of errors, and that is also the fear of truth. We will return to these topics.

## 6. Context of Justification and Context of Discovery: The Character of Methodology

The principle of critical examination, like the principle of sufficient justification, can be expressed as a general postulate to be invoked wherever solutions to problems are sought. To begin, however, it is appropriate to scrutinize the consequences of this principle for the theory of science, for in this realm there are relatively well-developed and detailed suggestions for the methodological conquest of interesting questions. After all, the sciences are the sphere of human life in which the principle of critical examination has hitherto been most consistently applied in practice. Freedom from dogmatism is taken for granted, at least in the central scientific disciplines, although that of course does not preclude the occasional deviation from this norm. In their commentaries, theory of knowledge and theory of science often seem to lag behind the actual practices of scientific life.

Although in today's theory of science a consistently critical point of view is beginning to prevail, it nonetheless still displays traits that appear intelligible only within the framework of classical foundationalism. Among them are the theoretical monism which is often, at least implicitly, present; the emphasis on the axiomatic method, by which one can develop and justify a privileged theory; and in general an emphasis on the static, the structural, and formal aspects of knowledge, at the expense of its dynamic aspects, which means ignoring developments, conflicts, and the need to choose between alternatives, which are as much a matter of course in science as in other realms of societal life. A methodology of critical examination, however, cannot have as its object merely abetting scientific practice in the justification and confirmation of already dominant views. Instead, it must presume that it is more important to further critical evaluation and revision of such views, to facilitate the advancement of knowledge.

One might object that this is a purely pragmatic point of view, to which theory of science, as a theoretical—as, indeed, a formal—discipline, ought not be subjected; but to that there is a relatively simple answer: theory of science insofar as it is directed to solving *methodological* problems can be no more *neutral* than moral philosophy.[14] One could of course develop a philosophy of science that is neutral, one that is restricted

---

[14] For a critique of the neutrality thesis endemic in analytical thought, cf., e.g., Joseph Agassi, "Epistemology as an Aid to Science: Comment on Dr. Buchdahl's Paper," *The British Journal for the Philosophy of Science*, vol. 10 (1959), pp. 135 ff. See also my essay, "Ethik und Meta-Ethik. Das Dilemma der analytischen Moralphilosophie," mentioned above.

to attempts to analyze and clarify the factual relations in the realm of scientific life, including the actual practices, customs, and habits of representatives of the sciences. But this philosophy would be nothing more than a sociological discipline, a sociology of science in a sense that already exists. It would not be a methodology in the sense required by our discussion.[15]

In order to distinguish these two disciplines and the problematic complexes treated by each, it has become customary to distinguish between the *context of justification* and the *context of discovery* of scientific knowledge.[16] This distinction may in fact be of some use here, although this way of expressing it is misleading in several ways. It suggests, on one hand, the acceptability of the idea of foundations, and on the other hand, the identification of heuristics and psychology, and thus intimates that psychological problems, social circumstances, and factual matters in general are methodologically uninteresting—a view that is quite explicit in the formalism currently dominating philosophy of science. Three things are to be noted:

1. Critical rationalism is not concerned with the justification of statements or systems of statements, even in the so-called context of justification; but rather with their critical examination and evaluation.

2. After the idea of foundations has been abandoned, the problem of heuristics can no longer be excluded from methodology—even though one particular presupposition often made in connection with the treatment of heuristic prob-

[15] The investigations of Kuhn in *The Structure of Scientific Revolutions* have a largely historico-sociological character. Cf., on the other hand, Karl R. Popper's criticism of methodological naturalism in his above-mentioned *Logic of Scientific Discovery*, as well as Viktor Kraft's plea for a critically normative concept of knowledge in his *Erkenntnislehre* (Vienna, 1960).

[16] Cf. Hans Reichenbach, *Experience and Prediction: An Analysis of the Foundations and the Structure of Knowledge* (Chicago, 1938), pp. 3 ff. His distinction corresponds more or less to that previously drawn between *quaestio facti* and *quaestio juris*.

lems has been shown to be untenable: the assumption that there must be a secure route to discovering knowledge.

3. All relevant aspects of the human cognitive situation, including the factual relations that play a role in that situation, must be taken into consideration in methodology, and that means that a usable scientific method may not, for example, be constructed on a utopian basis.

The concentration of modern investigations in philosophy of science on the analysis of formal relations between statements of different types has created the impression that theory of science, even in the factual sciences, is nothing more or less than an application, or even a part, of formal logic, including the relevant portions of mathematics and some components of the semantics of nonnatural languages. Now, there is no reason to object to the thesis that logic and mathematics play an important role in philosophy of science. But to narrow the focus exclusively to these elements, as is characteristic of the formalistic tendency, is another matter. However important logical relations of all sorts might be for the evaluation of scientific statements, a meaningful analysis and criticism of knowledge is quite impossible if one neglects the extralinguistic context in which these statements occur. To this context belong not only the factual matters to which the relevant propositions refer, but also those that characterize the circumstances and relationships of human cognitive activity. This includes not only the activities of thought and observation in isolated individuals, but also critical discussion as a pattern of social interaction, and the institutions that support or weaken, advance or hinder it. Thus it is not formal logic alone that is of interest, but the logic of science as a social institution as well.

In our criticism of classical epistemology we encountered theses that transcend pure logical relations, as, for example, our discussions of some of the vacuum fictions contained within that doctrine, such as the fiction of the existence of context-independent observations and unprejudiced intuitions, or the utopian postulate of the elimination of all prejudices. One might be tempted to fasten upon exactly this point and declare that it is just the application of psychological ideas to the solution of epistemological problems which is the *proton pseudos* of such theories and that the point is completely to exclude considerations of this sort from epistemology or scientific theory in favor of formal and semantic analyses. But that would be a very dubious and hasty way of coping with this problem, for it would mean that one, say, as an empiricist, would have to declare methodologically irrelevant the problematic of the human activity of observing, or as an intellectualist, problems of the human activity of thinking; thus it would be exceedingly difficult to make explicit the difference between the two views. Furthermore, there would still be no escape from the possible application of the results of linguistics to particular considerations, at least as long as one is occupied with linguistic facts, which is practically impossible to avoid. Once the epistemological relevance of pragmatic relations is admitted, in the sense of the common contemporary distinction between syntax, semantics, and pragmatics, then the narrowing of the focus of theory of science, mentioned above, disposes of itself.

An analysis of the classical problem of justification alone reveals the necessity of going beyond formal relations and paying more attention to pragmatic points of view. The same is true of the attempt to overcome classical foundationalism by the application of the idea of criticism. The choice between the principle of sufficient justification and the principle of critical examination is a pragmatic choice which must be made with due consideration of logical relationships, among other things. That the problem of rationality is not only a formal, but also a pragmatic, problem, by no means implies that in solving it one can restrict oneself to the analysis of factual relations in the realm of scientific life, or to attempts to explain such relations, as a sociology of science might. The primary task to be accomplished here is the determination of scientific method, a method that has not only formal but also factual— e.g., social—aspects, as we shall see. Elaboration of a method of critical examination then demands, above and beyond attention to formal considerations, attention to linguistic and other factual relations that are relevant to human problem-solving behavior. Incorporation of pragmatic considerations, however, does not mean sanctioning the naturalistic fallacy in philosophy of science, arguing from factual statements concerning the sciences to normative statements in this realm, but only requires attention to human possibilities in developing a methodology of human knowledge. Methodology is in principle nothing but a fundamental technology for problem solving, which is oriented on certain normative points of view—on values that are connected with the human striving for knowledge of reality and for truth. The adoption of any specific method, including the method of critical examination, involves a moral decision,[17] for it signifies the adoption of a methodological praxis with many consequences for social life. It is of great importance not only for theory building—the formulation, elaboration, and testing of theories—but also for their application, and thus for the role of knowledge in society. The model of rationality found in the critical point of view is the sketch of a way of life, a social practice, and therefore has ethical, even political, import. It is not an exaggeration, but the identification of a simple and easily understood relation, when one points out that the principle of critical examination establishes, among others, a connection between logic and politics.

If we now return to the distinction between context of discovery and context of justification, we may conclude that so far as our investigations are concerned it is only usable if combined with the rejection of methodological naturalism and a transcendence of the methodological formalism that is often connected with it. The methodology of science can contribute

---

[17] Cf. Karl R. Popper, *The Open Society and Its Enemies* (Princeton, 1950), p. 243: "Ethics is not a science, but although there is no rational scientific basis of ethics, there is an ethical basis of science, and of rationalism." In chapter 23 of the book is to be found, incidentally, an analysis of the social aspects of the scientific method. Dingler, too, recognizes an ethical basis of science; cf. his *Philosophie der Logik und Arithmetik*, p. 32.

critical points of view for judging scientific practice, and can thereby introduce the practice of a critique that advances the progress of human knowledge by making possible the revision of erroneous views. It formulates the morals of scientific thought and work, though without necessarily using normative sentences.

## 7. DIALECTICAL THINKING: THE SEARCH FOR CONTRADICTIONS

We have seen that the orientation toward the classical idea of justification leads to a preference for conservative strategies in cognitive processes, putting a premium on behavior designed to protect old errors against relevant criticism and innovations, and thereby to conserve them. This hinders the advance of knowledge, which often develops and succeeds in counterintuitive and counterinductive ways, that is, against what had formerly been considered well-grounded truths. A criticist methodology can start from the assumption that the advance of knowledge requires the overcoming of old and well-rooted habits of thought and perception—habits which, according to a psychic and social principle of inertia, have the tendency to respond with resistance to any such alterations, and indeed with a resistance whose strength is directly proportional to the thoroughness and comprehensiveness of the innovation concerned. The demand of classical doctrine, that one must put aside all prejudices before knowledge can begin, initially appears to counter this inertia effect in a particularly radical way; but this is only an illusion. That dictum arises out of a utopian evaluation of the human cognitive situation, one which drastically underestimates the possible positive effect of available presuppositions for the process of cognition.[18]

[18] Cf. Popper, *The Open Society and Its Enemies*, chapter 23, and "On the Sources of Knowledge and Ignorance" in *Conjectures and Refutations*; also Charles Sanders Peirce, "Some Consequences of Four Incapacities," *Journal of Speculative Philosophy* 2 (1868), pp. 140-157; reprinted in vol. 5 of *The Collected Papers of Charles Sanders Peirce*, ed. C. Hartshorne and P. Weiss (Boston, 1934).

So-called prejudices, as they are expressed in habits of thought and dispositions of comprehension, are after all nothing else than theoretical points of view which have been developed in earlier problem-solving behavior—partly in earlier generations—and which form the groundwork for the solution of later problems. The idea that they are false just because they are inherited, whether handed down by tradition or developed in earlier situations, and must therefore be radically rejected is hardly acceptable.[19] It represents a *negative genetic fallacy*. The belief that one can radically purge the mind of prejudices is an illusion, which takes its revenge by the fact that in cognitive enterprises embodying such attempts to purify our belief systems "down to the bare boards," the old presuppositions tend to reappear, but now in the guise of more self-conscious, more self-evident, and thus apparently better grounded truths.[20] The striving after knowledge conducted under the influence of foundationalism then basically is nothing more than an attempt to produce good reasons for old prejudices, to anchor that which one already believes or holds as self-evident even more deeply in thought and action.

The methodology of critical examination must abandon the vacuum fiction of classical epistemology, which does not correspond to the real characteristics of the human learning situation, and replace it with the attempt to make so-called prejudices useful for the advance of knowledge. That means that one should not attempt to eliminate them all—a utopian enterprise, in any case, for one often does not even recognize

[19] Cf. on this problem also Karl R. Popper, "Toward a Rational Theory of Tradition" (1949), in *Conjectures and Refutations*, pp. 120 ff., and my contribution, "Tradition und Kritik," in *Club Voltaire*, II (Munich, 1965), pp. 156 ff.; cf. also P. B. Medawar, "Tradition: The Evidence of Biology," in his volume of essays, *The Uniqueness of the Individual* (London, 1957), pp. 134 ff.

[20] One should think, for example, of Descartes, to whose "universal doubt" Peirce refers in his work; and of the proofs of God or of "transcendental" efforts, which often are only attempts to justify habitual patterns of thought as "necessary," and thus rest on the inconceivability of the unfamiliar—that is, on a lack of imagination.

deep lying prejudices. Nor should one attempt to produce justifications for them, for they can always be found; rather, so far as is possible at any point, one should make them testable, and concern oneself with examining them in view of their consequences. It is a matter, in short, of treating them not as *dogmas*, but as *hypotheses*, which could in principle— in situations that are relevant to their testing—break down, and then so far as is possible, to find or to invent such situations. Not recourse to a final and certain *foundation*, but the search for relevant incompatible instances—that is, the search for *contradictions*—is consequently the necessary recommended route for one who wishes to approach the truth.

If one wishes to specify the *role of logic* in such a process, then one can say that it enters not as an *instrument of positive justification*, but rather as an *organ of criticism*.[21] Accordingly, this methodology is not, like the classical, oriented upon the *principle of sufficient justification*; but rather it is oriented upon a methodological version of the *principle of noncontradiction*, which one could express something like this: search constantly for relevant contradictions in order to expose present convictions to the risk of refutation, so that they will have a chance to prove themselves. This quest is not recommended because contradictions are desired in themselves and must be preserved; nor, indeed, because one can thereby better take into account the contradictory nature of reality; but simply because when relevant contradictions emerge one has occasion, in accordance with the principle of noncontradiction, to revise one's convictions.[22] This principle is applied here in a somewhat roundabout way, that is, not in a way so that every noncontradictory system is considered acceptable—that would be a relatively simple and comfortable situation. But rather,

---

[21] Cf. Karl R. Popper, "Science: Conjectures and Refutations" (1953), reprinted in *Conjectures and Refutations*, pp. 33 ff., p. 64.

[22] Popper has emphasized this point in his criticism of dialectical thought; cf. his essay, "What is Dialectic?" (1940), in *Conjectures and Refutations*, pp. 312 ff.; cf. also Eduard von Hartmann's criticism of Hegel's dialectical method in *Über die dialektische Methode* (Berlin, 1868), pp. 38 ff.

contradictions are explicitly sought in order to force the development of thought. The need for revision results from the fact that one cannot suspend the principle of noncontradiction without generating the extremely unpleasant consequence that any conceivable arbitrary claim would thereby be rendered possible.[23]

If one applies the principle in this way, the resulting method can with some justice be called "dialectical" in a clear and univocal sense that corresponds to an old philosophical tradition.[24] The confusions sown by the philosophical escapades of German idealism under the name of "dialectic"[25] could serve as our excuse if we wished to avoid this word, but it is not necessary to refuse to use it so long as no confusion arises. Pre-Socratic dialectic—more precisely, that of the Eleatic school —already operated with the formulation of "hypotheses" and the so-called method of indirect proof, which was directed

[23] Cf. section 2, chapter 1, above. Freedom from contradiction is in itself merely a logically minimal requirement of knowledge. Consequently a pure coherence theory of truth is inadequate. The demand for freedom from contradiction only becomes methodologically interesting when the active search for ideas and observations that are relevant but incompatible with previous cognitions is incorporated into it.

[24] Cf. Eduard von Hartmann's chapter, "Die Dialektik vor Hegel," pp. 1 ff. Popper's critical philosophy is nothing but a development of this old dialectical method—together with a critique of its degenerate Hegelian form— in which it is revealed that this method is at the same time that of natural science; cf. the early reference in his *Logic of Scientific Discovery*, p. 55, and also his analysis in "Die Zielsetzung der Erfahrungswissenschaft" (1957), reprinted in *Theorie und Realität* (Tübingen, 1964), pp. 73 ff. See also Paul K. Feyerabend's "Problems of Empiricism," in *Beyond the Edge of Certainty*, ed. Robert G. Colodny; Joseph Agassi, "Science in Flux: Footnotes to Popper," in *Boston Studies in the Philosophy of Science*, vol. 3, ed. Robert S. Cohen and Marx W. Wartofsky (Dordrecht, 1967), pp. 293 ff. For a dialectical treatment along these lines of mathematical problems, cf. Imre Lakatos, "Proofs and Refutations," *British Journal for the Philosophy of Science*, vol. 14, nos. 53-56 (1963-1964).

[25] Cf. Ernst Topitsch, *Die Sozialphilosophie Hegels als Heilslehre und Herrschaftsideologie* (Neuwied and Berlin, 1967), and also the pertinent sections of his *Sozialphilosophie zwischen Ideologie und Wissenschaft*, 2d ed. (Neuwied and Berlin, 1966).

toward the derivation of contradictions in order to prove the falsehood of certain claims;[26] this method then found acceptance in mathematical thought. The idea of utilizing methodologically the fact that a valid deductive argument allows a negative truth value to be transferred backward from the conclusion to the premises can be generalized; and, after the principle of sufficient justification has been abandoned, this alternative may be elevated to the basic idea of scientific and, beyond that, of all critical method. This method is dialectic in that it ascribes a great importance to the search for and elimination of contradictions—a procedure that may have developed out of a dialogue or discussion between interlocutors. It is a *negative* method in that what matters in it is not positive *justifiability* and the associated attempts to seek foundations, but rather *refutability* and attempts to find counterexamples—from which, occasionally, a provisional corroboration can result. Of course, the simple elimination of contradictions is not an adequate characterization of this method, for this end is easily attainable in any case if one is prepared to forgo content and explanatory power. What is needed is the capacity to construct theories that are refutable and therefore confirmable, that is, theories that have no characteristics making them epistemologically uninteresting.

It is clear, then, that thinking in the sense of this principle is not, as is the observance of a foundational postulate, suited to conserve convictions and to fix knowledge at the stage it has currently reached. Rather, it aims at overcoming the present state of knowledge and revising established convictions. It is not the justification of the "given" through recourse to

[26] Cf. the works referring to this by Árpád Szabó, "Anfänge des Euklidischen Axiomensystems," in *Zur Geschichte der griechischen Mathematik* (Darmstadt, 1965), pp. 355 ff., and "Greek Dialectic and Euclid's Axiomatics," in *Problems in the Philosophy of Mathematics*, ed. Imre Lakatos (Amsterdam, 1967), pp. 1 ff., where evidence is produced that the method of Greek mathematics, as revealed primarily in Euclidean axiomatics, derives from Pre-Socratic dialectics, a connection not suspected when one listens to post-Hegelians talking about dialectic.

firm foundations that is striven for, but rather for its refutation through the discovery of contradictions. Thus, one can in fact say that here in a very precise sense *dialectic* and *development* hang together; while on the other hand, *axiomatic* thinking of the sort associated with theoretical monism, because it strives for a firm foundation, easily tends to set a premium on the *preservation* of what has already been achieved. In this connection it might be interesting to learn that in Greek mathematics[27] the term "axiom"—like the term "hypothesis"—is of dialectical origin, and that it originally by no means meant indubitable and self-evident truth, nor even "plausible assumption" but simply "claim," which means a statement, "disagreement with which is suspended by the partners in the dialogue"[28]—that is, an assumption for purposes of argument. The axioms of Euclidean geometry, the paradigm of a well-organized system of knowledge that offered for centuries the ideal for the construction of a science, were clearly only later endowed with the claim of indubitable truth, and thereby were dogmatized until the discovery of non-Euclidean geometries once again removed this status. Despite this shock undermining the status of knowledge accepted as certain until that time, the ideal of axiomatization remained until now mostly associated with the idea of justification. It was believed that greater certainty could be expected through a *"deeper grounding of the foundations* of particular areas of knowledge" with the help of the axiomatic method.[29] At least within the narrow confines of mathematics and metamathematics, the ideal of certainty remained for the most part uncontested. Only re-

[27] Cf. Árpád Szabó, "Anfänge des Euklidischen Axiomensystems," pp. 401 ff.

[28] Ibid., p. 405; he comes to the conclusion that in its beginnings deductive mathematics was a special branch of philosophy—more precisely, a special branch of Eleatic dialectics (p. 458).

[29] Cf. David Hilbert, "Axiomatisches Denken" (1918), reprinted in *Hilbertiana* (Darmstadt, 1964), p. 3 and passim; on the criticism of the various programs for the foundation of mathematical knowledge, see Imre Lakatos, "Infinite Regress and Foundations of Mathematics," pp. 165 ff.

cently has fallibilism seemed to encroach upon this area of knowledge, after all foundationalist programs have failed.[30] Mathematics no longer seems to be an island of certainty in a sea of our otherwise fallible knowledge. So we have every reason to consider anew the role of axiomatic thought and the meaning of the axiomatic ideal for the development of all areas of knowledge.

We have been considering the ideal of the axiomatic construction of all science, of its construction as a calculus, in which all logical relations are transparent and controllable. In most cases, behind this ideal stands the fundamentalist view, that through its realization contradictions, differences of opinion, and controversies will once and for all be avoided, that all decisions within the realm of knowledge, or even beyond, can be replaced, so to speak, with calculations—an idea which, as is well known, has played a considerable role in philosophical thought, for instance, in the philosophy of Leibniz[31] and his followers. We have here an epistemological utopia before us, which, in fact, despite the intentions of its defenders, can be seen as a consistent expression of a static model of rationality, a model which is, in essential respects, irreconcilable with the ideal here advocated of a critical and—in the sense specified above—dialectical method. To be sure,

[30] In addition to the essay by Lakatos cited in the previous footnote, see the contribution by László Kalmár, "Foundation of Mathematics—Whither Now?" in *Problems in the Philosophy of Mathematics*, ed. Imre Lakatos (Amsterdam, 1967), pp. 187 ff., and the subsequent discussion.

[31] See, for example Leibniz's statements about his planned *scientia generalis*, linked to a *characteristica realis* in an unfinished work containing the following typical passage: "car cette même écriture seroit une éspèce d'algèbre générale et donneroit moyen de raisonner en calculant, de sorte qu'au lieu de disputer, on pourroit dire: comptons . . . ." ("for this very script would be a species of general algebra, and would provide a means of reasoning by calculating, so that instead of disputing, one could say: let us calculate . . ."); printed in *Die philosophischen Schriften von Gottfried Wilhelm Leibniz*, vol. 7, ed. C. J. Gerhardt (Hildesheim, 1961), p. 26; see also p. 65 of the same volume. Leibniz's idea seems to be the inspiration behind the thought of Bertrand Russell and the neo-positivists.

within the framework of this method, axiomatizations are completely possible as provisional stages of the progress of knowledge, for the obligatory principle of noncontradiction is not abandoned by this method, but rather methodically exploited in a certain way. As we have seen, it is not a question of a dialectic that is supposed to overcome logic, but rather of a dialectic that utilizes logic in ways which serve the advance of knowledge, without thereby starting from the presupposition that meaning, truth, and decidability are inseparable, and that a decision about what is true must always ideally be reached through a kind of calculation, when we have succeeded, that is, in finding the proper basis for such an operation.

## 8. CONSTRUCTION AND CRITICISM: THEORETICAL PLURALISM

When examining the consequences of critical rationalism in the sphere of philosophy of science, one may start from the fact that in scientific thought one is striving for knowledge of the nature of the real world, and thus for theories that possess the greatest possible explanatory power and penetrate as deeply as possible into the structure of reality;[32] and which, we may conjecture, come as close as possible to the truth, although we may never be certain about it. What is important, then, is not the origin of such theories but their efficiency and the possibility of testing them. That means, among other things, that in the framework of a criticist theory of science, the derivation of a theory from a metaphysical conception is not to be regarded as a blemish, particularly since such conceptions—one needs merely think of those of the Pre-Socratics[33]—

[32] Cf. Karl R. Popper, "Die Zielsetzung der Erfahrungswissenschaft," in *Theorie und Realität* (1964) and idem, "Truth, Rationality and the Growth of Scientific Knowledge," in *Conjectures and Refutations*, pp. 215 ff.

[33] Cf. Friedrich Nietzsche, *Philosophy in the Tragic Age of the Greeks*, trans. M. Cowan (Chicago, 1962); also Karl R. Popper, "Back to the Presocratics" (1958), in *Conjectures and Refutations*, pp. 136 ff.

have proven themselves, in part, extraordinarily fruitful from the scientific point of view. Science progresses neither by the derivation of certain truths from self-evident intuitions with the aid of deductive processes, nor through the derivation of such truths from self-evident perceptions using inductive processes: it advances, rather, through speculation and rational argumentation, through construction and criticism. In both respects metaphysical conceptions may acquire importance by providing counterintuitive and counterinductive ideas in order to break our usual habits of thought and perception and to sketch alternative possible explanations for real relationships, thus facilitating a critical evaluation of previous convictions.[34] In contrast to such a constructive and critical metaphysics, a dogmatic metaphysics, developed either merely to preserve the status quo of scientific thought or to cut itself off completely from scientific thought in order to preserve, untouched, a world picture immunized against all possible results of research of whatever kind, renders no service to science, nor to knowledge of any sort. Now that the positivist's theses of meaninglessness have turned out to be questionable, it is advisable to put the connection between science and metaphysics into the right light, as well as the factual significance of philosophical speculation for knowledge. It is not a question of evaluating metaphysical conceptions per se as a whole, but merely of seeing the relevant distinctions between them so as to have the chance of exploiting their speculative and critical potential for the advance of knowledge.

If it is important to develop theories that are as comprehensive as possible and possess great explanatory power, then

[34] With regard to the starting point of modern natural science, the scientific revolution of the seventeenth century, Alexandre Koyré has pointed out the great importance of metaphysical ideas, with whose aid the old cosmos-metaphysics was destroyed, and in its place a metaphysical framework for building the new science was created. See his *Galilean Studies* and his *Newtonian Studies*; see also Edwin Arthur Burtt's interesting book *The Metaphysical Foundations of Modern Physical Science* (London, 1924; 2d ed., London, 1932).

one possible use of metaphysical speculation emerges immediately: for in such speculation comprehensive theories for the interpretation of reality frequently arise, even though in a sketchy form—theories which may be of interest for the formation of scientific theories. They may not be immediately applicable, and thus not testable without further ado, but they nevertheless contain explanatory viewpoints and thus research programs for science that can lead to substantial and testable theories.[35] To this end, of course, it is necessary that one not conceive of metaphysical ideas as intuitive insights possessing an a priori validity, because, for example, they cannot be refuted by facts. Rather, one should endeavor to develop such ideas to theories refutable in principle, which can compete with hitherto accepted scientific theories; for the fact that such conceptions appear to be above competition should doubtless be regarded, in the light of the principle of critical examination, as a defect worth eliminating. On the other hand, this means that all attempts to inhibit the working-out of such conceptions at an embryonic stage of their development— because they do not accord with hitherto well-established theories, for instance—are counterproductive. The fact that metaphysical conceptions cannot be immediately disproved by experience is not an adequate reason for not taking them seriously, particularly when they prove incompatible with scientific theories; for to reject them out of hand would mean leaving the critical potential contained within them unused, and thus declaring the present state of knowledge to be sacrosanct.

This brings us to an important part of the methodology of

[35] Cf. Nietzsche's impressive description in *Philosophy in the Tragic Age of the Greeks*; see also Karl R. Popper, "The Nature of Philosophical Problems and their Roots in Science" (1952), in *Conjectures and Refutations*, pp. 66 ff.; Paul K. Feyerabend, "How to be a Good Empiricist—a Plea for Tolerance in Matters Epistemological"; J.W.N. Watkins, "Confirmable and Influential Metaphysics," *Mind*, vol. 67 (1958), pp. 344 ff.; Gerard Radnitzky, "Über empfehlenswerte und verwerfliche Spielarten der Skepsis," *Ratio* 7 (1965), pp. 109 ff.; Joseph Agassi, "Science in Flux." See also my introduction, "Die ökonomische Tradition im soziologischen Denken" in my volume of essays, *Marktsoziologie und Entscheidungslogik* (Neuwied and Berlin, 1967).

critical testing: *theoretical pluralism.* As we discovered from our critical analysis of the foundation postulate, one can never be certain that a particular theory is true, even when it appears to solve the problems for which it was designed; so it is always worthwhile to *search for alternatives,* for other theories that may be better because they have greater explanatory force, avoid particular errors, or in general overcome difficulties that previous theories were unable to master. As the history of the sciences has shown, every theory has weaknesses of some kind.[36] Particular facts with which it cannot cope must be regarded as anomalies, exceptions, or deviations in the light of its explanatory ideas, however much one hopes, in the long run, to be able to encompass them within the framework of the theory. But one is normally not inclined to abandon a theory totally because of such difficulties, for it at least affords a structuring of problem situations that would otherwise remain unstructured,[37] a frame of reference within which problems and possible solutions may be articulated. "La pensée abhorre le vide; une théorie scientifique ne disparaît que si elle est remplacée par une autre."[38] But it is of course by no

[36] This applies also to the sphere of the most advanced sciences; cf. Kuhn's *The Structure of Scientific Revolutions.* No one who knows the subject well will dispute that it applies to the social sciences, e.g., to the theories of the economic tradition with their relatively highly developed internal structure; see also my book, *Marktsoziologie und Entscheidungslogik,* and my essays, "Zur Theorie der Konsumnachfrage," *Jahrbuch für Sozialwissenschaft* 16 (1965), pp. 139 ff., and "Erwerbsprinzip und Sozialstruktur," *Jahrbuch für Sozialwissenschaft* 19 (1968).

[37] We possess a certain amount of information from psychological research concerning the significance of the drive toward the structuring of unstructured situations; cf., e.g., Muzafer Sherif and Carolyn W. Sherif, *An Outline of Social Psychology* (rev. ed., New York, 1956); Muzafer Sherif and Carl I. Hovland, *Social Judgment: Assimilation and Contrast Effects in Communication and Attitude Change* (New Haven and London, 1961); Leon Festinger, "A Theory of Social Comparison Processes," *Human Relations* 7 (1954), pp. 117 ff. That the results of such investigations are also interesting for the theory of science can only be denied by a person who wishes to keep this discipline uncontaminated by any empirical admixtures; this is, of course, the case with the formalism that is so very widespread.

[38] Alexandre Koyré, in "Galilée et la Loi d'Inertie," reprinted in his *Galilean*

means certain that all difficulties may be resolved within the framework of the existing theoretical conceptions, of the old paradigm. In order to overcome anomalies, a radical change in the metaphysical frame of reference may be necessary, such as was effected in the transition from the Aristotelian to the modern image of the world. It is this that gives rise to the constructive and critical role of metaphysics in the progress of knowledge.[39]

If we assume that theories seek to demarcate the range of possible events, then we might conclude that any redefinition of this range by altering the theoretical interpretation means that a certain number of once impossible events become possible, and similarly hitherto possible events are rendered impossible. In this sense, then, a metaphysical conception can assert the *impossible*: that is, it can outline possibilities that, although there is no reason to preclude them from the outset, are not available according to the present state of knowledge. One may assign to critical *metaphysics* the same function with respect to *science* as *utopia* has for *political* thought:[40] just as utopia aims at a radical alteration of the present condition of human society,[41] metaphysics aims at a radical transformation of the present state of knowledge. Both therefore contain a negation of the status quo, a critical potential which, if it is to be exploited, requires the elaboration of a concrete alter-

---

*Studies*, in which he draws attention to the fact that at that time *it was insufficient* to oppose Aristotelian physics with a metaphysics like the bold and radical system of Giodano Bruno. What was needed, in addition, was a new physics based upon such a metaphysical conception.

[39] It is therefore not a valid objection to Marxist sociology or the Marxist epistemological program to suggest that Hegelian metaphysics acted as midwife at their birth, as Robert C. Tucker seems to assume in his interesting book, *Philosophy and Myth in Karl Marx* (Cambridge, Eng., 1961). On the other hand, the retrogression of Marxism to a sterile metaphysical scholasticism in dialectical materialism merits a thoroughly negative verdict from the criticist viewpoint, since what we have here is a classic example of a dogmatic metaphysics.

[40] I am indebted for this hint to Paul Feyerabend.

[41] Cf. Leszek Kolakowski's very instructive description in "Der Sinn des Begriffes 'Linke,' " in his book, *Der Mensch ohne Alternative* (Munich, 1960), pp. 142 ff.

native; for it is no more possible to replace scientific knowledge as it exists at present by a metaphysics than it is to replace the present state of society by one anticipated in a utopia, that is, one constructed in a social vacuum. A metaphysics is made concrete by the working-out of a theoretical alternative, a utopia by the working-out of an institutional alternative.[42] In both cases one needs to be prepared to accept the fact that testing against the resistance of reality compels unpredictable revisions. Any attempt to avoid this critical dialogue with reality—any attempt to attain the perfect state in one leap—leads in both cases to the suppression of criticism and to domination by an inflexible, incorrigible system. Thus it is not merely a matter of exploiting the critical potential of such conceptions; one must also seek to subject them to a realistic critique, to develop them to the point where they have a chance of being shattered by the nature of reality. In the case of a utopia, one should reflect that by using our knowledge of actual relationships we may conduct the test in a way that will keep the costs of a possible failure within reasonable limits.

This consideration returns us to the critical function of thinking in alternatives and, thus, to theoretical pluralism. The methodology of sufficient justification, as has already been said, tends to be bound up with a theoretical monism that from the very outset gives the prevailing theoretical conception such an advantage over other possible—and possibly still undeveloped—alternatives that they are scarcely considered as rivals. Such a methodology is concerned with elaborating and establishing ever more securely the one approved theory. This may in some circumstances involve strengthening the foundations, should they hitherto have proved inadequate, or making minor modifications that help to adapt the theory to reality. As we know, this aim is perfectly attainable if one is ready to bear the costs of the undertaking,[43] which consist

[42] Cf. the final chapter of this book.

[43] Cf. the exhaustion method proposed by Dingler, which is frequently used in scientific practice, as Kuhn's investigations seem to show.

of a diminution of the content and explanatory force of the theory, and its calcification into a rigid, dogmatic metaphysics.[44] All relevant facts are interpreted finally not merely *in the light of*, but also *in the sense of* the particular theory. This may always be done if we introduce appropriate ad hoc assumptions, particularly since the power of theoretical thought to impress its character upon the process of observation is beyond question. From the critical point of view, one may remark here, such theories are withdrawn de facto from the realm of scholarly intercourse, even if they still circulate within the institutional sphere of learning; after all, the institutions of knowledge—universities, research institutes, academies— are in themselves no guarantee of the preservation of critical thought. To a certain extent they protect the sphere of knowledge against outside influences and facilitate a relatively undisturbed scientific discussion; but they cannot always prevent a voluntary renunciation of criticism.

A theoretical monism can thus very easily have the consequence that facts are employed merely to illustrate or support the prevailing theory and are, therefore, interpreted in a manner that conforms to it, while the critical significance of contradicting facts is overlooked. This is connected with what I described above as the *impossibility of a theoretical vacuum*, which seems to follow as a special case from the above-mentioned tendency toward the structuring of unstructured situations. The scientific activity of solving problems depends for its preservation upon the successful structuring of problem situations, and this in its turn requires the existence of a theoretical frame of reference, however inadequate. As a result, in cases where only one theory is present, this almost automatically assumes the function of such a frame of reference. Even if one follows the ideals of critical empiricism and emphasizes the testing of this theory; even if one actively searches for contrary cases, which may even include an attempt to create such cases experimentally; even if diverging facts emerge,

---

[44] Cf. Paul K. Feyerabend, "How to be a Good Empiricist," pp. 3 ff.

it is still almost impossible to avoid continuing to think in terms of this frame of reference. In the absence of alternatives, a theory liable to criticism on the basis of facts that contradict it is nevertheless retained, because there is a need for a frame of reference to articulate those phenomena, situations, and problems for which the theory does afford interpretations and solutions. Where only a single method of structuring is present, it enjoys in some measure the status of a monopoly. So it is not surprising that it is easy to take a negative view of existing criticism, and to overcome difficulties by means of the method of exhaustion.

The methodology of critical examination will then, for this reason, regard as necessary not merely *the search for contrary facts*, but above all the *search for alternative theoretical conceptions*, in order to facilitate the construction and application of competing frames of reference as well as novel solutions to problems. Within the framework of such competing theoretical attempts, it often happens that previously discovered anomalies that have not been theoretically "digested" become significant for the explanation of real events.[45] Further, often it is not until one or more theoretical alternatives are present that it becomes possible to determine or even create situations that are incompatible with the theory in favor and can thus contribute to its collapse.[46] An alternative theory can, for example, lead to experiments that show how phenomena incompatible with the old theory may be produced. An experiment whose result not only calls into question an existing theory but also represents the success of a theoretical alter-

[45] Cf. Kuhn's above-mentioned investigations; J. W. Atkinson's expositions in criticism of the learning theory law of effect within the framework of an expectation theory of behavior in J. W. Atkinson, *An Introduction to Motivation* (Princeton/Toronto/London/New York, 1964), pp. 292 ff.; or the treatment of the Giffen anomaly in economic thought—although the latter is open to certain objections; see my above-mentioned essay on the theory of consumption (note 36).

[46] Cf., e.g., Paul K. Feyerabend, "A Note on the Problem of Induction," *The Journal of Philosophy* 61 (1964), pp. 349 ff.

native has a far greater chance of being seen as a critical instance. In the face of a conception which, in addition to the cases already explained, also explains cases at variance with the accepted theory, and which, moreover, explains, say, why the latter in some situations offers an excellent approximation to the true solution, but in others a more or less striking divergence—in the face of such a theory, it is very difficult to save the old theory from collapse by applying immunizing strategies, for its comparative contribution to knowledge is less. Theoretical pluralism, then, is a means of preventing the dogmatization of theoretical conceptions and their consequent transformation into metaphysical doctrinal structures immune to criticism; and it is here that the *critical* use of alternative metaphysical conceptions can make its contribution.

These are the basic features of that reform of empiricism which proves to be necessary within the framework of criticist philosophy. This reform does not minimize the important role of experience in forming theories, which empiricism has always, with some right, stressed. But it eliminates the dogmatizing of experience, which is the basic danger of empiricist thought, just as the dogmatizing of intuition or reason may be said to be the permanent danger for intellectualism. It does so by taking into account the theoretical imprint—of which we are often only dimly aware—on the so-called facts of experience. It is precisely when this is forgotten that the danger arises of overestimating the autonomy of the factual basis of theoretical thinking, and thus of contributing to the uncritical treatment and the conservation of the very theories whose conceptual apparatus had determined the articulation of that basis. Only when the empiricist myth of the "given" has been eliminated by this means may the critical function of facts in the construction of theories be properly exploited. Paradoxically, this myth—quite contrary to the actual intentions of empiricism—has the effect of withdrawing certain theories from factual testing. In practice, then, it turns the empiricist tendency into its opposite, in just the same way that the intellectualist myth of the "given," which refers to self-evident

69

intuitions, de facto impedes the formulation of theories by favoring, in the last resort, only familiar already existing theories, to the detriment of theoretical speculation and the criticism it makes possible.

With regard both to the forming of theories and the use of observation, our suggested revision overcomes that passivity which, in classical doctrine, dominates the interpretation of the cognitive process. The place of sensible or intellectual intuition is taken by construction and experiment, that is, by human *activity*, which articulates the products of the imagination in symbolical constructions and tests them in thought experiments as well as actual ones, i.e., by active interventions designed to assess their performance and thus their comparative corroboration. Knowledge thus alternates between construction and criticism. It is a part of human praxis, in which decisions must continually be made. Epistemology, and thus also the theory of science, is the theory of this praxis, which provides methodological points of view, and at the same time, therefore, critical points of view for the judgment of its results and methods and reference points for rational decisions. If, however, knowledge is a part of human praxis, there is no point in distinguishing between theoretical and practical reason, or constructing an antithesis between cognition and decision, as would appear plausible for an epistemology which conceived knowledge as a revelation, either of the reason or of the senses. Epistemology and theory of science, insofar as they have a methodological character, are concerned with promoting the rationality of decisions and thus of human praxis within a particular sphere of social life. This they do by making relevant criticism possible within this sphere. To do this, however, is to fashion a conception of rationality that has consequences for every sphere of social life.

# THREE

# Knowledge and Decision

## 9. THE PROBLEM OF FOUNDING ETHICAL CONVICTIONS

IN OUR analysis of the problem of knowledge we have now reached the general problem of value, which from our present perspective presents itself at first as the problem of the relationship between knowledge and decision. This problem, in the form in which it must be tackled today, seems to have emerged relatively recently. One may presume that in early times it was not stated in that form because the natural value-Platonism of the everyday view of the world tends, by a linguistic fusion of values and facts, to transpose the problem of decision to the level of cognition,[1] and it does this in such an imperceptible manner that the questionable nature of the operation does not become obvious. For the most part, even a sharp distinction between knowledge of facts and knowledge of values is not drawn, particularly as long as a sociomorphic interpretation of the world transfers normative categories without any inhibition to the cosmos as a whole. The cognitive interpretation of value judgments is taken to be natural and uncontestable; so there can be no question of making a corresponding distinction within the realm of knowledge itself. At this stage, values have the same character of givenness as facts themselves; knowledge of them can be thought of, as in the case of factual connections, in accordance with the reve-

[1] Cf. Ernst Topitsch's investigations in *Vom Ursprung und Ende der Metaphysik. Eine Studie zur Weltanschauungskritik* (Vienna, 1958); Hans Kelsen's work in the volume, *Aufsätze zur Ideologiekritik*, ed. Ernst Topitsch (Neuwied and Berlin, 1964); Hans Reichenbach's critique of cognitive-ethical parallelism in his book, *Der Aufstieg der wissenschaftlichen Philosophie* (Berlin-Grunewald, undated); and Ernst Gellner's analysis in his book, *Thought and Change* (Chicago, 1964).

lation model, as a passive and nonarbitrary comprehension of existing features of the cosmos. This anchoring of values in a sociomorphically interpreted reality assures their dogmatization in the most natural manner possible. Today this fusion is still observable in the idea of natural law, one of the surviving remnants of this world view.

It is only at a more advanced stage that the dualism of is and ought, of theoretical and practical reason, emerges,[2] and makes possible the autonomous treatment of ethical problems, posing the problem of foundation in this sphere in a manner that seems to render its explicit treatment necessary. A situation has thus arisen which, as may easily be seen, must of necessity lead to the same difficulties we already encountered in our analysis of the problem of foundation. After all, the Münchhausen trilemma arises from any attempt to carry through the idea of foundation irrespective of whether it is cognitions or values and norms that are to be secured. An ethical system that claims to be based upon intuitions expressing ultimate normative principles will have to face two objections: first, not only are the intuitions of members of differing social systems frequently quite out of harmony with one another, but also they tend to be determined by the traditions of the cultural milieu in which the persons concerned have grown up—which may be adduced in explanation of this divergence; and second, the recourse to such intuitions in the process of justification is nothing but the dogmatizing of traditional norms. Any attempt to construct an ethical system *more geometrico*, i.e., to treat it in accordance with the Euclidean ideal of axiomatization, does not improve matters in this respect, even though through such an attempt the logical relationships within the approved system of norms may be more clearly expressed. A more empiricist version of this type of justificational thinking in moral philosophy, which might have recourse to such things as immediate experience of value,

[2] Cf. Karl R. Popper, *The Open Society and its Enemies*, chapter 5, "Nature and Convention."

or to feelings, is vulnerable to the same objection that these are largely determined by cultural influences; in addition, it would confront problems analogous to those of induction if it wished to advance beyond the casuistic level of individual decisions to the level of systematizing of ethical thought. One cannot see how such a recourse to particular sources of valuations, no matter whether these be intuition or feeling, conscience or practical need, can lead to anything but a dogmatic ethic in which these authorities figure as uncriticizable "givens," although we now know that they are all determined de facto by the sociocultural milieu and are thus changeable. This shows that even an autonomous ethics that has disengaged itself from the old socionormative world view is still not protected against dogmatic thought.

Furthermore, the dualism of is and ought introduces difficulties, insofar as it can contribute to the generation of a deep rift between knowledge and decision, between analysis of facts and evaluation. This does not emerge very clearly so long as cognitive interpretations of normative statements dominate the field; that is to say, so long as one can postulate the existence of specific types of insight that underlie value judgments and norms. Philosophical orientations that proceed in this manner are forced to assume ad hoc the existence of corresponding entities[3] that usually have no explanatory function in relation to actual events. Moreover, they are faced with the difficulty that value statements that are cognitively interpreted in this way, and consequently possess a descriptive character, can produce no normative conclusions, that is, no

---

[3] One might think here of Max Scheler's "value qualities" and "value states" ("Wertverhalte")—cf. his book, *Der Formalismus in der Ethik und die materielle Wertethik* (1916), 4th ed. (Bern, 1954), pp. 35 ff., 107 ff., 205 ff.—which are "grasped" by quasi-cognitive acts of feeling and preference; cf. Viktor Kraft's criticism in his book, *Die Grundlagen einer wissenschaftlichen Wertlehre*, 2d ed. (Vienna, 1951). G. E. Moore's "non-natural" properties also belong here: cf. his *Principia Ethica* (1903) (Cambridge, 1960), as well as the critique in W. K. Frankena, "The Naturalistic Fallacy," *Mind* 48 (1939), reprinted in *Readings in Ethical Theory*, ed. Wilfrid Sellars and John Hospers (New York, 1952), p. 103.

CHAPTER THREE

statements that contain directives for attitudes and actions.[4]
This means that such a system could only be used normatively
at the cost of committing the *naturalistic fallacy*, unless for
practical purposes one explicitly introduces a normative principle. Such a principle would not be itself amenable to cognitive interpretation, however, so that, at this point at least,
the problems of interpretation and justification emerge once
more.

An ethical cognitivism that postulates no new kinds of insights or entities but undertakes to reduce ethical statements
to cognitive statements of the usual sort certainly avoids the
arbitrariness of the ad hoc procedure described above, but
not the problem of the naturalistic fallacy. Moreover, in such
a conception the autonomy of ethics would disappear once
more, although that would certainly not be considered a disadvantage by those who strive for a scientific ethics—above
all when they are of the opinion that it is only thus that moral
problems are capable of rational solution. In such a case the
difficulty would lie in the fact that a moral science of this type
would admittedly perform a useful service in describing and
explaining facts that are interesting from the ethical point of
view; but it would have to leave the establishment of moral
directives to other authorities, which would then have taken
over the proper business of ethics.The results of sociological
and psychological research may certainly be relevant to the
solution of moral problems; but it would be difficult to demonstrate that they themselves afford solutions to such problems. In any case, anyone who advocates a methodology of
sufficient justification in moral philosophy could not be satisfied with this form of cognitivism.

At this point it becomes clear that the dualism of is and
ought may be difficult to overcome; but emphasizing the complete autonomy of the ethical by no means removes all difficulties, because the problematic nature of the so-called nat-

[4] Cf. my essay, "Ethik und Meta-Ethik, Das Dilemma der analytischen
Moral-Philosophie."

uralistic fallacy, by revealing an especially wide gap between knowledge and valuation, appears to make the problem of justification particularly difficult in this field. As soon as the assumption of the existence of an autonomous realm of values or a pure sphere of validity and obligation proves to be an illusion (a survival from the age when moral thinking was rooted in an interpretation of the cosmos that claimed objective validity—an illusion certainly bolstered by our habitual linguistic usage but eventually falling victim to modern linguistic criticism)—as soon as this happens, any mode of thought that seeks a secure foundation will find itself without a clue as to how to prevent the incursion of pure arbitrariness into moral philosophy. The distinction between grasping reality and imposing obligation is radicalized in such a way that on the one hand we have objective, neutral, disinterested knowledge free from all arbitrariness, while on the other we encounter radically subjective decisions, subject to the will, engaged and thus not neutral. As a result, knowledge and commitment seem to suffer a total separation.

This development reached an extreme stage with that polarization in philosophical thought when two philosophical movements arose, each of which seemed almost totally uninterested in the other: *existentialism* and *positivism*.[5] These are orientations that differ hardly at all on the dichotomy between knowledge and decision, but adopt radically different points of view in their evaluation of it. Whereas existentialism stresses decision with its free and undetermined nature, emphasizes its irrationality, and declares scientific knowledge essentially uninteresting precisely because of its objectivity, positivism places the emphasis upon knowledge and objectivity, stressing its foundability and rational character, while dismissing decision and commitment to the realm of subjectivity and arbitrariness as philosophically uninteresting. One side seeks to eradicate objective knowledge because it allegedly

[5] Cf. the interesting comparative analysis by Walter Kaufmann in his book, *Critique of Religion and Philosophy*, chapter 2, section 11 ff.

fails to make contact with existence; the other seeks to avoid subjective decision because it appears to lie outside the sphere of rationality. However little they may have to say to one another, it is nevertheless clear that both movements start to some extent from common presuppositions. Both opt for a view in which rationality and existence part company,[6] but one emphasizes the rational analysis of facts, while the other glorifies irrational existential decisions.[7] Both are inclined toward a *facticist* conception of knowledge, one outgrowth of which is an instrumentalist interpretation of science; science is seen only as a source of relevant predictions and as providing means to practical ends. Similarly, both tendencies incline toward a *decisionist* treatment of value problems, a correlative to the foregoing insofar as it leaves the assignment of moral ends at the mercy of irrationality, which, since reason is restricted to technical problems, is afforded an unlimited field of activity.[8] Any discussion between these two trends seems not merely unnecessary—since they have no need to dispute about the presuppositions they share—but actually impossible, because each party, by virtue of this shared ground, is

[6] Ludwig Wittgenstein's thesis, "We feel that even if *all possible* scientific questions can be answered, problems of life have still not been touched at all" (*Tractatus Logico-Philosophicus* [London, 1933], 6.52, p. 187), could just as well come from a supporter of existentialism.

[7] It goes without saying that this simple characterization can only isolate a pervading *tendency* in these two trends, and cannot characterize in detail the ideas of each philosopher who is commonly assigned to one or the other.

[8] On this point Jürgen Habermas is undoubtedly right, though, characteristically, he himself goes along with the instrumentalist interpretation of science, as do many philosophers who derive their views from Hegelian ideas; cf. Habermas, "Dogmatism, Reason and Decision" in his volume of essays, *Theory and Practice*, trans. J. Viertel (New York, 1973). In this work one may see what misunderstandings can arise when one forces the analysis of other conceptions into the convenient scheme of a critique of positivism because one cannot shake oneself free from a Hegel fixation—a fixation that, politically speaking, is among the most dubious characteristics of the German philosophical tradition; cf. the above-mentioned book by Ernst Topitsch, *Die Sozialphilosophie Hegels als Heilslehre und Herrschaftsideologie*, and Ralf Dahrendorf, "Die deutsche Idee der Wahrheit," in his book, *Gesellschaft und Demokratie in Deutschland* (Munich, 1965), pp. 175 ff.

obliged to concede to the other a sphere of influence that its own methods render inaccessible—the sphere either of "pure" fact or of "pure" decisions.

Inevitably, this situation fundamentally changed when the shared presupposition was itself questioned, which happened primarily as a result of the discovery, made more or less simultaneously in many places, that ultimately decisions lie "behind" all knowledge. Indeed, this discovery was made before the opposition between positivism and existentialism began to dominate the philosophical scene.[9] This incursion of decision into the sphere of knowledge could be seen as representing a considerable danger to the objectivity of the latter, because radical subjectivism in the treatment of problems of value might also extend to the sphere of knowledge and leave it at the mercy of subjective arbitrariness and whatever type of commitment is in favor at any given time. As soon as one has seen through the stipulative character of positivistic criteria of meaning and other cognitive criteria and has thereby acknowledged their relatively arbitrary nature—in the sense of the above-mentioned common presupposition—then knowledge as a whole seems to slip, or at least its objectivity seems to become questionable. And on the other side, as a consequence of this discovery, not only does the radical distinction between knowledge and decision seem to become problematic, but so does the hitherto unanalyzed and unexplained equation of decision and arbitrariness—the thesis of the fundamental irrationality of all decision.

That the process of cognition is shot through with regulations, valuations, and decisions seems to be an observation that needs only to be stated clearly to be assured of general recognition.[10] We choose our problems, evaluate solutions to them and decide to prefer one of the available solutions to

[9] I am thinking here primarily of the studies of Karl Popper, Hugo Dingler, Hans Reichenbach, and Herbert Feigl.

[10] Cf. my essay, "Wertfreiheit als methodisches Prinzip. Zur Frage der Notwendigkeit einer normativen Wissenschaft," in *Logik der Sozialwissenschaften*, ed. Ernst Topitsch (Cologne and Berlin, 1965), pp. 181 ff., reprinted in my volume of essays, *Aufklärung und Steuerung* (Hamburg, 1976).

the others—a procedure that is certainly not lacking in components of an unambiguously evaluative character. Since philosophy of science is concerned with the criteria that play a part in such processes, one could without more ado assign the controversies that occur here to the sphere of valuation. Many would undoubtedly find this attribution strange: some, because they consider philosophy of science to be an analytical enterprise and thus value-neutral and are unwilling to leave it at the mercy of arbitrary subjective choice; others, because they believe that in discussions about value the commitment of the participants must always express itself in easily identifiable value judgments with an existential tinge. But all this is by no means the case. Theory of science—and in fact the whole theory of knowledge—is not neutral; but it would be rash to draw from this the conclusion that it is particularly characterized by its use of value judgments. Rather, discussion in this field clearly demonstrates that one may debate problems of value without casting one's own commitment into the scale through formulation of corresponding value judgments. This is relatively easy to understand, since, as soon as commitment begins to operate in the discussion, arguments *ad hominem* come to the fore. Be that as it may: epistemology and philosophy of science may be regarded as that branch of value theory concerned with the development of viewpoints designed to promote the rationality of our problem-solving behavior within the sphere of knowledge.

From the point of view of sufficient justification, an attempt has been made to demonstrate that there is an essential distinction between statements of fact and statements of value, and thus between science and ethics.[11] This attempt suffers from the fact that, on the one hand, for factual statements it is quietly permitted to break off the foundation regress at the usual points, while on the other hand, it is not realized that the "vertical" continuation of this regress may in some cir-

[11] Cf. Walter Dubislav, "Zur Unbegründbarkeit der Forderungssätze," *Theoria* 3 (1937), pp. 330 ff.

cumstances lead to demands of the very sort that we have already seen to be incapable of justification—quite apart from the fact that the demand for justification seems itself to be of such a type. If this is the case, however, then in the last resort this unfoundable nature of value statements must itself color knowledge. To recognize this fact, it is an advantage if in the first instance the question of the foundation of ethics is placed parallel to the analogous question in the sphere of philosophy of science, not in that of science itself. It may be remarked in passing that the idea of justification, no matter on what level, leads, as we are aware, to the well-known trilemma. Thus, we have every incentive to abandon the idea for statements of all kinds, normative as well as descriptive.

Let us return to our problem of knowledge and decision. Our discussions so far clearly show that the dichotomy between rational knowledge and irrational decision suggested by the polarization of philosophical thinking into positivism and existentialism is inadequate, because of the reason that behind every piece of knowledge—conscious or unconscious—stand decisions. It is therefore impossible to base a thesis of the irrationality of decisions upon their unfoundability without this thesis necessarily being extensible to the whole realm of knowledge. Furthermore, it has now become clear that the distinction between rationality and irrationality, since it is a *methodical* distinction, must have reference to praxis, and must consequently find its proper place *within* the sphere of evaluation and decision. It relates to the sphere of cognition insofar as the latter is dominated not by passive contemplation and revelation, but by intellectual activity and shaping, which includes selection, evaluation, and decision; and over and above that, it plays a role in all those spheres in which problems have to be solved, and, therefore, among which construction and criticism have their place. We have already seen that a conception of rationality is possible which takes account of the unfoundability of knowledge and decision, to the extent that in abandoning its striving for certitude, it also sacrifices the idea of foundation, without giving up the possibility of criticism. It should now be clear that this conception is just as significant for ethics as for epistemology. Before returning to it, however, we should deal with a problem that has long played a considerable role in the discussion of method in the social sciences, and that indubitably belongs in this context: the problem of the value neutrality of science.

## 10. SCIENCE AND PRAXIS: THE PROBLEM OF VALUE NEUTRALITY

If scientific knowledge is indeed a branch of social practice in which valuations and decisions play a significant role, then the question arises as to whether this fact does not have consequences affecting the principle of value neutrality of science formulated by Max Weber. What has been said so far might suggest that this principle is hopelessly discredited; for there can be no doubt that the conception of rationality developed here is intended to have a normative function, and its application is intended to lead to the judging, and thus also to the evaluating, of the results and methods of scientific work from such particular points of view as absence of contradiction, content, explanatory force, and corroboration. We also know of course that in this social sphere, as in other spheres, ideals, norms, and programs are of great significance; ideals of truth, norms for testing and corroboration, programs for knowledge and research are just as much subject to critical discussion as, for example, the theoretical conceptions advanced, or the experiments planned and carried out. Can this sphere be distinguished from other spheres of social life in such a way that an otherwise unknown and unserviceable principle of value neutrality may be postulated in its case—a principle that might be able to guarantee the strict neutrality of scientific statements or even the neutrality of science as a whole as against these other spheres? If such should be the significance of Max Weber's principle, then one could only concede its uselessness and join the chorus of critics who have been so numerous to date.[12] But that, as will be shown, is by no means the case.

The postulate of value neutrality, as one can easily see, is in the first place—like certain versions of the principle of noncontradiction, as for instance the one formulated above—a methodological principle, which to that extent possesses a normative function. If one were to formulate it as a normative principle and at the same time ascribe an unrestricted validity to it, it would come under its own jurisdiction and thus lead to a self-contradiction, so a version of the postulate formulated in this manner would not be of much use. There is no reason to believe that Max Weber was thinking of a principle of this kind. Rather, he characterized a principle that can without any real difficulty be maintained for large areas of knowledge, so that his opponents in the debate on value judgments generally do no more than claim a methodological exception for particular sciences, on the grounds that the principle would be of no use in these special cases. Thus, for example, in the humanities (the so-called *Geisteswissenschaften*) a claim to methodological autonomy is often made, which is intended to suspend Max Weber's postulate. Let us consider what we should make of such claims.

First, one may ascertain that the paradoxical character of the above-mentioned principle disappears immediately when it is restricted to the realm of discourse about which Max

[12] For Max Weber's treatment of value problems, cf., above all, the following works: "Die 'Objektivität' sozialwissenschaftlicher und sozialpolitischer Erkenntnis" (1904); "Der Sinn der 'Wertfreiheit' der soziologischen und ökonomischen Wissenschaften" (1917-18), and "Wissenschaft als Beruf" (1919), in *Gesammelte Aufsätze zur Wissenschaftslehre*, by Max Weber, 2d ed., ed. Johannes Winckelmann (Tübingen, 1951). The latter essay appears in *From Max Weber: Essays in Sociology*, trans. and ed. H. Gerth and C. Mills (Oxford, 1946) as "Science as A Vocation." For an analysis and criticism of objections to Max Weber's principle, cf. my contribution, "Theorie und Praxis. Max Weber und das Problem der Wertfreiheit und der Rationalität," in *Die Philosophie und die Wissenschaften. Simon Moser zum 65. Geburtstag*, ed. Ernst Oldemeyer (Meisenheim, 1967), pp. 246 ff., reprinted in *Konstruktion und Kritik*.

Weber was most likely thinking when he formulated his claim. In the social sciences—and after all, this was the group of sciences for which he formulated the principle—one can distinguish between (1) the level of *objects* to which the statements of these sciences refer, e.g., the social facts; (2) the level of the *object language*, e.g., the scientific statements about these objects; and (3) the level of the *meta-language*, e.g., the relevant methodological statements involved. If one does this, the question of value neutrality breaks into three separate questions that can be discussed separately. Their analysis might well give rise to relatively unambiguous results: the problem of valuation in the object sphere of the social sciences; that of value judgments in the object language; and that of the value basis of these sciences.[13]

Now it is indisputable that the social sciences cannot help but make valuations the object of their statements. But such statements, as Max Weber already saw, can have a cognitive informative character. They can describe, explain, and predict the valuations of the individuals and groups analyzed, without themselves possessing any evaluative content. Nor need the problem of the value basis cause any difficulties, for the dependence of scientific activity on evaluative points of view—the normative background of the sciences—need not be disputed by an advocate of the value-neutrality principle. Of course, one can also make this value basis in its turn the subject of a cognitively objective and, in this sense, value-free analysis, as has long been done in the social sciences.[14] The field of statements, then, to which Max Weber's postulate primarily relates is that of the social sciences' object language. The real

[13] Since I have analyzed the problem in depth elsewhere, I shall limit myself here to summarizing the results; cf. my essays, "Wissenschaft und Politik. Zum Problem der Anwendbarkeit einer wertfreien Sozialwissenschaft," in *Probleme der Wissenschaftstheorie. Festschrift für Viktor Kraft*, ed. Ernst Topitsch (Vienna, 1960); "Wertfreiheit als methodisches Prinzip," reprinted in *Aufklärung and Steuerung*; and "Theorie und Praxis."

[14] One of the most famous examples of this is, of course, Max Weber's essay, "Science as a Vocation," cited above.

point at issue in the controversy over value judgments is, therefore, the necessity or possibility of value judgments in the context of object-language statements of the social sciences themselves; it is the problem of a normative social science that formulates value judgments about its field of objects, the social facts.

It is clear that the solution to this problem depends on the aims of scientific activity and on the nature of the means it employs. On occasion those who support a normative social science employ the expedient of representing such a science as being inevitable.They do so for the simple reason that it is not possible—as they say—to neutralize the language of social science, i.e., that the means to achieve a value-free social science in Weber's sense are not available.[15] This thesis can nowadays retain a certain plausibility only for those who are prepared to disregard more than half of the literature of modern social science. It accounts for ordinary language with its natural value-Platonism, but pays no heed to the fact that in the course of the development of the sciences, one discipline after another—beginning with the physical and mathematical sciences—has gone over from the sphere of value-based treatment to that of value-free analysis. In the face of this fact one can only regard Strauss's thesis as an attempt to justify an already partly superseded status quo—an attempt, incidentally, which characteristically employs essentialist methods.

When establishing the goals of scientific activity, the question arises as to whether one wishes to remain content with the knowledge of reality, its structures, and relationships, or if one proposes aims for science that go beyond this. For the task of knowledge, one can get by with a science for which Max Weber's postulate of value neutrality is no obstacle. This result is independent of the nature of a science's domain of objects, and is thus achievable for other branches of the humanistic sciences. It does not require neglect of the great significance of norms, value judgments, and decisions for all

---

[15] Cf., above all, Leo Strauss, *Natural Right and History* (Chicago, 1953).

kinds of human activity, including knowledge and thus the sphere of science itself, nor a neglect of their significance within the object field of certain sciences concerned with human activity. On the contrary, it takes express account of these facts. What must be kept clearly in view is that precisely those facts and contexts which, from the viewpoint of particular values, appear most relevant—and these frequently include facts from the sociocultural sphere, especially those relating to morals, law, and politics—must often be subjected to objective analysis of a cognitive character in order to achieve a rational solution to practical problems.

The postulate of value freedom under discussion here belongs, as I have already mentioned, to the sphere of regulative norms. But it is precisely because of the possibility that its significance for science may be objectively analyzed that it becomes possible to make relations from the sphere of evaluation the object of knowledge and thus treat them in a non-valuative manner. The acceptance of this principle is doubtless a matter of decision; but this is also true of the acceptance of the principle of noncontradiction and all other methodological principles, including the choice between the principle of foundation and that of critical examination. However, it applies not only to these principles: it is also true of the acceptance or rejection of theories, hypotheses, research techniques, the choice of problems, criteria, viewpoints, and perspectives—all of which are the order of the day in scientific practice. Cognition is replete with valuations and decisions of all kinds. Its rationality is expressed precisely in the manner in which these valuations are made and these decisions are reached; rationality is always a matter of method and thus of praxis—of cognitive and scientific practice, but not restricted to this area.

At this point the question arises about the application of science to life in society, and whether the demands of the latter do not necessitate the introduction of value judgments into the context of scientific statements. The contemporary defenders of normative social science frequently support their position by reference to the need for a science that is useful in practice.[16] For practical application, it is in their view nec- essary, or at least expedient, to make systems of social-sci- entific statements normative by introducing suitable value premises, even if pure knowledge may be able to do without such normative components. This position is based upon the fact that with the logical means at our disposal it it not possible to deduce normative or otherwise prescriptive conclusions from statement systems of a purely cognitive and informative char- acter. If one wishes to avoid the naturalistic fallacy, the only way out seems to lie in the explicit introduction of appropriate value premises. This argument appears at first cogent; but nonetheless it does not suffice to demonstrate the necessity of a normative science.

It is no doubt correct that for the practical application of scientific statements we need to be clear about what we want. Nor can it be denied that in themselves statement systems of a purely cognitive and informative nature afford no answer to this question. Admittedly, in some circumstances it is pos- sible to transform them into technological systems that pro- vide information about the possibilities of human action; but at most this gives us an answer to the question of what we are able to do. Pure science, then, when applied to practical problems, provides us with the means of investigating prac- tical possibilities and ascertaining how far we can master the situation before us; but it does not tell us that we ought to actu- alize any of these possibilities; it does not, therefore, prescribe our decision for us. So the results produced by a value- free science can never suffice for the mastery of practical situations. In other words, the necessities of action always transcend what knowledge has to offer us. We thus see that

---

[16] Cf. the works of Gerhard Weisser, e.g., *Politik als System aus normativen Urteilen* (Göttingen, 1951), and my criticism in the works mentioned in footnote 13 to this chapter; cf. Klaus Lompe's recent book, *Wissenschaftliche Beratung der Politik. Ein Beitrag zur Theorie anwendender Sozialwissen- schaften* (Göttingen, 1966), and my criticism in "Sozialwissenschaft und pol- itische Praxis," in *Konstruktion und Kritik*.

decisions are crucial for cognitive practice, and practical decisions cannot be derived from knowledge alone.

To infer from the above that science should be made normative for practical reasons would be to draw a false conclusion. The application of science does, it is true, require additional decisions—decisions about aims and the admissibility of means; but this alone does not make it necessary to create a normative science containing ready-made judgments waiting to be applied to each and every concrete situation, judgments out of which the concrete decision is logically deducible in each case. To turn the above-mentioned ideal of Leibniz in a normative direction is just as utopian as to try to realize this ideal in the sphere of pure cognition, especially since its claims go beyond Leibniz's idea. Its realization would make it possible not only for the decisions in the sphere of cognition, but also for those in the other spheres of social practice to be replaced in principle by calculations. This idea overestimates the completeness and certainty of knowledge that is attainable and also our capacity to make decisions; it recalls the epistemological optimism of the Enlightenment and of the ideal of an ethics *more geometrico* in which Euclidean thought is applied to moral problems. If one abandons the methodological ideal of sufficient justification that lends plausibility to this ideal, then one cannot see where the advantages of such a conception lie. As soon as one grasps that an ideal normative science of that type cannot be realized, one is naturally confronted with the question of the advantage of maintaining this ideal in principle, but so weakening the demands made upon it that the system can no longer perform any of the functions originally expected from it.

In this situation it is worth remembering that normative systems of the sort proposed here are not needed for the practical application of knowledge. Generally speaking, decision in practical situations, especially in novel ones, requires considerations specific to the situation in question, which cannot be anticipated in a general manner. Science can contribute by analyzing what choices are possible within the limits set by the relevant normative viewpoint, thereby making it possible to realize projects stemming from practical imagination. For the laws of the theoretical sciences should be regarded, in practical terms, as *limitations* imposed upon the imagination when problems are to be solved. Neither science or a normative system of prior decisions can replace the creative imagination required by the solution of new problems.[17] This fact alone is sufficient to guarantee the failure of any attempt to anticipate human practice *more geometrico*. The practitioner, insofar as he is not following an established routine, is in the situation of the artist who utilizes the laws known to him in order to realize creations of his own imagination. His activity advances by alternation of construction and criticism, just as does the cognitive activity of the researcher and the formative activity of the artist.

## 11. THE CLASSICAL MODEL OF RATIONALITY AND THE DISCUSSION OF VALUES

We have seen that the foundation postulate leads to exactly the same difficulties in the sphere of moral philosophy as in epistemology and theory of science. The search for an Archimedean point in ethics is just as useless and misdirected as in other disciplines. From the fallibilist viewpoint it cannot be the task of philosophy to justify the present state of knowledge or morals by providing it with a "transcendental" or any other kind of substructure, thus dogmatizing it. On the other side, the search for a perfect system containing within itself ready-made decisions appropriate to all morally relevant situations is a utopian undertaking that pays no heed to the importance of uncertainty, risk, and imagination in the solving of practical

[17] The role of the imagination, which tends to be neglected in views that operate with the idea of axiomatizing human practice, is rightly stressed by G.L.S. Shackle in his book, *Decision, Order and Time in Human Affairs* (Cambridge, Eng., 1961), pp. 8 ff.

problems.[18] The utopian version of the striving for certainty takes just as little account of real human possibilities as does the conservative. The one constructs problem solutions in a vacuum and ignores the importance of tradition for human progress; the other preserves previously achieved solutions and thus underestimates the possibility of learning. Both ignore the possibility of reacting to new situations with creative answers—answers that cannot be anticipated by calculations made within the framework of abstract systems of rules laid down once and for all.

In response to the weakness of a moral philosophy based on the idea of foundation, a new trend has emerged recently under the influence of analytical and hermeneutic modes of thought; it reduces philosophizing in this sphere to the analysis of problems of meaning. Philosophy, so the advocates of this solution by resignation maintain, is not concerned with explaining real relationships: let science look after that, insofar as it is possible. Nor does it have the task of providing foundations—that would exceed its power. No, philosophy is merely concerned with understanding, with disclosing the meaning of human action, or at least of its linguistic components. Analytical moral philosophy, following the later philosophy of Ludwig Wittgenstein, wishes, as a neutral meta-ethics, to analyze the language games in which moral expressions occur.[19] Philosophical hermeneutics, following Martin Heidegger, postulates the universality of the hermeneutic viewpoint, and even goes so far in a spirit of conscious nonneutrality as to legitimize prejudices transmitted by tradition by rendering them understandable, thus throwing overboard the tradition of crit-

[18] Cf. Leszek Kolakowski's criticism of the ideal of a perfect code of morals in "Ethik ohne Kodex," reprinted in his volume of essays, *Traktat über die Sterblichkeit der Vernunft* (Munich, 1967), pp. 102 ff.

[19] For criticism of this trend, see my essay, "Ethik und Meta-Ethik"; see also Hans Lenk, "Der 'ordinary language approach' und die Neutralitätsthese der Meta-Ethik," in *Das Problem der Sprache*, ed. Hans-Georg Gadamer (Munich, 1967), pp. 183 ff.

ical thought.[20] These tendencies in analytical and hermeneutic thought reveal a skepticism about the possible power of human reason, which one can understand if one starts from the fact that it was long the custom to regard the model of rationality presented by classical methodology as the only option. The difficulties inherent in this model were then interpreted as the natural limitations of rationality as a whole, with the result that a philosophy that did not wish to proceed dogmatically seemed obliged to confine itself to inquiries into meaning.

This attitude can already be clearly recognized in Max Weber, whose ideas, as has been observed with some justice, have influenced both positivism and existentialism, although he himself cannot readily be assigned to either camp. As is well known, Weber was not content merely to postulate the principle of value freedom for the social sciences; rather, he expressly concerned himself with the question of how far science can make a contribution to the discussion of value problems,[21] and in this connection he propounded the thesis that value judgments should certainly not be excluded from the field of scientific discussion. Criticism ought not stop short of value judgments, he maintained, but it is necessary to clarify the meaning and purpose of such criticism.[22] His investigations of this question make it clear that he regarded the function of a rational discussion of problems of value to be the clarification of all the logical and factual relationships involved, as well as the disclosure of the fundamental normative positions that act as starting points in deciding such questions. But the decision to adopt one of these positions over another, and therefore the concrete decision that resulted in the given practical situation, must be left by science to the agent. The ultimate "value axioms" adopted by those involved can, in

[20] See chapter 6 of this book.

[21] See Weber's essays, "Die 'Objektivität' sozialwissenschaftlicher und sozialpolitischer Erkenntnis," pp. 149 ff., and "Der Sinn der 'Wertfreiheit' der soziologischen und ökonomischen Wissenschaften," pp. 406 ff.

[22] Weber, "Die 'Objektivität,' " p. 149.

Max Weber's view, be explicated and understood through rational discussion, so that the concrete decisions that result from them also become intelligible; but in the last analysis, they themselves are inaccessible to criticism. The discussion, therefore, contributes to the clarification of the various positions and to the illumination of the contexts that serve to justify the decisions; but there the matter ends. The limits of critical argumentation have been reached in expressing the consistency of the various possible standpoints.

This view is obviously based on an implicit acceptance of the classical rationality model, but combines it with the experience, deriving from actual value controversies, that differing "ultimate attitudes" are not merely logically possible but often actually present. Once these have been made explicit, it is hard to see how one can get any further by means of rational analysis. At any rate, it seems more honest to concede the situation than to expect science to support one of the solutions over the others without any adequate justification for doing so, or to find a formula that will harmonize and cover up the conflict in values instead of letting it be fought out. Since Weber was unable to accept the relativity of values as a way out of this dilemma, his combination of ethical fundamentalism and pluralism led him to the conclusion that the various irreconcilable value attitudes were in fact the consequence of convictions based on belief; one had to choose between these without being able to appeal to science for assistance. Connected with this was his view that "every scientific discussion between proponents of opposed beliefs . . . really serves only to test and consolidate each party's own beliefs."[23] There are many indications that Max Weber held "ultimate value assumptions" to be basically incorrigible, or at least not open to the influence of rational criticism. By his attempt to clarify what contribution scientific discussion might

[23] Eduard Baumgarten, in his introduction to Max Weber, *Soziologie: Weltgeschichtliche Analysen-Politik*, 2d ed., ed. Johannes Winckelmann (Stuttgart, 1956), p. XXXV.

make to the solving of value problems, he sought to advance the frontier of rational criticism as far into the territory of credal convictions as seemed consistent with the classical model of rationality. What became clear in the process, of course, was that, given the prevailing pluralism of ethical standpoints, it was necessary to concede the irrationality of the highest normative presuppositions if it was not to look as if one's own position should be preferred on rational grounds. Since no rational authority could be found to which one's own attitudes could be referred as being demonstratively the only correct one, it was also necessary to concede to those who held different views the sovereignty of their own conscientious decision.

We have seen that the thesis of the irrationality of genuine decisions is an assumption common to the positivist and the existentialist movements that developed since the time of Max Weber. The polarization of thought that occurred in the course of this development ensured that the components he had united in his existential rationalism move apart. Positivism cultivated the rational analysis of science, in the course of which, it must be said, the role of decision in scientific solutions to problems remained at first very much in the dark; existentialism sought to make clear by hermeneutic methods the irrational character of existential decisions, and in doing so, neglected the possibility of deciding in favor of rationality in thought and action. In a situation such as this, it was not to be expected that the problems raised by Max Weber would be taken up again and reconsidered from fresh points of view. Weber's critics, who sought to vanquish him by starting from theological or quasi-theological premises,[24] could find no valid objection to his assumption that ultimate presuppositions and fundamental decisions were a matter of faith and thus, although intelligible, certainly no longer amenable to criticism—an assumption

[24] For a survey of the various tendencies in Max Weber criticism, cf. Guenther Roth, "Political Critiques of Max Weber: Some Implications for Political Sociology," *American Sociological Review* 30 (1965), pp. 213 ff.

which nowadays, presumably, is deeply rooted in everyday thought as well. Such critics had a great fondness for using the immunity to criticism of ultimate presuppositions for their own purposes, without being prepared to allow him the same privilege.

As was shown above, the discovery that ultimately decisions of some kind lie "behind" all cognitive acts—a discovery that is already at least implicitly present in Weber's analysis of science[25]—has to some extent created a new problematic, in that the difficulties which had arisen concerning value problems and which led to the assumption that there was a limit to rational discussion, must be carried over into the sphere of cognition. Cognitive claims, like moral and political claims, incorporate evaluation and decisions under whatever point of view one adopts. If one adopts a foundationalist position, then immediately the question of the ultimate value presuppositions of knowledge arises; and evidence that demand statements are ungroundable can also be extended to those demands that specifiy the requirements usually accepted for valid knowledge. One who criticizes Weber's views on the status of ultimate value assumptions must realize that he is attacking a much more general problem, and that his criticism strikes at a conception that is at least implicitly common to the fundamental convictions of otherwise very heterogeneous philosophical, theological, and ideological tendencies: the position that *so-called ultimate presuppositions are immune to criticism*. So we have now characterized the problem situation in a way that shows the precise parallelism between the problem of foundation in moral philosophy and in epistemology.

Our criticism of the classical methodology of sufficient justification may now, in principle, be applied to the problem of

---

[25] Cf. Weber's essay, "Wissenschaft als Beruf" ("Science as a Vocation"), which analyzes the decision in favor of rationality that is implicit in scientific work and underlines the contrast to theological thought, which always, according to Weber, demands the "virtuoso achievement of 'sacrificing the intellect.'" Cf. ibid., p. 595. Cf. also Karl Löwith's observations on this in his essay, "Die Entzauberung der Welt durchWissenschaft," *Club Voltaire*, II (Munich, 1965), pp. 134 ff.

the basis of ethics, for it applies to the general structure of foundationalist thinking, regardless of the kind of convictions discussed. Whoever seeks a sufficient justification for concrete value judgments and moral decisions in accordance with the classical model will be obliged to fall back on ultimate standards of value in the manner proposed by Max Weber—standards not capable of further foundation, if the other two horns of the trilemma are to be avoided. But that is nothing more or less than a retreat to dogmatic principles no longer subject to criticism, to the incorrigible ultimate attitudes evidently considered necessary by Max Weber. Now one may object that his whole exposition of the problem of values already contains a prior decision in favor of the classical type of rationality, modeled on the Euclidean ideal. But to opt for this ideal is to exclude attitudes that do not, without further ado, conform to it. The participants he envisions in a discussion of values are so characterized as to be amenable to criticism from logical and factual points of views, while anything that goes beyond that encounters their resistance. There is no doubt that Weber was not thinking of this characterization in psychological terms; rather, he presupposed the objective validity of logic and the factual sciences, without considering the possibility that the "ultimate presuppositions" of these sciences might also be drawn into the discussion.

Immediately, however, the question arises: Why should only Max Weber's "ultimate axioms of value" be declared immune by the participants in such a discussion, and thus be dogmatized? They could easily do the same with other components of their convictions, for the rationality model presupposed by Weber permits in principle the dogmatizing of any part of one's system of beliefs, provided the laws of logic are not infringed in the process. To permit such infringements does, to be sure, leave the range of solutions favored by Max Weber, but it would open an even wider scope for such immunizations. One need only think of the suspension of the principle of contradiction found in certain champions of Hegelian dialectic, which if skillfully used can ensure their victory in every discussion—at least as long as their adversaries do not see through the strategy. It is thus by no means self-evident that only those possibilities of rational criticism envisaged by Max Weber are capable of realization. If one abandons his rationality model, therefore, the number of ethical positions possible may be multiplied still further.

In any case, if one wishes to subject his ideas to criticism, one can first of all admit that it is certainly possible to take any particular component of any view one likes and render it immune to any kind of criticism; and this includes so-called ultimate presuppositions of either cognitive or normative character. As we have already seen in our investigation of epistemological problems, such immunity is not an intrinsic characteristic of any particular component of our convictions; but it can certainly be produced, if one is prepared to use appropriate procedures. Depending upon the nature of the convictions in question and the character of the sphere in which they occur, their dogmatization may be associated with a variety of more or less serious difficulties. But as a fundamental possibility it may not be excluded from any field of the human search for orientation in the world, not even from the sphere of science; dogmatization is a possibility of human and social practice taken as a whole. It is an expression of the fact that the will to achieve certitude triumphs over the will to attain solutions that remain open to possible criticism— solutions subject to resistance both from reality and from other members of society, which must either prove their worth or come to grief in the process. The closing of systems of belief is not a command of logic or any other objective authority: it is a demand of the will and of the needs and interests that stand behind it. The openness of such systems, one might well say, is itself a moral question.

## 12. CRITICAL PHILOSOPHY AND ETHICS: THE ROLE OF CRITICAL PRINCIPLES

He who concedes the possibility of dogmatization can by no means be forced to accept this practice as necessary in any particular case, as the classical concept of rationality suggests, at least in the case of so-called ultimate presuppositions. Rather, one can regard the methodology of critical examination, sketched in our general treatment of the epistemological problematic, as a *general* alternative to the classical doctrine, and apply it to *all* kinds of convictions, including normative conceptions and standards of value. The impression that there must exist "ultimate" presuppositions that per se are beyond criticism arises only as a result of the fascination exerted by axiomatic thinking, which, after all, insures that assumptions of this kind are *created*. We know nowadays that axiomatizations are useful for certain purposes but certainly do not provide final and in principle uncriticizable solutions.[26] Above all, they certainly cannot show that any particular statement has per se the character of an "ultimate assumption" and is in *this* sense an axiom.[27] Apart from the fact that for each thesis there are in principle infinitely many possible premises,

[26] Cf. the interesting book by Alexander Israel Wittenberg, *Vom Denken in Begriffen. Mathematik als Experiment des reinen Denkens* (Basel and Stuttgart, 1957), and also the above-mentioned works by Imre Lakatos.

[27] In this connection it is interesting to consider Max Weber's remarks concerning the way in which he viewed the identification of "ultimate value axioms" of individuals. According to him, their elaboration is "an operation that starts from an individual valuation and an analysis of its meaning, rising to always higher and more fundamental value attitudes. This operation does not employ the means of an empirical discipline and produces no factual knowledge. It is 'valid' in the same way that logic is valid" ("Der Sinn der 'Wertfreiheit' der soziologischen und ökonomischen Wissenschaften," ibid., p. 496). In his contribution to the discussion of value judgments in a committee of the "Verein für Sozialpolitik" in 1913 (cf. *Max Weber, Werk und Person, Dokumente*, selection and commentary by Eduard Baumgarten [Tübingen, 1964], p. 102), Weber still speaks of a purely *logical* procedure, which is valid "by virtue of the validity of logic." This striking revision after four years of an otherwise little-altered text is doubtless attributable to Weber's subsequent realization that logic cannot provide the wished-for procedure. An inductive operation would be required, but there is no quasilogical canon for that, either. Moreover, the question arises as to when the regress he envisages may be broken off, i.e., when some presupposition may be identified as "ultimate." And here we again encounter our old problem: the foundation regress is in principle unlimited.

no point can be identified as that at which a foundation regress would have to be broken off. The most one can say, then, is that a person who, in a value discussion of the type cited by Max Weber, declares any one of his statements to be an "ultimate" presupposition *is not prepared* to open it up to discussion.[28] Thus the delimitation of critical discussion he postulates is dependent on the will of the partners involved. In discussions of value, too, the only limits of rationality are those imposed by the persons taking part. Here, too, the idea of critical examination may be applied as a matter of principle to all the component parts of the convictions in question; and, of course, it is not possible here either to force one of the participants to accept a critical argument.

As we have seen, a peculiar combination of fundamentalism and pluralism lay behind Weber's view of discussions of questions of value. Applying the criticist approach to the problems of moral philosophy certainly involves rejecting fundamentalism but not ethical pluralism, which is really a part of this approach as well. When we are concerned about treating ethical statements and systems not as *dogmas* but as *hypotheses*,[29] then it is crucial to be able to consider *alternatives* and to generate new perspectives yielding other solutions to ethical problems than those hitherto current. Thus, the "anarchy of values" now lamented by so many when they see the various competing ethical systems and attitudes should instead be regarded as a challenge; competing proposals should be subjected to a critical evaluation with reference to the problems of our present situation. A critical moral philosophy cannot be expected to provide the morality prevailing at any given

[28] In my critique of this aspect of Max Weber's view I concur, as far as I can see, with Eduard Baumgarten and W. G. Runciman; cf. Eduard Baumgarten's introduction to *Max Weber, Soziologie: Weltgeschichtliche Analysen-Politik*, pp. XXXV ff., and his *Max Weber, Werk und Person*, pp. 652 ff.; and W. G. Runciman, *Social Science and Political Theory* (Cambridge, Eng., 1963), pp. 156 ff.

[29] "Hypothesis" signifies in this context, of course, nothing more than an assumption that, in principle, is subject to criticism.

time with spurious justifications in order to anchor it more firmly in the consciousness of people and in social conditions. Its task consists rather in shedding a critical light upon it, throwing its weaknesses into relief and developing viewpoints through which it might be improved.

An important question arising in this connection is that of the role of knowledge and thus of science in this undertaking. At first sight it looks as if objections to the naturalistic fallacy would necessarily lead to such a sharp separation of factual statements and value judgments that an autonomously constituted ethics would be completely cut off from knowledge, which would thus become irrelevant to any criticism of ethical thought and morality. But that does not necessarily follow at all. As has already become clear from our earlier analysis of the immunization problem, it is certainly possible to isolate parts of a system of convictions from one another, if one so wishes. Ethical components can then also be shielded from knowledge to a certain degree, so that they may be protected for a time from the erosion with which the advance of scientific knowledge may threaten them. But that, again, requires a decision to apply procedures conducive to dogmatization. There is no "natural" or necessary isolation of this kind, as the history of thought and morals has shown. Whatever one means by autonomous ethics, it can in any case not mean that no cognitive criticism of our value orientation is possible—unless, that is, the earlier theonomous dogmatism is to be replaced by one of an autonomous character.

If the dialectical method described above is to be adopted for moral philosophy, then the main task is to shed a critical light on given value orientations by seeking relevant contradictions, aiming, if necessary, at a revision of the convictions involved. Insofar as the elimination of contradictions is demanded through this maxim, it is already contained in Weber's approach, which after all presupposes the validity of logic. Moreover, insofar as considerations are involved about how far ends pursued on the basis of assumed value principles are capable of realization, this maxim is adopted by Weber. In so

97

doing he concedes the possibility of rational value criticism to an extent that goes far beyond what would be permitted by an extreme ethical irrationalism. Only the fiction of ultimate presuppositions totally detached from the cognitive context suggests—unnecessarily, as we have seen—that there is any limit to criticism. Nor is the active search for contradictions expressly made into a maxim in Weber's thought, even though the context in which the problem of value is debated—a discussion between two people of opposing views—does contain an element of this type. One can see now that Max Weber's approach is obliged to make implicit use of a critical principle not found in pure science—the maxim that *ought implies can*.[30] Without this maxim one cannot see how, within the framework of Weber's conception of rationality, any kind of cognitive criticism can be brought to bear upon value convictions. What we have here is a *bridge principle*—a maxim to bridge the gap between ethics and science—which has the function of rendering scientific criticism of normative statements possible.

As soon as the possibility of using such bridge principles for critical purposes has been conceded, it is difficult to see why one should restrict oneself to this principle and permit only that criticism of value orientations which has an immediately technological foundation. In fact, a critical moral philosophy will need to set for itself the explicit task of discovering more such bridge principles that will allow knowledge to be utilized for purposes of criticizing normative conceptions. A further principle of this kind, in addition to the already-mentioned Postulate of Realizability might, perhaps, be a Postulate of Congruence. This would make the criticism of normative assertions possible, the meaningfulness of which involves the existence of factors or relations that we are not

[30] For analysis of this sentence, see Manfred Moritz, "Verpflichtung und Freiheit. Über den Satz 'sollen impliziert können,' " *Theoria*, vol. 19 (1953), pp. 131 ff. The sentence may be said to correspond to the old *ultra posse nemo obligatur*. Its meaning may become clearer if it is cast in the logically equivalent contrapositive form, "not-able-to implies not-obliged-to."

ready to accept as real in our cognition. The assumption, for example, that there are higher beings in heaven who have the right to issue commands of any kind to human beings, and that they have delegated this right to the head of a tribe or a state, is indeed compatible with certain sociocosmic world views; but according to our present state of knowledge, it would be subject to criticism on the basis of a Postulate of Congruence. The resulting criticism might well be so extended as to include the content of norms whose only support is an assumption of this or a similar kind. Many theses of modern Protestant theologians who have thrown overboard essential parts of the sociocosmic views that provided the framework for the growth of theology may well, for this reason, become extremely problematical.[31] There are incongruities between cosmology and ethics that cannot survive critical examination. The problem of the naturalistic fallacy need never arise in such criticism.

The belief that, because of their autonomy, ethics and actual morality cannot be subjected to criticism based in knowledge arises presumably from a vacuum fiction such as the one which played a role in our analysis of epistemological problems: from the assumption, that is, that at a certain point in time we have to make a decision about our fundamental system of values as a whole, and we must do this in complete isolation from all considerations unrelated to value, and thus from all considerations of knowledge. Only after this fundamental decision has been made might cognitions be introduced for practical applications, i.e., for so-called technical questions. But a situation requiring a decision of this kind never in fact arises. Particular value convictions always appear in combination with knowledge. They are intimately intermixed, "bound up with" factual convictions—a situation that everyday thought

---

[31] The reader will notice that the above-mentioned assumption is subject to criticism not because of its rough and simplistic formulation. Present-day refinements of expression are of no avail here unless they contribute to making such theses more vacuous, thus permitting other critical arguments to arise. See chapter 5 of this book for a discussion of this problem.

takes into account with its Platonism of value.[32] It is necessary, then, to make continual use of both kinds of conviction in solving the problems of our existence, to constantly test them and, if need be, to revise them. New ideas and experiences can lead us to restructure our cognitive system in some particular manner and in this way also to change our system of values. It is true, as we know, that one cannot without more ado deduce a value judgment from a factual statement; but particular value judgments can certainly turn out to be incompatible with particular previously held value convictions *in the light of a revised factual conviction*. A critical application of the above-mentioned bridge principles is one means of exposing such incompatibilities.[33]

Yet another kind of criticism may arise from the fact that new moral ideas are developed that make earlier solutions to moral problems appear questionable. It is often in the light of such new ideas that problematical elements in these solutions that were hitherto disregarded or taken for granted be-

[32] For this reason Gellner says, with some justification, that such Platonism is, indeed, a somewhat worthless philosophy but an excellent sociology; cf. Ernest Gellner, *Thought and Change*, pp. 84 ff.

[33] With regard to the possibility of objective criticism of value convictions, there is an obvious agreement between the view developed here and that expressed in Viktor Kraft's treatise, *Rationale Moralbegründung* (Vienna, 1963); cf., e.g., pp. 33 ff. Admittedly, Kraft links the idea of criticism with the foundation postulate in a manner that, in my view, leads inevitably to the difficulties exhibited above. In concrete terms, these difficulties appear in his analysis of the problems primarily in his proposed recourse to natural needs as ultimate realities; on this problem, see Karl Acham, "Rationale Moralbegründung. Einige Bemerkungen zur analytischen Moralphilosophie im Hinblick auf Viktor Krafts gleichnamiges Buch," *Archiv für Rechts- und Sozialphilosophie* 53 (1967), pp. 387 ff., esp. pp. 402 ff. Since I cannot see how the above-mentioned trilemma can otherwise be avoided, I would therefore—in complete harmony with the rational attitude underlying his aim—abandon the goal of a rational foundation of morality postulated by Kraft in order to support a consistent critical philosophy; such a philosophy would certainly permit one, for purposes of criticizing given moral conceptions and morally relevant social conditions, to operate in the spirit of Kraft's naturalism with arguments in which satisfying the needs of the members of a society would play a part.

come visible. Thus a new problem situation arises, as is also frequently the case in science when new ideas emerge. Hitherto unheeded possibilities of problem solving become apparent, making new decisions necessary. In earlier times, such ideas very frequently, although not exclusively, developed in the context of religious interpretations of the world. It is by no means certain that moral philosophy must here exercise abstinence, as the program of analytic philosophy would demand. Since the analytical program has been shown to be inadequate anyway, it is perhaps appropriate to point to the speculative and constructive side of critical philosophizing. This is a side which is, as in the field of knowledge, combined with another aspect already to be found in Max Weber, i.e., with an ethical pluralism that takes account of alternative problem solutions. Weber was completely right when he saw that the rational discussion of value problems does not necessarily lead to a consensus. But he did not consider the fact that situations of this kind are to be found also in the discussion of cognition problems. If he had realized this, it might have saved him from assuming in the discussions of values a limit of rationality that does not occur in his discussions of cognitive questions.

Thus it is possible to overcome positivist resignation in questions of moral philosophy without lapsing into the existentialist cult of commitment, which replaces rational discussions of such problems with irrational decisions. Criticist philosophy, which presents us with this opportunity, has a moral content itself. Whoever adopts it does not decide for an abstract principle with no existential significance, but for a way of life. One of the immediate ethical consequences of criticist philosophy is the conclusion that unshakable faith, impervious to rational argument, valued so highly by many religions, is not a virtue, but a vice.[34]

[34] Cf. Richard Robinson, *An Atheist's Values* (Oxford, 1964), pp. 118 ff.; but above all, Walter Kaufmann, *The Faith of a Heretic* (Garden City, N.Y., 1961).

# FOUR

# Mind and Society

### 13. THE PROBLEM OF IDEOLOGY IN CRITICIST PERSPECTIVE

THE genesis of the problem of ideology can be traced back to the insight occurring in various conceptions that the problem of knowledge has a social dimension. This fact, for which the phrase "the mutual involvement of thought and being" (Seins-verbundenheit des Denkens) was coined not so long ago, provided the inducement, especially under the influence of Marxist ideas, to so intermingle sociological and epistemological questions that from the logical point of view the objection was raised that problems of the genesis of knowledge were not being kept sufficiently separate from problems of its validity. This objection was offered with particular fervor by thinkers close to the positivist tradition, that is, to a way of thinking in which it is important to protect science from ideological influence of all kinds. From the perspective of positivism, there is a close connection between the problem of value neutrality and the problem of ideology, insofar as it seems impossible to demarcate ideology from science without reference to value judgments. The critique of ideology that springs from this tradition, which argues from an epistemological point of view and which represents the ideological character of statement systems as a cognitive blemish, customarily makes the emergence of more or less hidden value judgments in such systems the cardinal point of analysis.[1]

[1] Compare, above all, Theodor Geiger, *Ideologie und Wahrheit: Eine Soziologische Kritik des Denkens* (Stuttgart-Vienna, 1953); and in reference to the economic tradition, see Gunnar Myrdal, *The Political Element in the Development of Economic Theory* (1932), trans. Paul Streeten (Cambridge, Mass., 1961), and my book *Ökonomische Ideologie und politische Theorie* (Göttingen, 1954).

This approach does not seem, in fact, inappropriate, for the paradigms of religious or secular ideologies most frequently used as starting points for an examination of this problem, such as the Catholic or Communist systems, are distinguished by the fact that in them more or less concealed value judgments are presented as components of a science, and cognitive value is claimed for them. This practice clearly contradicts the principle of value freedom, and thus contributes an important direction to the solution of the problem of demarcation, if one is prepared to acknowledge this principle for the formulation of scientific results. The fusion of cognitive and normative components in systems of statements which as a whole present cognitive claims is apparently a very successful way to influence attitudes and modes of behavior, and to legitimize—and thus to stabilize—institutional arrangements. So from there one also seems to have access to the question of the effectiveness of ideologies. The actual import of such systems of statements from this point of view seems to consist chiefly in this: that they convey the impression that one is dealing with objective and unrevisable knowledge, and thus contribute to the dogmatizing of specific value judgments and norms in the social groups for which they are authoritative.

Thus, it is understandable that Theodor Geiger, in his attempt to demarcate ideology and science, treated the value judgment as the paradigm of ideological statement, in accordance with his view that judgments of this sort in general are disguised as cognitive statements without possessing true cognitive content.[2] His paratheoretical statements, which have the same character without necessarily being reducible to valuations, are conceived of as extensions of this category for purposes of ideology critique, in order to include, as no less ideological, certain nonevaluative utterances that are among

[2] The Platonic analysis of value judgments used by Geiger is in any case extremely problematic; for my criticism of this and some other aspects of Geiger's thought, see my article, "Ideologie und Wahrheit. Theodor Geiger und das Problem der Sozialen Verankerung des Denkens," in *Konstruktion und Kritik*, pp. 168 ff.

the components typical of ideological statement systems. They are extremely loosely characterized, however—so much so as to cast doubts upon the adequacy of Geiger's solution to the problem of demarcation. Above and beyond this, fundamental objections can be raised to any treatment of the problem of ideology in which demarcation stands in the foreground, especially one that attempts to solve this problem through logical analysis of categories of statements. To begin with, the way the question is formulated is directed explicitly toward the problem of *illegitimacy*. That is to say, Geiger's objective is to demarcate cognitively illegitimate statements and the systems in which they are contained from genuine cognitive statements. His concept of ideology purports to be an epistemological concept. The demarcation suggested by him corresponds to some extent to the positivistic distinction between science and metaphysics, except that for him the positivistic thesis of meaninglessness is replaced by the thesis of the epistemological illegitimacy of certain statements—namely, statements that are anything other than the result of a processing of observations according to rules of logic.[3]

Geiger's attempted demarcation is thus subject to the same objections that confront the analogous attempts in the camp of philosophical positivism, all the more so as his formulation is less subtle and therefore considerably easier to attack. Furthermore, the thesis of illegitimacy can hardly be interpreted otherwise than to be itself subsumable under the negatively characterized category of value judgments. Thus one must conclude that Geiger has in effect based his demarcation of ideology on a thesis he himself would have to characterize as ideological. Furthermore, the thesis that value judgments are cognitively illegitimate is of course self-reflexive, and thus establishes its own cognitive illegitimacy. This weakness is not as easily curable as one might think if one considered it to be only a question of wording. For any reformulation—adequate in Geiger's sense—of the thesis underlying his demarcation

[3] Compare Geiger, *Ideologie und Wahrheit*, p. 47.

attempt would undoubtedly have to be constructed to reveal the evaluation—according to Geiger's own account, fully subjective—that conceals itself in that "pseudo-objective" thesis. That alone is sufficient to make his demarcation attempt highly questionable. Apart from that, the manifest intention of his demarcation, oriented as it is toward definitional stipulations, is to spare the critic of ideology any discussion with those whose products fall under his verdict.[4] We are presented, then, with a reproach of cognitive illegitimacy whose basis is secured by stipulation and is, thereby, purportedly exempt from all discussion. But precisely this circumstance can be turned into an object of criticism if one begins with the principle of critical examination and thereby rejects the dogmatization of statements. Geiger's solution to the problem of demarcation, as we can clearly see, may be traced back to an epistemological dogma.[5]

Let us for the moment turn away from this recourse to dogma, and ask ourselves how in general we ought to view attempts to resolve the demarcation problem primarily by logical characterization of various categories of statements, which means, in practice, through the logical analysis of particular propositions. An attempt of this sort is not satisfying from an epistemological point of view, because it pays no heed to the importance of context for the interpretation of statements and because it furthermore implies that one can resolve the question of the rationality of conceptions independent of problems of methodical strategy. Geiger's way of posing the problem shows a certain logicism in its treatment of the problem of ideology and leads no further, even from

[4] That seems to me to be clearly suggested by his discussion on pp. 46 ff., for example.

[5] That is not to deny that in many of his works Geiger has shown himself an extraordinarily critical thinker, from whom one can learn a great deal—above all because of the clarity with which he formulates his theses. Many have stumbled over the snares of such problems; but in the case of unclear thinkers who use esoteric vocabulary it is not so easy to see.

the sociological point of view; that is, it does not contribute anything toward the explanation of the phenomena.

But Geiger calls attention to yet another aspect of the problem of ideology, although it is hardly compatible with the approach sketched above. It concerns not the *fusion* of evaluation and knowledge through the formulation of *crypto-normative* statements, but rather the *motivation* of *factual-informative* statements by the evaluations that underlie them.[6] Here, then, we no longer face the epistemological problem of demarcation, but rather the sociological problem of *explanation* which refers to questions of causation and forces one to develop a theoretical approach. The interplay of these two problems in Geiger's analysis becomes apparent through certain absurdities that cannot be resolved within the framework of his approach. An ideological determination of statements of the sort he envisions—the motivation of cognitive statements by evaluations—might well be difficult to demonstrate in particular cases, although one might hope that psychological research will help to solve such problems sooner or later. But be that as it may, the inclusion of this problem calls into question the demarcation of science from ideology on the basis of specific types of statements; for one cannot expect that a demarcation derived from motivational considerations will converge with one resulting from logical analysis; all the more as one cannot categorically exclude the possibility that motivation of the sort Geiger describes could under some circumstances generate empirically testable, perhaps even true, statements. According to Geiger's own distinctions, however, such statements would under no circumstances have an ideological character. To be sure, Geiger makes a sharp distinction here between the motivation of questions and the determination of statements, and he restricts his suspicion of ideology to the case in which the evaluation influences the answering

---

[6] Compare Geiger, *Ideologie und Wahrheit*, chapter 7, "Frage-Antriebe und Aussage-Steuerung."

of the question, not its posing. But even such an influence need not necessarily produce false answers.

The examples analyzed by Geiger show that his emphasis gradually changes in the course of his investigations from the logical *structure* of the propositions considered to *strategies* applied to statements and statement systems. Thus, an interesting problem shift occurs, moving him from his initial approach in a direction which, in my view, is significantly more fruitful for the problem of ideology. While in the beginning the problem of *demarcation* plays the central role and produces attempts to expose a type of statement that can be characterized as ideological, later, particularly in the analysis of particular examples, *procedural* problems move into the foreground, and, with them, attempts to distinguish strategies peculiar to ideological thinking. But since these strategies are applicable to statements of any type, Geiger's conception loses its unity of focus.

Once one agrees to approach the problem of ideology as a question of sociological explanation, and thereby allows problems of motivation and of social causation, Geiger's demarcation problem may not simply retreat to the background as a secondary problem. On the contrary, it might well emerge that epistemologically inspired and logically implemented demarcations of the sort initially attempted by Geiger have no real basis whatsoever. Nomological hypotheses invoked to explain social phenomena in the realm of ideology formation could presumably serve also for the explanation of social events in the realm of science, and vice versa—and this not only in the ideologically compromised social sciences and humanities, but in mathematics and the natural sciences as well. The quasi-ontological distinction between science and ideology, from which the analysis of ideology frequently proceeds, has a certain resemblance to the Aristotelian distinction between "natural" and "externally imposed" motion,[7] a distinction which

[7] Compare the analysis of Alexandre Koyré in his *Galilean Studies*, pp. 17 ff.

107

might seem plausible to common sense but was completely banished by the scientific revolution of the seventeenth century.

That theoretical illumination and explanation of states of affairs in different social areas that are institutionally and culturally delimitable from one another should require one to call upon different laws is a very curious epistemological idea. In our case, it might be associated with differences of valuation,[8] or it might as likely be associated, as is often the case, with certain obvious differences of actual functioning in virtue of special social regulations. There is some inclination to elevate such modes of functioning to the rank of explanatory laws, although we know that one and the same theory—for example, one in the natural sciences—can explain even very differently functioning machines,[9] given dissimilar conditions of activity. Such conditions in social areas might be traced to different types of institutional rules—for example, regulations that contribute to competition of ideas and to the generation and spread of innovations, versus those that contribute to monopoly and regimentation of spiritual production and to the conservation of traditional patterns of interpretation. However, insofar as one is in a position to offer explanations

[8] That one can explain completely different valued things by applying the same principle is a thesis that often arouses strong resistance. We instinctively prefer to believe that good things must come from noble sources, bad things from questionable ones; thus for example, we think of error as arising out of rather disreputable interests, while truth, on the other hand, must stem from noble, pure contemplation, or perhaps even from divine inspiration.

[9] This distinction between the patterns of functioning—i.e., natural and social mechanisms—and the lawlike regularities that explain the existence of such patterns under certain circumstances is in no way dependent upon questionable analogies of content between the different realms of explanation. In any case, one finds a thoroughly apposite analysis containing this distinction, associated with a comparison of natural and social mechanisms, in Max Weber's extremely interesting article, "R. Stammlers 'Überwindung' der materialistischen Geschichtsauffassung" (*Gesammelte Aufsätze zur Wissenschaftslehre*, pp. 324 ff.), a work that also contains an examination of the rules of games that deserves at least as much attention as Wittgenstein's remarks on this subject.

for such phenomena, one commands a knowledge that can be made technologically fruitful in influencing events through creating institutional arrangements that are effective in producing the desired results—for instance, by providing optimal conditions for theoretical speculation and for critical discussion of its results.

If we now return to Geiger's attempt to analyze and resolve the problem of ideology, we can more clearly see, from the position we have reached, exactly what is problematic about this interesting undertaking. The two problems whose interplay produces the difficulties in Geiger's solution, are those of demarcation and of explanation. The *demarcation problem* here is only a modern refurbishing of the *essentialists'* question of the *essence* of ideology—a question in which, as often happens, definitional and normative intentions are bound together, although its answer would not yield any real knowledge.[10] The *problem of explanation*, on the other hand, has reference to *causal connections* in this area and its solution demands a *nomological* basis. But the range of application of the relevant laws is not restricted to those phenomena picked out by the essentialist inquiry. The answer to the question of essence as dictated by an evaluative point of view has little to do with the solution to the causal problem. And in any case the latter, even in epistemological respects, is more important than the solution to the demarcation problem at least as long as one is prepared to broaden the *methodological* problematic to include questions of *social technology*. One can be restrained from such an extension only through a demarcation dogma constituted a priori, according to which it is forbidden to burden the solution of philosophical problems with considerations of factual, or even worse, of social, relationships, although it is not obvious why philosophy should have more to do with logic—undeniably a very important special disci-

---

[10] On the criticism of essentialism, compare the relevant sections in Karl Popper's books, *The Open Society and Its Enemies, The Poverty of Historicism*, and *Conjectures and Refutations*; compare also my above-mentioned book, *Marktsoziologie und Entscheidungslogik*.

pline—than with physics or sociology.[11] In opposition to all that, we ought to emphasize that the critical method has not only logical facets, but, for instance, psychological and sociological ones as well, to whose analysis the relevant sciences could contribute.

## 14. IDEOLOGY AND METHODOLOGY: THE PROBLEM OF JUSTIFICATION AND THE CRITICISM OF IDEOLOGY

Before we turn to the social science aspects of the problem of ideology, we should consider the extremely interesting connection between ideology and science, which becomes clear when one considers the typical strategies that play a role in each field. Relationships seem to exist between the problem of ideology and the problem of method in sciences, which make it quite understandable how demarcation attempts of the sort described above can easily lead to a dead end.

We saw that Theodor Geiger's method of argument drew him into a paradoxical situation: the situation of a critic of ideology who has based his criticism on a thesis that necessarily must itself fall victim to the criticism. That is, the demarcation problem Geiger wishes to resolve, is de facto a part of a typical ideological question, the *problem of justification*. It makes no great difference to the general character of this

[11] After the positivistic program was proved unrealizable, the clean demarcation between philosophy and science on the basis of the division of all cognitive statements into logico-analytic (or contradictory) and factual-empirical could not be maintained. Even if we were to succeed in showing that the problematic sentences about the incompatibility of colors qualify as analytic according to a revised classification (compare Harald Delius, *Untersuchungen zur Problematic der sogenannten synthetischen Sätze* a priori [Göttingen, 1963]), certain sentences with mixed quantifiers are nevertheless left over—for instance, "all-and-some statements"—which cannot be so treated. Compare J.W.N. Watkins, "Between Analytic and Empirical," *Philosophy* 32 (1957), and "Confirmable and Influential Metaphysics," *Mind*, vol. 67 (1958). For a criticism of "pure" philosophy in the sense of the analytic tradition, compare Karl Popper, "The Nature of Philosophical Problems and their Roots in Science" (1952), in *Conjectures and Refutations*.

question whether it is posed as a query about the legitimacy of knowledge or as a problem of the justification of social orders and the structures of sovereignty. But this problem is identical with the *problem of foundations* discussed above, as it was usually posed in classical methodology. What is at stake is a conception that cannot be restricted to the realms of science or even of knowledge, but is to be conceived of much more universally, in that it can be applied in all social realms— to the legal order, to economic life, to questions of morals and politics: in short, everywhere that legitimation of statements, systems, ways of behaving, institutions, and orders comes under consideration.

From these considerations, however, a serious consequence arises for the epistemological problematic of ideology: anyone who accepts the classical methodology that has its origins in the principle of sufficient justification cannot possibly *distinguish ideology from knowledge* in a convincing way; for the only solution to the problem of validity considered practicable by this methodology, as we found through our earlier analysis, is recourse to a more or less camouflaged dogma—the route, in other words, typically attributed to ideological thinking. The methodical approach, characterized by the foundation principle, thus exhibits, even when it is in fact combined with a critical attitude, an intrinsically authoritarian-dogmatic structure; for every justification of the type demanded by this approach falls back in the last analysis upon some foundation whose authority is established and must be somehow transferred—through deductive or inductive procedures or some other device—to the statements or states of affairs to be legitimized. The dogmatic model of rationality that comes to expression in the corresponding interpretation of scientific method is *eo ipso* the model of ideological thinking. The fact that in order to achieve justification, differing ultimate authorities and various transfer procedures might be called into play, does not affect the character of this method, which is directed toward attaining *certainty*, and thereby also *validity*, through recourse to a court of appeal that possesses unconditional authority.

The significance of the methodology of critical examination as a general alternative to this practice of delimited rationality thereby becomes clear. For this methodology, in which justification is replaced by permanent critique, provides a model of rationality which can fundamentally take the place of justificationalism in all social areas, and can replace the typical ideological style of thinking, even if one has no illusions about the real possibility of completely eliminating this style.

If one accepts this revision in the formulation of the problem of ideology, one has reason to reconsider the possible tasks for the criticism of ideologies from this perspective. It becomes less tempting to concentrate on denigrating certain types of words and statements, such as value words or value judgments, less plausible to consider the critique of ideology an enterprise of language purification, as would be very natural to do from the positivistic point of view.[12] Indeed, the elevation of the language of pure science—in some respects a value-free language—to a model for reasonable speech in general is ill-advised; and the belief that this ideal could be put into effect is a utopian hope which rests on the problematic claim that such language, in fact a complicated and relatively esoteric special instrument created for the pursuit of knowledge, can provide the best solution of the communication problem in every situation. From the criticist point of view one can rather make a stronger case for setting the criticism of ideology the task of so reducing the irrationality of life in society that the results and methods of critical thinking can be made fruitful for the formation of social consciousness and of public opinion: the task, in short, of *enlightenment*. That

---

[12] In this respect one can certainly agree with Lübbe's criticism on this point; see Herman Lübbe, "Der Streit um Worte, Sprache und Politik," *Bochumer Universitätsreden*, vol. 3 (Bochum, 1967). Compare also my article, "Politische Ökonomie und rationale Politik," in *Theoretische und Institutionelle Grundlagen der Wissenschaftspolitik*, published by Hans Besters (Berlin, 1967), p. 61, reprinted in *Aufklärung und Steuerung*.

means, above all, promoting education by rational problem-solving procedures, furthering thereby a style of thinking that corresponds to the model of critical rationality sketched above. It is often less important to pass on detailed knowledge than it is to teach a method that allows the individual to form independent judgments[13] and to see through strategies of immunizing and obscuring, of obfuscation and confusion, and other dogmatic ways of proceeding. The object of such an education would be to give members of a society immunity to irrelevant types of argumentation, while making them more sensitive to genuine and relevant criticism.

Ideology critics might then devote themselves to the correction of certain prejudices which, according to the present state of knowledge, could not withstand critical objections, particularly socially and politically influential prejudices. From the point of view of the critique of ideology, one might say that the progress of knowledge consists in the revision of existing and influential prejudices, a revision that can advance only very slowly on all social areas. By the correction of questionable prejudices we of course do not mean anything like the complete purification of consciousness recommended by classical epistemology; we need not elaborate upon that here. Criticism of specific socially effective theoretical, moral, and political ideas cannot mean eradicating all ideas of this type; the criticism of dominant values does not imply the creation of a value vacuum, if only because such a vacuum, for psychological reasons mentioned above, could not be maintained. Nor is an ideology critique of this sort to be conceived of as a subfield of sociology; rather, the results and procedure of

---

[13] Bertrand Russell quite correctly points out that schools these days are often used simultaneously "to mediate information and to promote superstition," and that the spread of the knowledge of scientific achievements is not identical with the spread of the scientific way of thinking recommended by him. Against William James he maintained the critical thesis: "What is necessary is not the will to believe, but the will to discover. . . ." See his "Free Thought and Official Propaganda" (1922), reprinted in *Sceptical Essays* (London/New York, 1928).

all sciences come into consideration. Copernicus, Galileo, Newton, and Darwin are as much a part of the history of the critique of ideology as Helvetius, Feuerbach, Marx, Nietzsche, and Freud, and they are so insofar as the discoveries of all these thinkers have in large measure become socially significant. We do not thereby deny that the sociological investigations specifically directed to the problem of ideology might under some circumstances become significant for the criticism of ideology; nor is it necessary to demarcate it from criticism of knowledge, morals, law, or religion, or from other types of critical thought. Such demarcations are unimportant from our point of view. The criticism of the classical model of rationality is equally relevant in all these domains.

The question of the value-free character of science is also in no way particularly interesting from the point of view of the critique of ideology. First of all, a science that is in Max Weber's sense value-free can without difficulty contribute considerably to ideology critique. The explanation and analysis of circumstances, events, and causal connections as pursued by science today can be brought into social consciousness and used to good effect against prevailing prejudices. Moreover, ideology criticism, like science, can orient itself on the values inherent in the model of critical rationality and even further on other viewpoints, which, for example, could arise from the sort of critical moral and legal philosophy possible within the realm of criticist philosophy. That the critique of ideology is dependent upon the current state of knowledge is a fact, which need cause us no concern. An infallible authority that would guarantee a complete purification of the intellect from all socially influential errors, mistakes, and weaknesses is in any case, according to the criticist conception, nowhere to be found. We must also, in general, forswear such courts of appeal without lapsing into despair.

Since the critique of ideology must constantly battle against the processes of dogmatization, which, because of social inertia, reappear again and again, and, since in the process it must contend with views that have both deep psychic roots and strong social anchorings, it cannot rest content with the linguistic tools provided by science and philosophy. In the interest of the broadest and most penetrating results, it also draws on the means offered by art and literature, techniques that in fact have often been applied to this end. Even the sciences have had recourse to dialogue to present new ideas of great import to social conditions of the time to best effect.[14] The desire to use the theater in the service of ideology critique[15] might seem perverse to some, or at least a deflection from its usual purpose, especially if one considers it to be self-evident that either spiritual purification (catharsis) or, less pompously, enjoyment, is its natural purpose.[16] But there is no such thing as a "nature" of the theater from which one can necessarily infer the purpose for which it should be performed; indeed, its utilization for the critique of ideology seems very profitable. From the criticist viewpoint it is unnecessary to set limits upon the practice of criticism which would preclude exactly those tools that are most efficient for enlightenment and de-dogmatization. However, questions of efficiency—in semiotic terminology—are pragmatic, and thus technological problems that must be decided with reference to psychological and so-

[14] One thinks of Galileo's presentation of his theory in the form of a dialogue between three imaginary figures, Salviati, Sagredo, and Simplicio, in his *Discorsi e Dimostrazioni Matematiche intorno Due Nuoue Scienze* of 1638.

[15] Compare Paul Feyerabend's interesting article, "Theater als Ideologiekritik. Bemerkungen zu Ionesco," in *Die Philosophie und die Wissenschaft, Simon Moser zum 65. Geburtstag* (Meisenheim am Glan, 1967), pp. 400 ff., as well as the same author's section 6, "Theater," in his contribution "On the Improvement of the Sciences and the Arts, and the Possible Identity of the Two," to *Boston Studies*, III (Dordrecht-Holland, 1962), p. 406, where the classical theory of the theater is criticized and the possible role of the theater within criticism is elucidated with reference to Brecht.

[16] Brecht comments, in "Kleines Organon für das Theater" in his *Schriften zum Theater. Uber eine nicht-aristotelische Dramatik* (Frankfurt, 1965), p. 131: "Not even teaching should be expected of it . . . less than anything else do pleasures need a defense." The same author, however, as is well known, pleads for a critical theater (pp. 139 ff.), since criticism need not interfere with pleasure.

ciological viewpoints—that is, from perspectives that have always been decisive for the theory of the theater as well.[17]

## 15. The Mutual Involvement of Thought and Being as a Problem of Science

There can be no doubt that thinking oriented around the notion of justification, still prevalent in many areas of society, is not a fact of nature and hence unavoidable, but owes its supremacy to the presence of circumstances favorable to it. Should conditions change, this style of thought may recede or even vanish completely. This produces an interesting problem for the social sciences, one which can inspire theoretical, experimental, and historical investigations, and indeed, has already inspired many such studies in the past.

One of the most interesting results of these studies could be formulated as the thesis of the *nonexistence of "pure reason"*—that is, thought which is essentially free from all vital motivational and social influences—so that in order to understand its function one can in principle abstract from such factors. Human problem-solving behavior, even where the solutions it produces must meet certain standards or approximate certain ideals to be seen as *valid*, in fact depends upon the realization of certain conditions, whose absence would provide a different pattern of activity and hence different results as well. In this sense, the thinkers who have spoken of the "dependence of consciousness on being," or "the mutual involvement of thought and being," have undeniably seen something true, even though they have conjoined this insight with a cognitive program which was influenced by historism and therefore provided no incentive to seek out the general

---

[17] The criticist viewpoint thus consciously includes in its deliberations the pragmatic problem considered by Lübbe in his above-mentioned article. Compare Lübbe, "Der Streit um Worte," and Feyerabend, "Theater als Ideologiekritik," pp. 408 ff.

regularities that govern this relationship.[18] In the meantime, such theoretical sciences as biology, psychology, and sociology have achieved a plethora of results that are relevant to the explanation of such dependencies. Only a historist prejudice could prevent those interested in such phenomena from utilizing them this way. Various irrationalisms have long made profitable use of such regularities by exploiting the fear, the uncertainty,·and the striving for orientation of people to achieve the fixation of their behavior on certain ends, which have not seldom turned out to be incompatible with their fundamental interests. Even a rationalism that has no cause to suggest such goals should not ignore regularities of this type in its critical practice.

From the standpoint of modern research, what is characterized by sociologists of knowledge as the "being-bound" character of thought may be understood as the context-dependence of human problem-solving behavior. This activity is extremely selective with respect to thought, perception, and behavior, and appears, too, to be dependent upon certain frames of reference that are anchored in internal and external factors of different sorts—factors, for example, of a motivational and social character, whose contribution to the functioning of these processes can be determined.[19] As for the social anchoring of these cognitive patterns, which are relevant

[18] Consider in this connection Karl Mannheim and his concern—paradoxically to be understood only through his neglect of the history of natural science and mathematics—to establish a sociology of knowledge as a separate epistemology of the humanistic sciences, which correspondingly rejects nomological interpretations as a paradigm only of natural science. Cf. *Ideology and Utopia*, trans. Wirth and Shils (New York, 1966).

[19] Compare Muzafer Sherif and Carolyn W. Sherif, *An Outline of Social Psychology*, rev. ed. (New York, 1956); M. Sherif and Carl I. Hovland, *Social Judgment* (New Haven/London, 1961); Carolyn Sherif, Muzafer Sherif, and Roger E. Nebergall, *Attitude and Attitude Change: The Judgment-Involvement Approach* (Philadelphia/London, 1965). See also the survey of contemporary research in Martin Irle, "Entstehung und Änderung von sozialen Einstellungen (Attitüden)," found in the *Bericht über den 25. Kongreß der Deutschen Gesellschaft für Psychologie* (Göttingen, 1967).

CHAPTER FOUR

for the interpretation of situations, it is well known that reference groups—the social loci of this anchoring—exercise upon the individuals belonging to them a pressure to conform that is stronger or weaker, depending, first, upon the formal and informal sanctions available to them, and, second, upon the social importance of the problem under consideration—a pressure which is directed toward maintaining certain uniform standards for problem solving. Thus a change of social milieu—and hence of reference groups—generally has an influence upon the attitudes, convictions, and modes of behavior of the individuals concerned. The existence of social mechanisms that convey this pressure to conform has been frequently considered unconditionally negative; but such a valuation does not consider the possibility that the norms supported through such mechanisms might vary considerably in character. They can be of such a kind, for instance, as to provide protection for an arena of free creative activity against attacks that would destroy it. Anyone who is prepared to give up the utopian idea of a "pure reason" in the above-mentioned sense must come to terms with the fact that there are social factors of this sort which can indeed be shaped, but whose existence cannot be removed by decree. Reason in every form is a product of social and cultural forces shaping a living foundation.[20]

The anchoring of individual frames of reference, attitudes, and convictions in factors of the sociocultural milieu stems from the fact that in this way needs are satisfied—needs of all sorts, from the elementary needs of nourishment and shelter to those directed specifically to social relations, emotional security, intellectual orientation, or aesthetic satisfaction. The way in which the environment provides for the satisfaction of needs obviously determines, to some degree and in some

[20] Today we have some information about this physiological basis; see B.D.O. Hebb, *The Organization of Behavior: A Neuropsychological Theory* (New York/London, 1949), as well as P. B. Medawar, "Tradition: The Evidence of Biology" (1953) in his collection *The Uniqueness of the Individual* (London, 1957), and idem, *The Future of Man* (London, 1960).

118

direction, the ways in which individual problem-solving behavior develops, with earlier influences apparently exercising a relatively stronger force than later ones.[21] Clearly there are connections between need structure, structure of the belief system, and the individual style of problem-solving behavior; these connections go back to early experiences in problem solving. Above all, the dominance of experiences of fear seems to contribute to the tendency to construct closed belief systems, and thereby to the dogmatization of essential components of these systems.[22] An enduring sense of being threatened, particularly when it is inculcated early on through appropriate educational practices and environmental influences, is clearly an important condition for the generation of such belief systems. This condition can develop through the effect of early childhood experiences or later events and become a part of the structure of the personality; or it can be purely situational, and thus of a temporary nature.

People who have been formed in this way—who have an authoritarian, dogmatically structured belief system—display an approach to problem solving that suggests that their belief system is minimally coherent; that is, it consists of components that are sharply isolated from one another. The problem of creating a congruent system of beliefs, arising from the natural desire for a unified world view, is solved by such people through compartmentalization; they have no incentive for revision because they do not perceive the incompatibilities among the components of their belief system. This produces a heightened

[21] The extreme emphasis of the Freudian view on experiences of early childhood, however, cannot be maintained; see, for instance, Muzafer Sherif and Carolyn W. Sherif, *Reference Groups: Explorations into Conformity and Deviation of Adolescents* (New York/Evanston/London, 1964), pp. 180 ff. and passim; also see it for a criticism of the Freudian theory of conscience.

[22] Compare Milton Rokeach, *The Open and The Closed Mind: Investigations in the Nature of Belief Systems and Personality Systems* (New York, 1960). These studies support the psychoanalytic orientation of Pfister in essential points; compare Oskar Pfister, *Das Christentum und die Angst* (Zürich, 1944), in which he analyzes the connection between anxiety and dogmatism.

119

*immunity against relevant arguments*, combined with a willingness to alter certain components of the system under the influence of accepted authorities, even if that does not contribute to an improvement of the coherence of the system: in short, a certain *nonimmunity against rationally irrelevant arguments*. This is a style of thought that can be characterized as *"party-line thinking,"*[23] although it actually deserves a name that would take account of the legitimate theological claims for priority. We will see that thought patterns of this sort enjoy some institutional support; that they have had a certain importance for the development of the sciences; and that they can lead to extraordinarily subtle arguments, which nonetheless serve the sole purpose of concealing clear absurdities, in order to avoid surrendering dogmatized components of belief systems.

The emotional investment in belief systems that arise out of experience of fear contributes to the immunity of such systems to new ideas, experiences, and information of all kinds. To an emotionally anchored defensiveness, novelty appears threatening, so clinging to old convictions and deep-rooted prejudices is more prized than testing new ideas and methods; and specific components of beliefs, if sanctified by the social authorities to which the relevant individuals are dogmatically bound, become rigidly fixed. As is now well known, convictions that in no way correspond to reality—the inadequacy of which is readily apparent to a critical observer—can prove extraordinarily stable if they are supported strongly enough by the society. *Correspondence to reality* can be extensively replaced by *social anchoring.*[24] The loss of stable anchorings

[23] Cf. Milton Rokeach, *The Open and Closed Mind*, pp. 225 ff. and passim.

[24] This is shown to some extent by the study of certain sects that successfully compensate for the failure of prophesies through zealous proselytizing; see Leon Festinger, Henry Riecken, and Stanley Schachter, *When Prophesy Fails* (Minneapolis, 1956), where an explanation of such phenomena is attempted through the theory of cognitive dissonance—a theory that is also interesting for ideology analysis, and that is relevant to the analysis of millennialist and messianic movements such as early Christianity. The postponement of *pa-*

for a world view, and the associated condition of uncertainty, absence of norms, and disorientation, on the other hand, seem hardly bearable. In our analysis of the problem of knowledge, we have already indicated the impossibility of a theoretical vacuum. In the absence of alternative patterns of interpretation for the structuring of motivationally significant situations, dogmatically fixed attitudes remain in effect. In such mechanisms we discern the explanation of the fact that in social realms dominated by comparatively closed ideologies of a religious or secular character, innovators are very often castigated as heretics or renegades and persecuted, while acceptable innovations in matters of faith can at best be implemented in the guise of interpretations. Although errors, as we know, can have a positive effect on the advance of knowledge and the general improvement of our problem solutions, in these areas they are usually branded as sins, since people know they possess revealed truth, and this truth is considered sacred.

In certain circumstances, then, an emotionally rooted desire for certainty can create a situation in which the belief system that helps individuals orient themselves in reality can take on the character of a defense network against threatening information, so that the *protective function* overshadows the theoretical *function of orientation in the world*. We have here a situation—developed in classical epistemology into a conception of rationality of a certain sort—in which the drive for certainty overcomes the search for truth. The system thus becomes a closed one, so that information selection is increasingly oriented toward system-confirming, rather than merely system-relevant, information. Instead of paying attention to information that cannot be integrated into the system and seeking alternatives, people tend to collect confirming information, hoping by this course to minimize undesirable cognitive dissonances. If by chance *prima facie* contradictory in-

---

*rousia*, which leads to difficulties for theological thinking, may be rendered understandable through this theory, as are similar shifts in Marxist theory that represent the same strategy.

formation is encountered, the inclination is to reinterpret it appropriately and to rework it in system-confirming ways—applying, in short, immunization strategies that are directed toward maintaining the belief system, regardless of the epistemological costs of such procedures. Under some circumstances people are even prepared to sacrifice logic in order to keep beliefs safe from harm; in such decisions the authoritarian attitude of the believer toward certain institutionally defined authority figures sometimes plays a considerable role.

The closed nature of some individual systems of beliefs thus seems to be connected with an attitude that is favorable to the application of methods of positive justification; but it does not encourage the method of critical examination, which gives priority to the search for alternatives and for all relevant information, whether reconcilable with a particular system or not. *Critical rationality* of that sort and the *dogmatic rationalization* that is found in closed belief systems can be viewed as two limiting cases of cognitive functioning. Each of these extremes can be worked into a methodological model for problem-solving behavior in the various social realms, and the advantages and disadvantages of each from various evaluative standpoints can be investigated. This has to some extent been done in epistemology and in other parts of philosophy, such as ethics or political or legal philosophy. In the sciences the model that has largely prevailed is the model that the criticist point of view would most prefer, that in which thought is largely emancipated from motives of security and protection. It has almost developed to a technology, so far as the formal, linguistic and some of the social aspects are concerned, but less attention has been paid to the psychological problems involved.[25] It can be assumed, in view of the fact that the structural relations at stake are essentially independent of any

[25] There is on the one hand, a formal methodology that treats of the structure, testing, and application of theories; and on the other hand, a way of constituting free scientific discussion. But the motivational and the learning- and perception-theoretical aspects of problem-solving behavior until now have been given hardly any methodological consideration.

special nature of the problem to be solved or of any special content of the desired solution, that the model can be readily extended to other areas. Such structural relations also appear where dogmatic rationalizations are at work through the independence of special contents. Thus it is not surprising that the typical convert often retains the authoritarian-dogmatic structure of his belief system despite radical changes in the content of his beliefs.[26] The authority is interchangeable, the particulars of the belief system dictated by it are equally so; and the change of authority works in a way analogous to change in a party line by a persisting authority figure. In such circumstances, the "mutual involvement of thought and being" is revealed.

## 16. Dogmatization as Social Practice and the Problem of Criticism

Among the social aspects of dogmatism are, above all, institutional arrangements made by groups with dogmatic belief systems in order to immunize their adherents as far as possible against the influence of deviant interpretations and dangerous ideas and information. So even in its social aspects, dogmatization has a protective function. The *purpose of the installation of dogmas* is not so much the solving of problems of knowledge or morality as it is the *rejection* of inadequate solutions, that is, *solutions viewed as dangerous* by the relevant authorities: in short, *the defamation of alternatives*. It is opposed to free consideration of alternative solutions, and serves instead to establish the solutions condoned by the authorities, and at the same time to perpetuate the institutions associated with the approved system of beliefs by excluding those who believe otherwise—those who will not subordinate themselves to the relevant authorities. Belief in the adequacy of certain solutions is thus raised to the status of a legally

[26] Compare Eric Hoffer, *The True Believer: Thoughts on the Nature of Mass Movements* (New York, 1958, 1960).

enforceable duty.[27] In institutional systems of this sort, then, one of the above-mentioned paradigms of cognitive function, the model of dogmatic rationalization, is established as official practice. As we suggested earlier in our analysis of the epistemological problematic, the inseparable connection of theory of knowledge and social theory here shows itself particularly clearly.

It is unnecessary to emphasize that institutional structures and social mechanisms of this sort are not restricted to a special belief system, nor even to theological conceptions in the narrow sense of the word.[28] As is well known, secular ideologies can also in this way institutionally anchor obligations to believe and demands to obey, and can attempt to protect their articles of faith—or the currently imposed interpretations of the legitimate interpreters—from criticism through strategies of logical, psychic, and social immunization. The provisions to be considered in this regard range from raising children with only one-sided information available, protecting them from alternative world views and dogmatic viewpoints, and secluding them from persons who could represent other points of view or promote dangerous ideas, to directive and protective devices for adults in order to achieve the same ends—such as bringing all intermediate groups into line with a belief.[29] In general, such practices can only be put into effect

[27] See Joseph Klein, *Grundlegung und Grenzen des kanonischen Rechts* (Tübingen, 1947), where the legally protected coupling of belief and obedience is analyzed, although the author fails to perceive the dubiousness of the revelation model that favors such conjunctions.

[28] See Paul Blanshard's book, *Communism, Democracy and Catholic Power* (London, 1952), where this institutional aspect of things is illuminated in a comparative analysis of the Catholic and Communist systems.

[29] These are all well-known procedures practiced equally in Catholic, Communist, and Fascist systems, which show a strong similarity, at least in this one essential respect, from the epistemological and social-philosophical viewpoints of critical rationalism. For an analysis of ideological practices of this sort, see the interesting article by Arthur Schweitzer, "Ideological Strategy," *The Western Political Quarterly* 15 (1962), which treats Fascist and Communist practices.

when there is a hierarchy of leadership that has a monopoly on the resolution of questions of belief and associated problems. In order to render their decisions immune to objections of members of the group, holders of certain positions in such a hierarchy are often invested with a factually or even a dogmatically supported claim to infallibility, which under some circumstances can be legitimized from the content of the relevant belief system.[30] Naturally such a charisma, which is sometimes hereditary, fits particularly well into a revelation model of knowledge, which presents the knowing process as the passive reception of inspirations, stemming from an indubitable source and thus provided with a guarantee of truth,

---

[30] Compare Blanshard's analysis in *Communism, Democracy and Catholic Power*. Fascism also operated with infallibility claims, and did so, indeed, in conscious imitation of theological thought patterns, as can be seen by a reading of Hitler's book *Mein Kampf*, in which a not inconsiderable influence of Catholic thought is manifested; see *Mein Kampf*, 270-274th printing (Munich, 1937), p. 507: "Political parties are inclined to compromise; world views never do. Political parties take opponents into consideration; world views proclaim their infallibility." This is a characterization that obviously applies only to certain world views. In the memoirs of the former leader of the Hitlerjugend, Baldur von Schirach, it becomes more clear to whom Hitler wished to attribute infallibility; see Schirach, "Ich glaubte an Hitler," *Stern*, no. 27, 2 April 1967, p. 44: "Hitler stepped to the window and looked out at the Papal embassy on the other side of the street. He said, 'I do not contest the claim of the Holy Father in Rome to be infallible in matters of faith. And no one can deny that I know more about political matters than anyone on earth. Therefore I proclaim political infallibility for myself and my followers.' " The Catholic model must have seemed attractive to him because of its authoritarian structure. See also in this connection, *Mein Kampf*, pp. 512 ff., where the importance of sticking to dogmas is positively evaluated. The structural affinities of Catholic and Fascist thought were correctly evaluated by those church officials and moral theologians who in 1933 saw Hitler as an ally in the fight against rationalism and liberalism; see the well-known article by Ernst Wolfgang Böckenförde, "Der deutsche Katholizismus im Jahre 1933," *Hochland*, vol. 53 (1961), pp. 215 ff., and also the pertinent passages of the book by Karlheinz Deschner, *Mit Gott und den Faschisten. Der Vatikan im Bunde mit Mussolini, Franco, Hitler und Pavelić* (Stuttgart, 1965), pp. 124 ff. and passim; this book is interesting for the problem of the relationship of Catholicism and Fascism.

to whose sources the bearers of certain roles are then considered to have privileged access.

In social systems of this type, conflicts with undesirable tendencies are stemmed through dogmatizing, through the formation of official orthodoxies that elevate the rejection of alternative problem solutions to a duty. In them, innovations, should they fail to impose themselves in the guise of interpretations of traditional doctrines, can appear only as heresy or apostasy.[31] However, where blind obedience and unconditional belief are elevated to the highest virtues, it is natural that heresies and apostasies are contested by all available means. In the case of the Catholic church, the mildness that currently dominates is often mentioned, which in fact contrasts with the earlier bloody persecutions that fill church history. But this mildness is mainly a consequence of the reduced power available to Catholicism in modern industrial society.[32] Even with reduced weaponry a system that is organized according to its official epistemology so as to devaluate deviant and alternative interpretations by subsuming them under categories such as heresy to combat and eliminate them, has social and political consequences that are not conducive to openness

[31] For the problem of innovations, which are, to be sure, to some extent necessary for the accommodation of such structures to altered circumstances, see the interesting remarks of the theologican Karl Rahner, considered "progressive" in Catholic circles, in his article, "Theologie im Neuen Testament," published in volume 5 of his *Schriften zur Theologie* (Einsiedeln/Zurich/Cologne, 1962), pp. 33 ff., about the historicity of revealed truth.

[32] It can hardly be doubted that in the time of the Franco regime the Catholic system in Spain treated Protestants, Communists, and other dissidents much more harshly than the Communist system in Poland treated Catholics. In both cases the power structure played an important role. That things can get fairly bloody in Catholic spheres of influence even in the twentieth century was shown by the cruel purge of the Croats in the fourth decade of this century, never officially acknowledged, in which the Catholic clergy, completely in the spirit of the Middle Ages, participated. See the instructive account in the above-mentioned book by Deschner, *Mit Gott und den Faschisten*, pp. 225 ff.; compare also Ladislaus Hory and Martin Broszat, *Der kroatische Ustascha-Staat, 1941-1945* (Stuttgart, 1964), pp. 72, 93 ff. and passim.

and tolerance.[33] "Revelation," as Kolakowski correctly remarked, "is a textbook for the Inquisitor,"[34] and the Inquisition, in one form or another, is a normal phenomenon[35] in social systems of this sort. In a way it has an epistemological basis, as judicial procedures in general tend to be connected with views that have an epistemological character.[36]

Institutionalized belief systems that function in this way are, as we know today, based on the exploitation of human anxiety, an anxiety that is to some extent produced by the methods of the system itself. The dogmatic-magical practice of the sacraments in Christian realms and the corresponding rituals of other cultures are hardly explicable without this emotional

[33] Cf. Karl Rahner, "Was ist Häresie?" in *Schriften zur Theologie*, V, pp. 527 ff., where the authoritarian-dogmatic structure of Catholic epistemology is revealed—a doctrine for the effects of which the author pleads a historical understanding. Characteristically, Rahner is in a position to see "the false and primitive application of a true basic insight" (p. 536) in Communist party-line thinking and the associated social practice. He thus reveals a complete incapacity to understand that behind a liberal epistemology, which does not presuppose that anyone in particular is in possession of an absolute truth, an ethos of truth might stand that may have at least some claim to respect, but not an indifference to truth—which might be dubbed amoral without further consideration. That is understandable, for one who places a premium on belief in particular views can have at best an ambivalent attitude toward critical thinking.

[34] See Leszek Kolakowski, "Der Priester und der Narr. Das theologische Erbe in der heutigen Philosophie," in his above-mentioned collection, *Der Mensch ohne Alternative*, p. 261; compare also Popper's criticism of the revelation model in his above-cited article, "On the Sources of Knowledge and Ignorance."

[35] Arthur Koestler, in his book on the history of science, *The Sleepwalkers: A History of Man's Changing Vision of the Universe* (New York, 1963), argues that the case of the Catholic church against Galileo proceeded in the same ways as the processes involving the Soviet police three hundred years later. The OGPU even seems to have copied the inquisition methods of the Church. To Koestler's criticism of Galileo in this book, compare the anticritical remarks of Benjamin Nelson in his article, "The Early Modern Revolutions in Science and Philosophy," *Boston Studies*, III, pp. 17 ff.

[36] See Paul Feyerabend, "Law and Psychology in Conflict," *Inquiry*, vol. 10 (1967), pp. 114 ff.

foundation.[37] In comparatively peaceful periods in which no crisis of any kind convulses the social structure and conjures up the danger of a normative vacuum and a threat to the total system, a balance can be attained that is relatively easily borne by the normal members of the society under the dominance of a more or less mild scholasticism, which contains the anxiety created within the system and utilizes it for its cohesion. In times of crisis, on the other hand, mass movements often arise in which, under increasing pressure of anxiety, appropriate elements of the ideological milieu are activated and transformed in the direction of actual needs and in such a way as to be irreconcilable with the dominant scholasticism and the social system protected by it. Utopian components usually sterilized within the scholastic system by appropriate interpretation procedures are drawn upon for the interpretation of the contemporary situation,[38] generally with the effect of proclaiming as imminent the forceful disruption of all relations and a total rebirth of the society. Such interpretations, even if they are disguised as scientific analyses, represent the de facto success of wish fantasies, amplified through emotional pressure, over every sober, realistic, and critical judgment of the situation. The certainty of being in possession of the truth that springs from revelation theory, and the accom-

[37] See the book by Pfister, mentioned above, *Das Christentum und die Angst*, and the studies of Rokeach and his collaborators. Max Weber had already shown that Calvinism, which had almost completely eliminated the sacramental rituals of Catholicism, has also exploited human capacities for anxiety; see his treatment in "Die protestantische Ethik und der Geist des Kapitalismus," in his *Gesammelten Aufsätzen zur Religionssoziologie*, vol. 1, 4th ed. (Tübingen, 1947).

[38] For an analysis of such processes, see Norman Cohn, *The Pursuit of the Millennium: Revolutionary Messianism in Medieval and Reformation Europe and its Bearing on Modern Totalitarian Movements*, 2d ed. (New York, 1961); Emanuel Sarkisyanz, *Russland und der Messianismus des Orients, Sendungsbewusstein und politischer Chiliasmus des Ostens* (Tübingen, 1955); and Wilhelm E. Mühlmann, *Chiliasmus und Nativismus. Studien zur Psychologie, Soziologie und historischen Kasuistik der Umsturzbewegungen* (Berlin, 1961). Christianity, Communism, and Fascism owe their origins to such movements.

panying intolerance, is common to both the acute ideological movements and those chronic scholastic systems from which their sacred truths are often drawn. The only difference between them lies in the call to their members for collective action, in order to attain through their cooperation that stage of fulfillment which the scholastic systems envisage only as the final goal of the development.[39] In such movements, revolutionary practice can acquire a magical character similar to that of sacramental practice in the static systems of scholasticized religion. The radical criticism of social structures from a utopian point of view without any mediation of realistic analysis, as it is practiced in such movements, is no closer to the ideal of critical rationality than is the absolute justification of the status quo on dogmatic ground, which dominates in conservative ideologies.[40] In both cases, the possibility of rational discussion of alternatives recedes equally into the background, while the conviction of possessing the only possible and morally justified solution of all important problems increases; so it is considered unnecessary to take seriously the solutions suggested by others.

The results of theoretical and empirical research into the problem of the mutual involvement of thought and being have provided some knowledge of the conditions of dogmatization and fanaticism, which can be used to further critical reason and critical-rational practices in social life; for to explain a

[39] See the interesting study by Michael Walzer, "Puritanism as a Revolutionary Ideology," *History and Theory*, vol. 3 (1963), pp. 59 ff., with a comparative analysis of the ideas and activities of Puritans, Jacobins, and Bolsheviks, pp. 86 ff. See also his book, *The Revolution of the Saints: A Study in the Origins of Radical Politics* (Cambridge, Mass., 1965), in which Max Weber's view of the Puritans is given a considerable revision, as it is in H. R. Trevor-Roper's book, *Religion, the Reformation and Social Change* (London, 1967).

[40] One thinks of Hitler's constantly reiterated anti-liberal criticism of "the system" and of "objectivity." On this rhetorical strategy of Hitler's, see Kenneth Burke, "The Rhetoric of Hitler's 'Battle,'" reprinted in *The Philosophy of Literary Form* (Baton Rouge, 1941), pp. 191-220. This same essay discusses the teachings that Hitler took over from the Catholics.

social phenomenon, as we know from the methodology of theoretical thought, is to show how it can in principle be avoided. We know today that structural traits of belief systems, as displayed in the pedagogical practices used to support them, in the procedures of indoctrination associated with them, in the types of sanctions chosen to secure them—the premium, for instance, on affirming the decreed article of faith despite one's own doubt—these structural characteristics have psychic and social effects, which are largely independent of their specific content and affect the problem-solving behavior of the members of the relevant social groups in a way that is extraordinarily significant, both ethically and intellectually. We are in a position to see the conditions and consequences of dogmatic convictions and attitudes more clearly than ever before. It is thus quite possible that we are getting closer to the solution of the sociotechnological problem of how the various areas of life in society, from education to politics, can be so organized as to allow, on the one hand, the greatest possible unhindered and constructive expression of the creative imagination of the participating individuals, while, on the other hand, allowing the free development of a rational criticism, as effective as possible, to advance the realistic solution of problems.[41] The solution of this sociotechnological problem, however, is in itself in no way sufficient to reform society in this direction, for in institutional systems interpenetrated with dogmatic-authoritarian beliefs there are strong interests, armed with political powers, devoted to maintaining those convictions and the attitudes associated with them. The various political theologies which dominate the largest part of the world—and which are warmly viewed even by intellectuals, whose freedom of discussion depends upon the fact that they live in a liberal climate—make it certain that the thought patterns of dogmatic rationalization, despite the fatal conse-

---

[41] For a treatment of a society that is "open," and thus to a great extent amenable to criticism, see Karl Popper, *The Open Society and Its Enemies*, as well as William Warren Bartley III, *The Retreat to Commitment*, p. 140 and passim.

quences that have historically been associated with them, nonetheless enjoy the highest respect. The tradition of critical thought originated in Greek antiquity and brought forth rich fruit for a period of time. Though it was not entirely vanquished in the power struggles of the Hellenistic period, it was nonetheless overshadowed and absorbed by other traditions. It has reawakened above all in scientific thought and the associated liberal tendency of modern culture. It is rooted in many social areas of this culture, and is an object of sympathy for many members of modern society, even some who are in some way involved in the political theologies of this period. The critique of ideology can contribute to the advance of the ideal of critical rationality in all areas by employing methods that are compatible with this ideal.

# FIVE

# Faith and Knowledge

## 17. THEOLOGY AND THE IDEA OF DOUBLE TRUTH

ALTHOUGH the idea of critical examination seems to be gaining ground in today's philosophical thinking, and justificationalism, in its cruder forms, is generally discredited, there is at the same time a strong tendency to restrict the application of the critical method to selected areas, while retaining older thought patterns and methods in others. There are attempts to protect certain areas against the encroachment of critical points of view, or to allow only their limited application, while in other areas of thought they are given a free rein; it is almost as if in some cases the approximation of truth or the elimination of errors, mistakes, and misunderstandings could be furthered by criticism, while in other cases critical thought might be damaging, or at least of only limited use. Such attempts at delimitation, though in themselves not particularly convincing, occur in all societies, for there are always beliefs or components of beliefs that are so important that they cannot be subjected to critical scrutiny without producing discomfort. Thus, one is often quite ready to justify using different procedures in different areas by reference to the "essence" of a discipline, or the "nature of the thing"—that is, to the peculiar nature of the objects or problems in question.

So, for example, a fundamental distinction is frequently drawn between faith and knowledge, by which a methodological differentiation can be legitimized. In the area of knowledge, particularly in that of science, reason seems to have a function completely different from that it performs in the realm of so-called faith, of religious or ideological convictions.[1] Science and world views are usually sharply distinguished from one another, even by people who claim to be religiously uncommitted. Although an unrestricted critical use of reason seems completely appropriate in the former area, in the latter people are often more inclined to advocate an interpretative or exegetic use of reason, or to completely disengage the procedure adequate for this area from reason, which is often characterized then as "mere calculating rationality."

Thus, one develops a dualistic metaphysics, including its own methodological bifurcation; conjoined with the idea of a double truth, this seems well designed to protect traditional views against some kinds of criticism, thus establishing an insulated realm of uncontestable truth. Within this realm its advocates are, under some circumstances, even prepared to unseat logic, in order to render contradictions acceptable, although usually without realizing completely the import and absurdity of such an undertaking.[2] For the abandonment of the principle of noncontradiction in favor of what is often called "dialectical" thinking[3] might indeed be extremely convenient in some cases; but as we know, it allows us to deduce any possible consequences, and thus constitutes a logical catastrophe, involving the collapse of every sensible argument. This means, however, that it is a thoroughly dogmatic procedure, a retreat into complete dogmatism, which means a retreat into complete arbitrariness. The motive for choosing such a strategy is easy to see: although one is in certain possession of the truth, one has a fear of critical examination and

[1] Views of this sort have become important in the context of the crisis in theological thinking brought about by the Reformation; see Popkin, *The History of Scepticism from Erasmus to Descartes.*

[2] For the implications of such a procedure, see chapter 1; also compare Popper's above-mentioned article, "What is Dialectic?"

[3] See chapter 2, as well as Morton White's article, "Original Sin, Natural Law and Politics," in his book, *Religion, Politics, and the Higher Learning* (Cambridge, Mass., 1959), pp. 111 ff., where the role of so-called "dialectic" in this context is discussed.

would rather sacrifice the elementary morality of thought—that is, logic—than risk the loss of this presumably certain possession.

In this way, by isolating different areas of thought and action from one another by temporary suspension of logic,[4] one can gain some degree of recognition of dogmatic procedures. This is not done without developing a mild form of schizophrenia, which allows one to ridicule as "naive" the consistent application of critical procedures to all areas, without exception. At this point it is appropriate to return to our treatment of the problem of the connection between ethics and science. We saw that by application of *critical bridge principles*, we could establish a connection between knowledge and the adoption of moral attitudes that allow the criticism of such attitudes. If one is prepared to apply such principles, then, ethics cannot have complete independence from science. Here we become acquainted with the opposite procedure. Particular viewpoints are introduced that supposedly allow the separation of some problem areas from others, with the intention of eliminating any possibility of criticism from that direction; in short, one applies *dogmatic shielding principles*. From the standpoint of criticism, any demarcation between problem areas ought only be used to better develop a type of possible criticism, and not for excluding possible criticism in order to reduce the realm of rational discussion. Demarcations never should be used for immunization against criticism. Theses of the autonomy of various realms that serve only this type of protectionistic purpose deserve our mistrust, even though they are often maintained by researchers who are extremely amenable to critical argumentation within their special areas of expertise.[5] Precisely scientific specialization, which

[4] Recall the investigations of Rokeach, who characterized this strategy of isolation as typical of the party-line mentality; cf. preceding chapter.

[5] Pierre Duhem, in his "Physics of a Believer," in *The Aims and Structure of Physical Theory* (Princeton, 1954), pp. 273 ff., defends an autonomy thesis for physics that is designed to isolate that discipline so thoroughly from

is favorable for the institutional support of such theses of autonomy, makes it easy for a member of any discipline to restrict his critical attitude to the area in which he feels most at home. Theology, which has long welcomed such self-restriction, constantly endeavors to encourage it through appropriate arguments.[6]

Hand in hand with such attempts at immunization one often finds, as analyzed above, that simple naive belief that admits no doubts, and is thus unshakable, is prized as a virtue; ac-

---

metaphysics, and thus from religious faith, that any objections derived from physics against the Catholic faith in which Duhem was a believer can be neutralized (cf. pp. 282 ff.). He achieves this end by construing physics as an artifact designed for a specific purpose, and contrasts it with metaphysics, which offers true explanations that explicate the nature of objective reality. Science is explicitly conceived of in a positivistic way, so as to leave room for faith. As is well known, the same strategy is already found in Osiander's preface to Copernicus' *de Revolutionibus orbium coelestium*, though the preface certainly does not correspond to the intentions of the author of that important work; cf. Hans Blumenberg, *Die Kopernikanisch Wende* (Frankfurt, 1965), pp. 92 ff. It is also latent in the recommendation of Cardinal Bellarmin to Foscarini and Galileo; cf. ibid., p. 131; for an analysis and criticism, see Popper, "Three Views Concerning Human Knowledge" (1956), in *Conjectures and Refutations*; and Benjamin Nelson, "The Early Modern Revolution in Science and Philosophy," *Boston Studies*, III, in which the protectionist function of such instrumental interpretations of science—also occasionally fashionable today—is made clear. Interestingly enough, one can also find the same strategy applied to natural sciences by Hegelians; see Benedetto Croce, *Logic as the Science of the Pure Concept*, trans. Ainslie (London, 1917), and passim; or the works of German defenders of dialectic who wish to make space for a faith other than the Catholic.

[6] Compare, for instance, Cardinal Newman's classical dualistic thesis: "And as theology is the philosophy of the supernatural world, and science the philosophy of the natural world; so theology, and science, in respect either of the particular ideas of each, or of their range of application, are completely without possibility of communication, incapable of collision; and they need at best to be combined, not reconciled" (from his lecture "Christianity and Science" [1855], published in John Henry Newman, *Christentum und Wissenschaft*, ed. Heinrich Fries [Darmstadt, 1957], p. 33). The whole lecture is a paradigm of such dogmatically inspired philosophies of demarcations of competences, which attempt to protect theology from any essential objection.

cordingly, one finds the defamation of critical thought in the relevant areas as immoral, disruptive, or at least inappropriate to the character of the problem, as if, just when important things are to be considered—and the theological side constantly insists on their importance—the elementary morality of thought must be abandoned.[7] Obedience in faith, religious zeal, and similar "virtues," whose historical efficacy we know all too well, are repeatedly emphasized as being morally valuable in connection with some special contexts. Within authoritarian systems the virtues of the fanatic and the inquisitor find the recognition due them for their role in the preservation of such systems. The odd notions that one is obliged to maintain a particular belief[8] rather than search unconditionally for the truth; that the suppression of doubt, which in such circumstances is typically termed a "temptation," is of positive moral value; that a belief that might possibly be revealed as questionable from a critical point of view must at all costs be protected from that sort of argument: these ideas, however intelligible they might seem to a party-line thinker and partisan, have a false ring when one brings them together with

---

[7] Good examples of the type of objection to rational argumentation that stem from such a stance are found in a book that is very interesting in this respect: Helmut Gollwitzer and Wilhelm Weischedel, *Denken und Glauben: Ein Streitgespräch* (2d printing; Stuttgart/Berlin/Cologne/Mainz, 1965). In one place, for instance, Gollwitzer castigates one train of argument as an example of an application of "intellectual violence" (cf. pp. 201 ff.), but later he himself proceeds to offer a form of *ad hominum* argument that can only be termed a rather shameless strategy of intimidation (cf. pp. 206 ff.). An ad hoc constructed method designed to assure the believer of privileged position right from the start, so that he basically need never subject himself to any criticism—a method, in short, that involves the very opposite of an unprejudiced striving for truth—is here described by a theological communicant in such a glamorized way that one is left with the impression that it must surely have sprung from the heart of the Christian ethic of love. For a criticism of such strategies as they characteristically appear in theological writings, see Walter Kaufmann, *Critique of Religion and Philosophy*, as well as his *Faith of a Heretic*.

[8] See also Karl Rahner, "Über die Möglichkeit des Glaubens heute," in the fifth volume of his above-mentioned *Schriften zur Theologie*.

the idea of truth and with an ethos of truth. A particularly easy way of establishing a cognitive privilege for the believer is the thesis that only the believer can properly understand; so the understanding of the content of the belief already implies its acceptance, and the person who declines the belief cannot have understood it.[9]

## 18. Demythologization as a Hermeneutical Enterprise

If one were to expect critical thought anywhere in contemporary theology, it would probably be among certain representatives of modern Protestantism who are still linked to some degree with the liberal tradition. Albert Schweitzer was not wrong when he termed the research into the life of Jesus an act of veracity of Protestant Christendom,[10] and one might well say of his contribution to this research that he did not hesitate to draw relatively radical consequences from prima facie thoroughly unpleasant discoveries—unpleasant, that is, for Christian belief. By revealing the radical error that underlay the actions of Jesus, this research, by disregarding the protectionistic principles characteristic of Catholic doctrine, showed the *critical* meaning *historical* research, if one agrees to take it seriously, can have for the solution of *theological* problems.[11] The cosmological views of Jesus, as well as his ethical views, which were tightly connected with them—his "interim-ethic," which was based on his belief in the imminent end of the world—were shown to be basically untenable through the result of this research, so that his hitherto-unassailable

[9] This perfect immunization strategy, which, as we will see, is much in the thoughts of the contemporary hermeneutical philosophers, is applied by Karl Rahner, among others; see p. 63 in his fifth volume.

[10] Cf. Albert Schweitzer, *The Quest of the Historical Jesus*, trans. W. Montgomery (London, 1910).

[11] Compare Schweitzer's view in his book, *The Mystery of the Kingdom of God: The Secret of Jesus' Messiahship and Passion*, trans. W. Lowrie (New York, 1964).

authority for the believer is called into question.[12] This suggests that an unconditional search for truth can be extremely dangerous not only for particular dogmas, but for the foundations of Christian teachings in general—a long-known fact, one might say, but nonetheless of historical importance in that it emerged from within theological research inspired by a scientific ethos of truth.

The emergence of neo-orthodoxy and the influence of philosophical irrationalism on theological thinking, which won acceptance in Germany after the First World War, gave a turn to theological thought that allowed this precarious situation to be controlled, though not without reducing dangerous criticism to a tolerable level.[13] This is seen chiefly in the debates about demythologization, sparked by the Bultmann theses. The demythologization of the New Testament is in no way a critical enterprise, as one might assume from the name, but is in the main a hermeneutic undertaking directed toward saving the core of Christian belief through an interpretation harmonious with the contemporary world picture: to put it precisely, *a hermeneutical enterprise with an apologetic intent.* Its aim is not to make the results and methods of science fruitful for the criticism of faith—as might result from an unhindered drive for truth of the sort recognizable in some researches of the liberal era—but rather, it seeks to keep science and faith as cleanly separated from each other as possible, in order to make them mutually immune.[14]

Within this view, criticism is indeed exercised on the New Testament world view, insofar as such criticism seems

[12] But then Schweitzer himself has drawn positive conclusions, which, as Walter Kaufmann correctly remarked, quite closely approximate the old credo quia absurdum, in that he declared his own ethic of social renewal to be Christian, although it was incompatible with Jesus' interim ethic; cf. Kaufmann, *The Faith of a Heretic*, chapter 8, "Jesus According to Paul, Luther and Schweitzer."

[13] For an analysis of this turn, see Bartley's *The Retreat to Commitment*, as well as the above-mentioned books by Walter Kaufmann.

[14] On this point see, for instance, Friedrich Hochgrebe, "Die Bedeutung des Problems," in *Kerygma und Mythos. Ein Theologisches Gesprach*, ed. Hans Werner Bartsch (Hamburg/Volksdorf, 1951), pp. 10 ff.

unavoidable[15]—on belief in miracles, for instance, which, in any case, is today considered sufficiently disavowed—but in the last analysis, it is only directed to the proper way of hearing the message, which itself is not called into question but is subjected only to an "existential interpretation." In the Bultmann conception as well, with respect to kerygma, the motive of obedience in faith[16] occupies the foreground, which of course has nothing to do with critical science, but rather flies in the face of the critical method as we have explicated it. Thus, it is brazenly announced that the "preached word is the legitimized Word of God," that it is encountered as such, but that its legitimization can under no circumstances be questioned. One hears of an "eschatological revelation event," to which the "Word of preaching, springing out of the events of Easter" belongs, as does "the Church, in which the Word is further proclaimed"; and of the fact that the Church, although a "sociological and historical phenomenon" with a historically intelligible history, is an eschatological phenomenon as well. To make it all perfectly clear, the reader is told that all these claims are a "scandal," which can be overcome "not in philosophical dialogue, but only in obedient faith."[17] In other words, Bultmann, with the help of normal theological procedures, suspends critical thinking completely arbitrarily at exactly the point at which he can no longer use it, because it

[15] Compare, for instance, Rudolf Bultmann, "Neues Testament und Mythologie: Das Problem der Entmythologisierung der neutestamentlichen Verkündigung," in Kerygma und Mythos, pp. 15 ff.

[16] See ibid., pp. 46-48, and Hochgrebe, "Die Bedeutung des Problems," p. 11, whose letter seems to have been included in this collection of essays by its editor for very good reasons.

[17] That is nothing else than the irrationalism of Kierkegaard, which has triumphed over liberal rationalism in modern existentialism as well—a radical-authoritarian way of thinking which, by the way, is completely incompatible with the critical attitude of Nietzsche; cf. Walter Kaufmann, Nietzsche: Philosopher, Psychologist, Anti-Christ (Cleveland/New York, 1956), pp. 98 ff., 105 ff., 304 ff., and Eduard Baumgarten, "The 'Radical Evil' in Jaspers' Philosophy," in The Philosophy of Karl Jaspers, ed. Paul A. Schilpp (New York, 1957). Nietzsche, whose enlightenment tendencies are overlooked, is often referred to as a congenial thinker by this movement.

would lead to unpleasant conclusions. This stands completely in the service of hermeneutical reason, and this, in turn, is the handmaiden of apologetics; a truly theological handmaiden, indeed, who takes pride in paradoxes.

It is of particular interest to see how Bultmann distinguishes himself from earlier attempts at demythologizing.[18] The liberal theology of the nineteenth and early twentieth centuries made attempts in this direction, but according to Bultmann their procedures were not appropriate to the subject matter, because "with the exclusion of mythology, the kerygma itself was excluded." While at that time the mythology of the New Testament was simply critically *eliminated*, it now—after the setback during the establishment of Protestant neo-orthodoxy—becomes a question of critically *interpreting* it, of treating it in such a way that the kerygma is not "reduced to specific religious and basic moral ideas," and thus de facto "*eliminated as kerygma*," as happened in liberal theological thought. The hermeneutic turn in theology is a phenomenon parallel to the philosophical movement that took possession of the German spirit after the First World War and contributed considerably to the decline of critical-rational thought, particularly with Martin Heidegger, Bultmann's philosophical reference person. This hermeneutical turn amounts to a *restriction of criticism* in order to rescue the kerygmatic core of Christian faith, that is, to a regression of the state of theological thought— from the point of view of the method of critical reasoning— from that which Albert Schweitzer represented. One motive for this turn was presumably an awareness that a consistent development in the old direction would lead to explicit atheism.

The inconsistency of Bultmann's demythologization shows itself most clearly in his treatment of the cosmological problem. His presentation of the mythology of the New Testament[19] makes its cosmological character, and at the same time its obsolescence, clear. At stake, obviously, is a world picture

[18] Bultmann, *Kerygma und Mythos*, pp. 23 ff.
[19] Ibid., pp. 15 f.

140

that is completely implausible for modern man, unless one does not reflect on its compatibility with the rest of man's knowledge. This world view, Bultmann claims, could only be assumed as a whole, or abandoned;[20] as a modern theologian, he recommends its abandonment. Should "the message of the New Testament retain its validity," there is "no other way except to demythologize it." But then comes a remarkable turn, which introduces Bultmann's deviation from liberal thinking. The *genuine sense* of the myth, he maintains, is not to give an objective picture of the world; rather, it expresses how man is to understand himself in his world. The myth is *not* to be interpreted *cosmologically, but rather anthropologically*—or better yet, *existentially*.[21] It is this existential interpretation that is to save the tenable kerygmatic heart of the faith. It arises against the background of the modern world view, that is, of a cosmology that corresponds to our contemporary knowledge. But this new world view, as we know, has replaced the old through a series of revolutionary innovations; it is to be understood as an alternative to the old world view that was associated with Christianity, meaning either the Biblical view or the predominantly Aristotelian cosmology of the Middle Ages. If one takes this alternative seriously, one has every reason to eliminate the mythology, as was also the tendency in liberal theology of the old style, *presupposing* that the mythology is taken seriously as well. But among other things, that means accepting the fact that the *existential understanding* of the period belongs to a *cosmological context* from which it cannot be easily freed through existential interpretation; and that we, thinking as we do in a different cosmological framework, must also have a different existential understanding.[22]

---

[20] Ibid., p. 21. Here the "theologian and preacher (owes) himself and the congregation, and those whom he wishes to persuade, absolute clarity and punctilio"; he may not "leave the auditors in doubt over what they have to consider true, and what not."

[21] Ibid., p. 22.

[22] Compare the analysis in chapter 3 of the critical function of knowledge for ethics.

Bultmann's separation of cosmology from existential understanding is a thoroughly artificial and dogmatic operation, presumably suggested to him as a feasible course by a philosophy that had lost all traces of any relation to cosmology and had fallen into a pure subjectivism. Through it Bultmann comes to completely arbitrary decisions about what is to be eliminated and what is not. He eliminates angels and miracles; but he seems to prefer to "interpret" images of God and holy events as though they might fit better into the modern world view than the cruder mythological images. Bultmann's interpretation of the holy event as an *act of God* that possesses meaning for men unquestionably belongs to the existential interpretation; but it is simply impossible to determine what this way of speaking might mean if it does not claim to have any cosmological meaning. Bultmann's language is loaded with cosmological import[23] if one takes him at his word; it shows that he has a theistic world view, a definite cosmology that shares many important traits with the Biblical world view. He acknowledges a self-revealing God who intervenes in historical events and does so with an eye toward the salvation of men. To be sure, he would like to reconcile this part of his world view with the modern view, and this he does by his existential interpretation of kerygma. It thus seems possible to integrate components of an old cosmology into the modern cosmological framework. Of course, one may also interpret his language as partly metaphorical, as often seems appropriate; but he himself always refuses a consistent purely ethical interpretation of the relevant passages—concerning God's action and so forth—of the sort that would be found in liberal theology.

The hermeneutical style of Bultmann's thought seems to have paved the way for his belief in the possibility of existential interpretations in the Heideggerian sense which have no existential implications in the logical sense—that is, no cosmological consequences; but which nonetheless differ advantageously from the pure ethical interpretations of liberal

---

[23] See Bultmann, *Kerygma und Mythos*, part B, pp. 31 ff.

theology. If he does actually hold this belief, one might quite justly attribute it to the corrupting effect of certain philosophical movements on thought, as well as to the fact that modern theologians seldom take issue with philosophical movements that are disturbing to them. In any case, demythologization is nothing other than a hermeneutical immunization procedure for that part of Christian belief that modern theologians wish to save at all costs from contemporary criticism. In the process they unfortunately overlook the fact that the strategy they apply, namely, the interruption of criticism at the decisive point—the point they consider important—can by its nature be applied anywhere one wishes.[24] With a bit of good will one could equally well save angels and devils, miracles, resurrection in the literal sense, and the ascension, except that such attempts can no longer be made palatable to everyone. Furthermore, they overlook the fact that a consistent search for truth is incompatible with this strategy. Anyone really interested in truth will proceed in such a way as to subject to the most stringent examination exactly those views he considers most important—not only those he is willing to abandon with a relatively light heart. The sublime dogmatism of Protestant theologians is not rendered more tolerable by the fact that they have not imposed their dogmas by force, but have instead sneaked them in by a hermeneutical back door.

Bultmann's treatment of kerygma and his interpretation of the holy event are themes that occur again and again as central points in discussions of his demythologization. Many of his critics feel he has gone too far;[25] others feel he should go

[24] See our general discussion of the dogmatization problem.

[25] See, for instance, Julius Schniewind, "Antwort an Rudolf Bultmann. Thesen zum Problem der Entmythologisierung," in *Kerygma und Mythos*, I, pp. 77 ff., particularly page 87, where the question is asked whether "theology has been overcome by anthropology" in Bultmann. Schniewind is prepared to admit that one can fall into conflict with the scientific world view if one takes Christian beliefs seriously (pp. 112 ff.), and he acknowledges with no apparent qualms that Christology is intimately connected with demonology (p. 113), that is, with a component of an earlier cosmology, which he does not believe can simply be declared antiquated. Since this theologian has

143

further and turn the demythologizing into de-kerygmatizing.[26] The whole controversy makes clear what quickly becomes apparent to every attentive reader of Bultmann—that he draws the boundaries of demythologizing completely arbitrarily, and indeed, he draws them from a completely dogmatic viewpoint: to retain that which he considers the core of Christian belief,

---

obviously spent no time on methodological problems, which could easily arise in connection with his superstition, he is prepared to make admissions that would undoubtedly seem painful to the more accommodating Bultmann. He therefore has to use the frequently invoked "scandal" as an epistemological last resort a bit more than does Bultmann. Another example is Helmuth Thielicke, who in his contribution to the *Kerygma und Mythos* volume, "Die Frage der Entmythologisierung des Neuen Testaments," pp. 159 ff., abruptly ascribes the status of brute fact (p. 172) to the resurrection, and claims that demythologization simply encounters a divinely established limit "where it dares not enquire further" (p. 174). This limit is "the mystery of the God-Man." Thielicke considers the myth indispensable, speaks of the inadequacy of scientific thought with respect to its content (p. 177), and offers his own procedure to accommodate theology to modernity: "trans-mythologizing," "translation into a mythos which is modernized with respect to its world-picture" (p. 179), but he seems to feel not very comfortable with this solution. He speaks about an *aporia*, in the face of which it would be important, "*to make the reality visible behind the mythical veiling.*" See also Karl Barth in *Kerygma und Mythos*, II (Hamburg/Volksdorf, 1952), p. 104 f.; W. G. Kümmel, ibid., p. 157, and Regin Prenter, ibid., p. 82.

[26] Also Fritz Buri, whose philosophical grounding is in Jaspers, not Heidegger; compare his contribution "Entmythologisierung oder Entkerygmatisierung" in *Kerygma und Mythos*, II, pp. 85 ff. Buri rightly sees in Bultmann's reliance on "the soterical act of God in Christ as the ground of possibility for Christian understanding," a "regression into mythology" through which he "falls into contradiction with his own presuppositions" (p. 91). Through his attempt to interpret the Christ event existentially, Bultmann runs into a second great difficulty, "that *kerygma, being a soterical act of God, threatens to collapse into a bare act of human self-understanding.*" A third difficulty shows itself in the relationship in Bultmann between historical research and proclamation of the Gospel, where a great obscurity that is not eliminated but elevated to a principle is found, in that he stresses the "scandalous" character of the gospel message, approves of its counterevidential status, and eventually ascribes to it an eschatalogical, soterical role. One can only concur in these critical remarks, even if, knowing theological thought, one cannot help but wonder at what point this theologian, too, will abandon the critical method. More later on this point.

kerygma, as kerygma. Now, from the point of view generally accepted in the sciences, that of an unbiased striving for truth, it is not clear why one should bring oneself to a *sacrificium intellectus*,[27] to an abandonment of *critical* method, simply because traditional articles of belief might have to be jettisoned, even though they may have grown dear to our hearts. Any scientist who is prepared to sacrifice the rules of the game when one of his pet convictions is at stake voluntarily excludes himself from the scientific enterprise, even if he is institutionally defined by it.

It is probably a commonplace that the scientific analysis of Christian faith, like that of other beliefs, can lead to radical criticism of its mythological content. But the same is also true of the demand not to interrupt demythologization at a particular point only because it seems comfortable to do so. Even if demythologization "cannot be systematically continued . . . without eliminating the whole mythology, and consequently the entire Christian kerygma,"[28] it must nonetheless be pursued, even to the point of the elimination of kerygma—to a

[27] The flirtation with scandal, paradox, and antinomy as something valuable that is found in theologians of various persuasions reveals itself most concretely when their thinking treads on thin ice. The word "mystery" has a similar role in theological immunization attempts; compare, for instance, Karl Rahners' instructive circumambulations with this word in his essay, "Über die Möglichkeit des Glaubens heute," in *Schriften zur Theologie*, vol. 5—a work that, because of the extent to which it exemplifies a combination of special pleading and metaphysics instead of true argumentation, might disconcert those not inured to theological discussions, although in this respect it does not stand out in work of this or any other theologians. On the *sacrificium intellectus*, see Morris R. Cohen, "The Dark Side of Religion" (1933), in *Religion from Tolstoy to Camus*, ed. Walter Kaufmann (New York/Evanston, 1964), p. 286. This article and other selections in this volume provide rich material for the critical appraisal of theological efforts.

[28] See Regin Prenter in his contribution, "Mythos and Evangelium," in *Kerygma und Mythos*, II, p. 80. From this point Prenter infers quite remarkable conclusions because he is determined to save the Christian picture of God at any cost, and sees mythology as "standing guard before (!)" this picture; ibid. (cf. p. 82). He therefore concludes that mythology must be strengthened (p. 84).

"de-kerygmatization" that shows the various revelations to be historical products, without feeling it necessary to construct an ad hoc explanation that provides for divine interventions. After all, we do not normally allow this kind of explanation when we analyze religious developments in cultures that are less familiar to us.

## 19. THE PROBLEM OF THE EXISTENCE OF GOD AND MODERN THEOLOGY

Modern theologians generally pride themselves on accepting no theories for the explanation of natural—and thus historical—occurrences in which the concept of God appears. In this respect they wish to be considered enlightened, and thus avoid collision with modern factual science. For the most part they wish to have nothing to do with natural theology,[29] since such theology is indeed rendered obsolete by scientific developments. If one believes, however, that in regard to theology, this is the removal of a burden, since *natural theology* as a component of a *cosmological conception* is in any case constantly endangered by scientific progress—then one does not wholly draw the correct conclusions from this situation. In particular, one overlooks the unpleasant consequences. So long as such a natural theology is believed to be a necessary explanatory component of a cosmology,[30] then there is some reason to believe in the existence of God; that is, the concept of God is not devoid of function within the accepted world view—even if strict proof of a God must fail because one cannot establish, by proof, any claims with content. But as

[29] When I speak of "modern" theology, I am of course excluding Catholic theology, which explicitly protects its theses dogmatically, and does so in obedient submission to an authority that officially sets limits to its thinking, so that it would be a waste of time to wish to demonstrate this fact.

[30] That was indeed the case within the Aristotelian world view, which was fused with Christian interpretations in the Middle Ages. After the scientific revolution of modern times, natural theology was implicated in the defensive retreat of the Aristotelian world view, and was gradually shown to be superfluous. See Charles Coulston Gillispie's *The Edge of Objectivity*, pp. 263 ff.

soon as natural theology proves to be superfluous, the maintenance of the old conception of God, no matter how certain human needs may seem to speak in its favor, appears objectively as nothing more than a component of a questionable ideological strategy, an ad hoc procedure that must necessarily lead to "scandals," "paradoxes," and "aporia."

Normally, modern theologians proceed here in the same way as is often done when one wishes to defend one's pet ideas against the progress of science: by applying an immunization strategy through which the relevant conception is so completely emptied that it could not possibly collide with any fact whatsoever.[31] We know from modern methodological discussions that such a procedure, through which all risk of collision with the facts is avoided, is virtually fatal for the content of the view in question. Only one who is not aware of these issues can consider the result attained by such a procedure acceptable and advantageous. But a careful perusal of modern theological literature, particularly the literature concerning Bultmann, reveals that modern theology is a playground for admirers of such procedures.[32] Not the least of the reasons is that German philosophy, on whose results and methods modern theology has heavily depended, has fallen into epistemological disrepair because of developments following the First World War. The irrationalism that established itself in Germany has served very well to shore up traditional beliefs and theological ways of thinking.

In science, problems of existence that tend to be solved through the development of testable and validated explanatory theories recur constantly. If theories of this sort that can

[31] For this point, it should suffice to consider the epistemological section of this book and the references included therein.

[32] To be perfectly clear, this remark is directed also, and explicitly, against famous theologians who, like Bultmann, Tillich, and Niebuhr, are well respected because of their accomplishments. Consider in this regard the seldom-acknowledged criticisms in the above-mentioned works of Walter Kaufmann and William Warren Bartley, and "Original Sin, Natural Law and Politics" and other essays in Morton White's *Religion, Politics, and the Higher Learning.*

adequately explain the real phenomena are available, one can generally assume that the hypothetical entities referred to in these theories also really exist. Conversely, belief in the existence of objects that play important roles only in outmoded and obsolete theories must be abandoned along with these theories themselves, if one makes any pretense of adhering to critical methods. Thus, today one does not believe in the existence of phlogiston, of ether, or of a special power of life—not because these beliefs are *in themselves* meaningless, but because the theories with which they were associated have been shown to be untenable. The same fate has befallen the belief in witches, angels, devils, and gods as they occur in polytheistic world views.[33] Such consequences of the progress of knowledge tend, in general, to be conceded by Christian theologians as well. But if the Biblical God is called into question, they usually offer a special strategy, for which they have no use in normal circumstances because it amounts to "special pleading." They are prepared for very extensive accommodations to the modern picture of the world, even to the explicit abandonment of supernaturalism, if residence in the theological building is thereby made more comfortable. But they will not go so far as to give up the idea of God, even though it plays no role in any theoretical conception plausible enough to make its retention seem acceptable from a critical point of view.

This is not to deny that this idea is completely sensible within a sociomorphic cosmology such as the one that essentially determined the human world view until the modern scientific revolution.[34] But this cosmology has long since be-

[33] Remember in this connection the fact, mentioned earlier, that demonology was a highly developed specialty within theology in the sixteenth and seventeenth centuries, and indeed, one with considerable practical import, though this is acknowledged only reluctantly today. Nonetheless this "science" not only seems to have a place in the Catholic world view, but it also meets with approval from some Protestants; consider footnote 25 of this chapter.

[34] Cf. the investigations of Ernst Topitsch in his book, *Ursprung und Ende der Metaphysik* (Vienna, 1958), and his other works.

come obsolete. If, as is recommended by critical method, one treats the assumption of existence as a hypothesis with a function within a given system then there is no good reason to cling to this hypothesis when the context within which it had explanatory value is abandoned. The objection cannot be raised here that this could not be a question of a "hypothesis" because there is a significant difference between faith and knowledge. This difference exists only if one suspends the method of critical examination for certain components of our convictions—those that fall within the realm of so-called faith. That is, if one adopts what we have seen to be, with respect to the content of the problem under consideration, an arbitrary methodological demarcation, that can have only one purpose: that of dogmatizing those components. It is uncontested that one *can* so proceed, and can do so, indeed, in any area of thought. But it is a mistake to think that, from the viewpoint of the search for truth, it makes sense to so proceed. This can be readily seen if one is able to free oneself from the prejudice that in important—especially in sacred—questions there is less reason for careful analysis and weighing of alternative solutions than in questions of narrower existential import, especially in view of the fact that here completely different conceptions are actually at stake. Thus it would be very remarkable if one wished to elevate precisely the assumption of the existence of God to a dogma, as de facto almost always is done; although the defenders of such dogmas are usually not even in a position to make clear the meaning of this assumption[35]— not, that is, within the framework of the modern world view, which they in general wish to accept in its essential characteristics.

One of the most curious strategies for immunizing the idea of God that has recently found a following is that of *defaming*

[35] For a critical analysis, see, in addition to the sources already cited, the work of Norwood Russell Hanson, "What I don't Believe," in *Boston Studies*, III, pp. 467 ff., and also the discussion, "Theology and Falsification" by Anthony Flew, Richard M. Hare, and Basil Mitchell in Kaufmann, *Religion from Tolstoy to Camus*. See also Herbert Feigl, "Modernisierte Theologie und wissenschaftliche Weltanschauung," in *Club Voltaire*, II (Munich, 1965).

the concept of belief that is oriented to the "mere" holding—as true—of a contention;[36] this is a procedure that seems to provide a higher epistemological consecration for the position of subjectivism. To simply hold as true the thesis that a God exists who has certain characteristics or who intervenes in the world in certain ways might in fact often not suffice for the believer; but it is certainly a minimum implication of any belief within which it is possible to speak meaningfully and substantively of God. The trivialization or elimination of this problem of existence does not mean that one favors a higher and less crude form of belief in God; but rather, it is an indication either that one is unclear about important implications of one's own world view, or that one has de facto become an atheist but prefers to use theistic language in order to sustain the old façade,[37] possibly in order to be able to retain possibilities of action connected with the old tradition. But a conception of God that has only rhetorical and moral functions is extremely problematic, especially when it raises

[36] See, for example, the response of Hans Conzelmann in his conversation with Werner Harenberg, reproduced in his book, *Jesus und die Kirchen. Bibelkritik und Bekenntnis* (Stuttgart/Berlin, 1966), pp. 184 ff.

[37] Consider, for example, the following passage from Fritz Buri, *Wie können wir heute noch verantwortlich von Gott reden?* (Tübingen, 1967), p. 28 f.: "God is the mythological expression of the unconditionality of personal responsibility. If it were not for the mythological language of a voice which calls us to responsibility, we would not be able to attain clarity about the unconditional nature of responsibility. Naturally it speaks our language, arises in our heart, addresses us from our context—and is nonetheless not simply the voice of our heart, of my neighbor, of my situation. In the objective concreteness of our inner and outer world there is no unconditionality, but only manifest relativities which we do not perceive as absolutes for the sake of the proper fulfillment of our personhood. But in the midst of these relativities comes the voice, without the sound of which we will not attain personhood. . . . What should prevent us then from speaking of this voice, which enables us to experience the freeing and creative reality of personhood, as the voice of God—and thus of speaking of God, and indeed, of a God in person?" But if it is actually only a question of a mythological paraphrase of the problematic of responsibility, then in fact there is very strong reason for anyone who does not wish to mislead to think twice about using such language.

the question of whether those to whom the term is addressed are intelligent enough to see through its use. The thesis of the nonobjectifiability of God, which constantly recurs in this context, does not advance matters.[38] To speak of "an insight into the inappropriateness of conceptual-objective scientific thinking, both with respect to Being as a whole and to the reality of Existence"[39]—an insight that leads to the claim that God reveals himself to conceptual knowing solely as a mystery—is to adopt a thesis that is obviously intended to set a limit to others, as so often happens in theological thinking. The propounder of such a thesis can thus continue to speak of God without embarrassment or disturbance, because he is clearly beyond mere conceptual knowledge; but he conjoins no assertion with even a shred of content with his discourse. That one could speak likewise of any other mythological being whatever seems to be of no concern. Any impartial person can easily see that nothing is at stake here but establishing a privileged epistemological position through a semantic trick—uncontestable, unless one has seen through this procedure.[40]

In this theology, self-described as "modern," the problem

[38] Compare, for instance, Fritz Buri, "Theologie der Existenz," in *Kerygma und Mythos*, III, *Das Gespräch mit der Philosophie*, ed. Hans Werner Bartsch (Hamburg-Volksdorf, 1954), pp. 83 ff.

[39] Ibid., p. 85.

[40] Anyone who wishes to trace the source of this style of thinking can read Karl Jaspers' contribution, "Wahrheit und Unheil der Bultmannschen Entmythologisierung" in the same volume (ibid., pp. 11 ff.), where the superstitious belief in science is discussed; through the distinction between correctness and truth, the notion of double truth, which is a constant motif of theological thought, is introduced; "demythologization" is described as an almost blasphemous (!) word, and mythological language is termed the "language of that reality which is not merely empirical, that reality with which we live existentially, while our bare Dasein constantly loses itself in empirical reality, as though it alone were truly reality . . ." as if one were forced to go along with this quasi-theological doubling of reality in order to rationally interpret one's own existence. Further, one learns here that myth is "the a priori form of reason of the transcending ascertainment." Sloppy forms of expression lead to a conflation of truth and truthfulness, and the notion of a bad enlightenment, which can be identified with unbelief, is introduced.

of existence, when it appears at all, is so obliquely addressed that one cannot achieve clarity about what the respective theological—or in some cases philosophical—author really believes. A special epistemology that speaks of subject-object cleavage, nonobjectifiability, nonobjective discourse, "chiffres" of being, and similar things, without making any effort to take into consideration the results of logic, semantics, linguistics, or modern theory of knowledge, and whose only apparent advantage seems to be that it helps some thesis escape critical discussion—such an epistemology is a pompously designed machinery of immunization for which German philosophizing, above all, is responsible. It assures that no assertions can be exposed to the risk of refutation. Nonetheless, much is said of the "wager of faith," as if anything in any possible intelligible sense of the word was risked.[41] In the face of this theology, one is inclined to ask if the relatively open dogmatism of Catholic thought is not preferable.

Protestant theology, because it has to a certain degree taken the result of scientific investigation seriously—especially the results of its own investigations, such as the rediscovery of eschatology—has run into difficulties that have brought it to the brink of atheism. Already in the debates over demythologizing, which revealed the partiality of the Bultmann solution to problems and the dangers that could arise out of it, some voices began to speak out in favor of a relatively open remythologizing. Without doubt, the Theology of Hope[42] as sketched by Moltmann, which invokes the Hegelian Marxist

[41] An equally problematic strategy can be found in Tillich, who among other things claims that all talk of divine things is meaningless unless it takes place under "circumstances of deep emotion"; see Tillich, *Wesen und Wandel des Glaubens* (Frankfurt/Berlin, 1961), p. 20—a thesis that is a fundamental component of his theologically based theory of symbols. For a criticism of this view, see Kaufmann, *Critique of Religion and Philosophy*, and Bartley, *The Retreat to Commitment*, passim.

[42] Compare Jurgen Moltmann, *Theologie der Hoffnung: Untersuchungen zur Begründung und zu den Konsequenzen einer christlichen Eschatologie*, 6th ed. (Munich, 1966), as well as the volume, *Diskussion über die "Theologie der Hoffnung,"* ed. Wolf Dieter Marsch (Munich, 1967).

tradition, especially Ernst Bloch, and thus reflects the retreat of existentialism and the recent renaissance of Hegel in European thought, represents the most radical attempt in this direction, an effort that seeks to overcome the Heidegger-oriented Bultmann approach and its associated concessions to the modern scientific world view. Moltmann quite properly directs his attack against Bultmann's attempt to isolate the world view from self-interpretation so that theology might seem cosmologically neutral[43]—an enterprise that, as we have seen, cannot be consistently carried out without falling into a more or less concealed atheism. The radical nature of Moltmann's theology does not lie in the fact that scientific knowledge that collides with theological propositions is taken seriously, but rather the opposite: that a virtue is made out of the unreconcilability of the two—the virtue of consistently disregarding scientific thought. Theologians of the Bultmann school, infected as they were with the rational attitude associated with liberal research into the life of Jesus, still had scruples about whether belief in the resurrection, belief in a God appropriate to the Christian tradition, could be reconciled with the modern world view; but this no longer seems to upset this innovator of eschatology in the least.[44] He contents himself rather with questioning the prevailing world view of modern historical thought, which in his opinion is similar to that of Greek cosmology, as if one could afford to ignore the results of the sciences in order to arrive at adequate solutions of theological problems.[45] The epistemological naiveté

[43] Moltmann, *Theologie der Hoffnung*, pp. 58 ff.

[44] Moltmann emphasizes, for instance, that Christianity "stands and falls with the reality of the resurrection of Jesus from the dead," p. 150; see the third chapter of his book on the subject of the problem of the resurrection, especially sections 5, 6, and 7.

[45] The problem of the resurrection actually involves not only biological but even broader cosmological problems, which are indeed "primitive" because of this very elementary character. Nonetheless, this does not justify ignoring them regarding other issues. A thinker who rejects any world view associated with Greek cosmology—and the modern view certainly has characteristics that connect it with the cosmological speculations of the Greeks—because of

of this dynamic theology can be explained only by the dominant orientation in the German-speaking world of philosophy toward such thinkers as Heidegger and Hegel, a fact that has almost completely isolated us from the development of modern epistemology and theory of science. This kind of theology might well make the "dialogue with Marxism" and many other useful projects easier, but that it is often already considered a new and promising alternative to the theology of the Bultmann school is evidence of the extent to which Protestantism has removed itself from the morality of critical rational thinking.

## 20. MODERN THEOLOGY, ECCLESIASTICAL FAITH, AND SOCIETY

Theological interpretations tend not to be treated as private matters when they stem from influential members of the discipline. As is well known, Catholic theologians are subordinate to the doctrinal authority of the Church; they can be disciplined and their obedience is to a certain extent an existential matter, if we may apply an unphilosophic sense of "existential" in order to do justice to their precarious situation. Likewise, Protestant theologians, even if they function as university professors, cannot completely free themselves from considerations of the Church; they must reckon with the fact that their teachings affect the social realm of the Church. As is well known, the theology of Bultmann, because of its great influence on theological education in Germany, had repercussions that presented some difficulties to his followers. More than a decade ago, it led the evangelical theological faculty

the difficulty of reconciling it with the resurrection and similar phenomena might well be expected to tell us more about this event from his own point of view. The carelessness with which Moltmann treats questions that are so important for his theology in some respects exceeds even that which one has learned to expect since the decline of liberal theology. Even those inclined to look with favor on the ethical-political impulse of this thinking would not dare ignore that.

of the University of Tübingen to present to the Congress of
the Church of Württemberg a pronouncement upon this theological tendency which was clearly designed to placate the
ecclesiastical organs.[46]

The proclamation is an interesting documentation of the
way theologians sometimes interpret the freedom of scientific
investigation and teaching that is guaranteed in liberal countries. It makes certain institutional aspects of methodology
apparent as it is practiced, and clarifies the particular situation
of theology within the universities. It states, among other things,
that the respective faculty[47] "does not intend to allow itself
or the Church to become a forum, in which all possible opinions can be expressed in untrammeled freedom of speech."[48]
It recalls that this faculty worked on the doctrinal disciplinary
law of the Church of Württemberg, and had testified in one
case that this case fell under this law. It then explains "in
accordance with this position," that "there are limits within
which the point to which theology is directed must fall, in
order to be acceptable to the Church, and that the location
of these limits is determined through scripture and confession." The faculty expresses its understanding that the moment can come "when the Church *must* make clear that these
boundaries have been transgressed in the development of theology." The faculty expresses itself prepared to cooperate in
the measures the Church might then be obliged to take.

The proclamation then turns to Bultmannian theology to
determine whether it provides preconditions for such measures. In so doing it says of the Marburg theologian that his
freedom in approaching the New Testament "did not derive
from a frivolous presumption, but rather from the certainty
of a faith which attributes to the Gospel the power to sustain

[46] Compare "Für oder wider die Theologie Bultmanns," in *Denkschrift der
Ev. Theol. Fakultät der Universität Tübingen*, presented to the Landeskir-
chentag on March 11, 1952, published in Tübingen, 1952.

[47] In this case, the faculty of Christian theology at the University of Tübingen.

[48] P. 16.

its truth against any criticism."[49] In connection with an analysis that indicates one-sidednesses and dangers of Bultmannian theology and points to different possible interpretations, it turns against rationalism and liberalism and speaks in favor of a kind of demythologizing that interprets myth, rather than eliminates it; in this connection, the faculty promises the Church to do anything within its power "to steer the development in the last-described direction," and then it speaks of the "central task of evangelical theology," that is, "to protect the indissoluble internal connection between Revelation, Word, and Faith."[50] Finally, the possibility is considered that Bultmann "denied the resurrection of Jesus Christ," and the faculty thereby confesses an obligation which both in its wording and in its meaning is as irreconcilable with the idea of freedom of research and teaching as are the rest of the passages quoted from this pronouncement.[51] Questions are then raised about the effects on Church and congregation and on the education of the clergy, and finally it is attested that with Bultmann "the starting point and goal of his theology do not lie outside the boundaries drawn by scripture and confession," so that a judgment of condemnation by the Church would not be appropriate. The demand that his theology be left within the domain of the faculty's discretion was then explicitly *not* justified by reference to "the abstract principle of freedom of inquiry as such," but "out of the recognition . . . that the *Church* has need of a theology working within it in independent responsibility."[52]

One might well ask what such a faculty would then say if at some point a theologian in "frivolous presumption" did

[49] P. 18.

[50] Pp. 29 ff.

[51] Pp. 33 ff. It was stated as a *very serious objection* against him that "the simple faithful Christian does not recognize his own beliefs as they appear in the statements of Bultmann," p. 37. What should one then say about researches into the life of Jesus, and their consequences?

[52] P. 42. "What a happy coincidence," the liberal reader exclaims upon encountering this passage.

attempt to use his "abstract" right to freedom of instruction in such a way that the limits recognized by the faculty were breached—if, for example, in less ambiguous language the Resurrection were not "interpreted" but simply denied, leaving no range of meaning that could be invoked on the theologian's behalf.[53] The faculty seems not to have cared in the least for one thing in dealing with the Bultmann issue—the above-mentioned freedom of research and teaching. Instead, they concerned themselves primarily with the danger to the Church and to the simple faith of its members that may be caused by the free expression of certain interpretations by the members of the theological faculty. This document seems to show, in any case, that even in states that guarantee freedom of teaching and research, theological faculties are sometimes officially prepared to abandon this freedom, and if necessary, even to help assure that their members, when they exploit this freedom, will be disciplined—to lend their support, in short, to inquisitorial proceedings, however mild.

Freedom of research and instruction belongs to the legal aspect of the critical method, which one must take into consideration in the critique of ideology. The case just discussed shows that the institutional autonomy of science, which can go some way toward securing the possibility of an unhampered search for truth, is not necessarily sufficiently guaranteed by legal prescriptions of this sort so long as obligations of the kind described above still exist.[54] It has been justly pointed out in connection with the existence of theological chairs and faculties in universities, for which in general the principle of academic freedom holds, that the area of concern for holders of philosophical chairs is defined through certain

[53] Such developments have already begun.

[54] That shows itself here even through an association which, compared to others—for example, those in Catholic, Communist, or Fascist areas—is relatively weak. One might project from this how a "committed" university, of the sort that is being commended to us today by people who generally overlook the engagement represented by the liberal idea of unbiased search for truth and independent thought, might develop.

problems, not through particular solutions to these problems;[55] and that, indeed, it is not to be seen to what extent it should be otherwise for theologians. The indoctrination of clerical students with dogmatically prescribed solutions might well be in the interest of the church, but need not be in the interest of a state that has freedom of thought rooted in its Constitution. If the principle of academic freedom is strictly carried out throughout the entire body of the university—and a liberal democracy has, after all, no reason to grant privileged status to representatives of special beliefs in its universities—then it should be possible to appoint agnostics and atheists to theological chairs.[56] It is obvious that they would offer different solutions to theological problems than their Christian colleagues. But a faculty in which such appointments were normal would at least be well protected against producing documents of the sort analyzed above.

One must understand that the churches have worries other than those concerned with the freedom of inquiry. They are organizations that in large part depend for their existence upon satisfying, in certain ways, the needs of their members, and this includes, as it always has, the primordial need for refuge in the certainty of a faith that provides edification, comfort, and help. The Catholic church has long benefited from its authoritarian structure in its efforts to render its believers immune to influences that undermine their faith, but in recent times there seems to be a softening of the Catholic position as well. The Protestant churches, on the other hand, lacking a well-established authoritatively managed office for doctrine, now seem to be encountering difficulties whose consequences cannot be anticipated. The explicitly conservative theolgians, who have always been more concerned with faith than with relevant criticism, have a much easier time with these difficulties than their colleagues who have been fasci-

[55] Compare Morton G. White's "Religious Commitment and Higher Education," in *Religion, Politics and the Higher Learning*, pp. 98 ff.
[56] And not only when they camouflage their atheism as religiosity.

nated by the superficialities of demythologizing and who consider themselves less dogmatic because they are prepared to extend the limits of criticism somewhat wider. But the difference in method between the conservatives and the demythologizers essentially lies only in the fact that the former openly acknowledge their apologetic-dogmatic methods,[57] while the latter dress it up in a hermeneutic guise. The conservatives are more concerned with the preservation of the identity of the Christian tradition as anchored in the practices of many congregations, than with accommodation to the modern world view—not least because they seem to recognize that the substance of faith of this tradition might otherwise be completely lost.

One committed to the tradition of enlightenment and critical thinking can view the development of this controversy with equanimity. However, he will be better able to sympathize with certain utterances of conservative theologians who represent the standpoint of simple faith than with the purportedly modern smokescreens of many of their opponents.[58]

[57] A somewhat painful acknowledgment for a university teacher, one imagines.

[58] As, for example, when Walter Künneth explains that there are "central statements . . . with which the Gospel either stands or falls," by which he means statements about "the soterical reality of the crucified and resurrected Christ"; see the dialogue between Künneth and Werner Harenberg in Harenberg's *Jesus und die Kirchen*, pp. 191 ff. "The modernistic theologians," he maintains, "talk all around the resurrection, but at this point"—by which he means the empty grave—"it becomes concrete." He refers here to the concrete corporality, dealt with by the Modernists through reinterpretation. To the question of whether he did not mean "that the majority of theologians share the idea of God, as well as the belief in God" (p. 202), he answers, not unjustly, "that is a difficult, even a painful, question. . . . I can only judge by what they have written; and on that basis I would hesitate to answer yes to your question." This reminds one of Bultmann's claim that to believe in the resurrection of Christ means "to encounter the Gospel and to respond to it with belief" (p. 203 of the same book) and other utterances that an impartial reader can only perceive as an attempt by Bultmann to associate himself, through grotesque rephrasing, with a faith he has essentially abandoned long since.

And the way the latter sometimes manage to dismiss simple and obviously meaningful questions *a limine* will give him something to think about.[59] Considering the spate of nonsense such questions prompt, it is easy to understand why conservatives must consider the incursion of modern theology into a congregation equivalent to the confusion of that congregation,[60] "for modern theology produces no genuine Biblical enlightenment." Whatever a "Biblical enlightenment" might

[59] See for example the above-cited exchange between Conzelmann and Harenberg in Harenberg's *Jesus und die Kirchen*, pp. 185 ff.; consider, for instance, his reply to the question about the divine status of Jesus, or the question of whether Christ has risen or not. "One who asks such a question," Conzelmann responds, "isn't really asking anything, but already knows what resurrection is"—a truly astounding sentence, semantically! One who asks whether Spartacus led an insurrection, presumably "knows in advance" what an insurrection is—knows, that is, how the term "insurrection" is to be used. "The question whether the Resurrection is an historical fact, whether it occurred in time and space," he continues, "is absolutely senseless. The only factually significant point is that the crucified One has not been annihilated ... that he is there, that he is God, and thus that the world stands under the determination of the Cross. For the resurrected One is the crucified One. Only as such does he appear for us." I do not know from which perspective— except that of obfuscation—this position could be preferable to Künneth's. The arrogance with which the question is rejected is staggering. It could, after all, arise from the simple desire to figure out what a Christian should believe today. Possibly, too, the term "resurrection" is associated with a relatively definite—although possibly naive—image of the sort probably held by most Christians up to modern times. It is snubbed by an expert with the claim that the question is meaningless. The theologian here adopts the blustering tone of conviction of a representative of the Vienna Circle in Philosophy, although probably without knowing what difficulties lie ahead if he wishes to maintain that position. What is proposed as factually significant is certainly not clearer than the question about the resurrection. That it is not meaningful can be claimed only by one who is fully indifferent to the issue of whether Biblical expressions contain any truth value in the usual sense. From a semantic perspective, the Conzelmannian answer is at least as naive as the question he so consciously denigrates. Each of his sentences invites extremely painful questions, which can be ignored here only because the slovenliness that has begun to encroach under the influence of hermeneutical irrationalism prevents such questions.

[60] See the conversation of Harenberg with Gerhard Bergmann, pp. 175 ff.

160

be, we can nonetheless agree that in fact it is usually much more a question of befogging.[61]

Theologians of the demythologizing camp, as well, of course, deliberate about how they can convey their interpretations to believers without encountering incomprehension. And so there, too, the dogmatic objective can break through the critical overlay. One learns, then, that *critical* theology subordinates itself to the *authority* of the Word of God, and from *that* standpoint examines "the text of Biblical authors with critical expertise."[62] In light of this thesis one can understand very well why Bastian defends himself against the confusion of criticism with destruction, dissolution, or lack of respect, and maintains that what is destroyed by critical examination are "as a rule the decayed patterns of our understanding," for one does not expect such an enterprise to ever call into question matters of faith considered important by a theologian. Criticism, as is frequent in theology, stops short of the essential; there is difference of opinion only over what is essential, and that justifies the concern of churchmen and the laity. The controversy concerns *the point* at which the critical method should be jettisoned, and *not* the question of *whether* it should be. The slogan that the Bible demands critical readers is usually only hermeneutically intended.[63] Such things as mere truth,

---

[61] Of course the Conservatives also cannot avoid some strained interpretations, for the naive beliefs of earlier times are no longer valid for them, either. See, for instance, G. Bergmann's remarks on the Assumption, p. 183.

[62] Compare Hans-Dieter Bastian, "Zwischen Bibelforschung und Bibelignoranz," the foreword to Günter Klein, Willi Marxsen and Walter Kreck, *Bibelkritik und Gemeindefrömmigkeit*, Vorträge auf dem 12. deutschen evangelischen Kirchentag (Gütersloh, 1966), pp. 7 ff.; see also Walter Kreck's contribution on pp. 48 ff. of that volume.

[63] See Günter Klein, "Die Bibel braucht kritische Leser," in ibid., pp. 11 ff. Here he offers an example of biblical textual criticism which at first seems to represent a castastrophic result: the story in question is a complete fabrication; then he asks whether faith is strong enough to tolerate that. The reader is referred to the attitude of the first Christians who perceived the living growth of their tradition as an aid to faith, not a hindrance. At this point Klein poses the final, the "decisive" question—the question of the *vitality* of the text for us today. The *test*: "Does it give us the pleasure that

or mere facts, in the simple ordinary-language meaning of those words, is of complete indifference to these critics; or to put it another way, it is the propaganda value of particular textual passages that matters to them, as much as if it were a Communist, Catholic, or Fascist text. The beliefs of the witch-hunters and other fanatics were also sincere; their texts made them enjoy their faith, its profession, and the social effects it produced.

When the question of truth arises, it is treated in a very special way by representatives of modern theology. The reader might be confronted, for instance, with the question of whether the Gospels are true;[64] but at the same time anyone who might be tempted to institute a critical test of the relevant utterances is discouraged from doing so by introduction of the convenient fiction of unprovability, whereby any suggested possibility of examination is suppressed.[65] That one must without further ado emulate the faithful of the early period of Christianity is a demand we can hardly take seriously in the light of what we know today about the psychology of belief, particularly since the theologian has no scruples about treating believers of other traditions quite differently. That which is recommended by religious experts seems suspiciously like a demand that we should not be so precise about investigations of truth. And when in this context the danger of absolutizing and dog-

---

may make us inclined to confess Christ?" It is obvious that it is a far cry from the simple question of truth to this question. A Copernican revolution is at stake: the introduction of the pleasure principle into epistemology, as it were. The whole "*critical*" procedure has had but one goal—the attainment of an "*understanding*" that produces the *desire* for faith and confession.

[64] See Willi Marxsen, "Jesus hat viele Namen," in *Bibel Kritik und Gemeindefrömmigkeit*, pp. 32 ff.

[65] Nevertheless, it is not irrelevant to a decision about the credibility of the words of Jesus that he himself was clearly mistaken about some questions that are of great importance to his position—a result of research into the life of Jesus that ought to be used critically. To invoke the "wager of faith" against this and similar facts, as Marxsen does, is pure irrationalism. See also his treatment of the problem of truth in his book, *Das Neue Testament als Buch der Kirche*, p. 133.

matizing the contemporary scientific world view is pointed out—a caution generally issued by people who are significantly less fastidious when theological claims are at stake—then we are confronted with a remarkable misinterpretation of the real problem situation. Modern epistemologists and even critics of theology are well used to emphasizing that all our knowledge is hypothetical. But that does not prevent us from using the result of scientific research to criticize superstitions and no longer defensible notions that are, therefore, no less problematic. The method of critical examination has its origin, after all, in the elimination of the quasi-theological notion of certainty and its consequences. In any case, the demythologizers themselves use this procedure when they criticize ideas, including Biblical ones, which they no longer wish to defend. When they then turn around and encourage reverence and humility in research into Biblical texts[66]—a demand that certainly strikes the right note from the standpoint of the believer, but in this context moves toward a corruption of thought—one asks oneself why a critical interpretation is sought at all. The answer does not seem difficult to find: it is because a compromise is sought between the standards of research in modern science and what it is believed can be demanded of the faithful, who are bound by the needs of the Church, which have little to do with the pursuit of truth and a corresponding open-minded attitude toward new solutions to problems.

All in all, these representatives of theology manage to be *critical but nonetheless dogmatic*, critical in the things that are not so important to them, dogmatic in those that seem to be more so—a position, one might well say, which is understandable in their situation. The method they use is very easy to represent in its basic lines: a clear demarcation is made between what one wishes to preserve because it seems terribly

[66] On this and the previous point, see Walter Kreck, "Die Gemeinde braucht die Kritik der Bibel," in Klein, Marxsen, and Kreck, *Bibel Kritik und Gemeindefrömmigkeit*, pp. 48 ff.

important—for one's salvation, for instance—and what one is willing to sacrifice as irrelevant. Then one proceeds so as to protect the nucleus against all criticism through appropriate immunization strategies, among which the demand for reverence and humility vis-à-vis some topics might well be counted, while subjecting the rest of the doctrines to radical criticism and eliminating them—to the outrage of people who, though. they employ exactly the same techniques themselves, nonetheless draw the lines differently. Such methods might well be associated with a progressive and liberal position on matters of morality and politics, so that one is easily persuaded to judge this theology not by its methods, but by whether its defenders adopt unembarrassing positions on such questions as sexual morality, education, or foreign policy.

Despite the internal tensions they seem to have with their churches, which show in these quasi-political concerns, the theological faculties are—in truly theological issues, though not necessarily in questions of Church history or the like—nothing more than institutional residues of apologetic and dogmatic thinking inside the realm of scientific research and teaching.[67] Their existence in the universities creates the impression that theology as such is in principle a science like any other, although the more or less strong denominational attachment of their members often precludes the consistent application of the method of critical examination of exactly those issues which are considered most important. In this respect they are workshops for the elaboration, refinement, and "scientific" propping of ideologies, and their methods and products can be warmly recommended to anyone interested in the study of methodology and of criticism of ideology—two areas of research which, as we know, are closely related as objects of analysis.

[67] Of course, the theologians in question are only doing what many representatives of other sciences also do about their general world view, *apart* from their area of specialization. But they do it *within* their area of scientific specialization, and often they are not even shy about making it explicit. That distinguishes them essentially from other specialists.

# SIX

# Meaning and Reality

## 21. THE PROBLEM OF MEANING IN THE TRADITION OF HISTORISM

MODERN theology, as we have seen, basically draws its support with respect to methodology from ideas developed and elaborated by hermeneutical philosophy. This school of philosophical thought has always had very little contact with the natural sciences and their methods; but it has had strong associations with the humanistic or cultural sciences, helping them to clarify their presuppositions and methods and to develop a methodological separatism whose traces are still evident today. Its dominating problematic has always been the problem of *meaning*; the methodology they sought to develop to solve their problems was a doctrine of *understanding*, and the phenomena upon which it had to prove its usefulness were the manifestations of human *cultural reality*—language, myth, religion and law, literature, art, and eventually philosophy and science.

The great importance of texts in these areas suggested the idea of taking the model of interpretation of texts as a paradigm of knowledge for all phenomena of this sort, and thus to attribute to the humanistic sciences the investigation of *contexts of meaning* as the essential task. At the same time, this would provide a procedure *more philologico* as a methodological model for them,[1] in contrast with the natural sciences, which explicitly concern themselves with causal rela-

---

[1] Regarding this point, see the critical analysis by Jürgen v. Kempski, "Die Welt als Text," in *Aspekte der Wahrheit* (1962), reprinted in his collection of essays, *Brechungen. Kritische Versuche zur Philosophie der Gegenwart* (Hamburg, 1964), pp. 285 ff., where he underlines the dubiousness of ontologizing the textual model in hermeneutic philosophy.

tionships. In the humanistic sciences it became a matter of course to assume that they require their own special epistemological foundation because they were differentiated from the natural sciences by virtue of the peculiarity of the object of their investigation. This ontological justification of the methodological demand for autonomy of the humanistic sciences ran into considerable difficulties because of the simultaneous incursion into this realm of the methods of the natural sciences—difficulties epitomized by the decade-long controversy over "understanding and explanation," and the attempts at defense and demarcation associated with that controversy.[2]

The development and spread of hermeneutics was closely tied to that of *historism*, that very complex phenomenon of the history of ideas that one can conceive of—in rather simplistic terms—as a consequence of German idealism and the Romantic reaction to the rationalistic and purportedly unhistorical thinking of the Enlightenment. This connection of hermeneutics with historism, of orientation on the textual model and the cult of historicity, brought forth the typical traits of the antinaturalistic and quasi-theological orientation of humanistic and philosophical thought which is still the dominant emphasis in German-speaking circles today. In its extreme form, this approach seeks to impose this textual model on the whole of reality, attempting to elevate the theological style of thought to a philosophical ideal,[3] and does so by explicitly denouncing the "concept of method" of modern science, which must be overcome in the humanities. In fact, one can understand this philosophy, as we have already suggested, as a

[2] This controversy has had a great influence on the discussion of method in psychology, sociology, and economics; it has had some effect on historiography as well and is now beginning to spread to philology via linguistics. In jurisprudence and theology, on the other hand—dogmatic-exegetical disciplines par excellence—there has been no noticeable effect of such discussions.

[3] See particularly the very influential book by Hans-Georg Gadamer, *Truth and Method* (New York, 1975), part 3, as well as the criticism by v. Kempski mentioned above.

continuation of theology through other means—by the influence, that is, of Hegel and Heidegger, and with the means furnished by the thought of both philosophers. When one considers the use which modern theologians tend to make of it, we see philosophy serving still as the handmaiden of theology.[4]

Within the tradition of historism, a program of knowledge was developed that sought to introduce the typical characteristics of historical thought, as epitomized by its evolution in the nineteenth century, into all other disciplines, especially the social sciences. In terms of content, the constant flux and the alteration of things—of social circumstances and structures, of values and norms—as well as the individuality, the uniqueness, and the particularity, and thus the unrepeability, of events were emphasized; or, as we finally learned to call it, the *historicity* of development and its agents, human beings. From the beginning, a methodological approach connected with this view was supposed to justify the particular methodological stance of the humanistic sciences, the sciences of historico-social reality. The representatives of this methodological historism directed their criticism predominantly against two procedures they considered intrinsically alien to the nature of historical thinking: first, against the imposition of *absolute* and hence timeless and ahistorical *standards* on historical events—as, for example, those postulated by *natural law*; and second, against the attempt to explain the course of history and, in general, social and cultural phenomena with the help of *general*, timeless *laws*, as done in the natural sciences—against, that is, *naturalism* in the humanistic sciences. They considered history a network of events that carry their meanings within themselves and whose meaning relationships

---

[4] One can see very clearly in Gadamer the capitulation of this school of thought before the demands of theology; see *Truth and Method*, where he describes some exegetical and dogmatic questions as being of the sort about which the "layman" can have no position—a remarkable development in face of a philosophical tradition in which criticism of theology and religion have played an important role.

must be grasped immediately, without the application of universal standards or laws. In the place of explanation—the goal of the natural sciences—should come an interpretation that comprehends uniqueness and individuality—an individualizing method designed to explicate the essence of the phenomena out of their historical evolution. "The essence of the historical method," said Droysen, whose works, especially his methodological views, are still constantly referred to, "*is to understand by research.*"[5]

This program also expresses the hermeneutical research program that was worked out, philosophically elaborated, and legitimized during the development of historism; it is a program which, in a way similar to that of scientific positivism, emphasizes immediate experience as the means of grasping the "given," and which, like scientific positivism, has a strong mistrust of theoretical conceptions. The *hermeneutical positivism* of the humanistic sciences—in part formed by the phenomenological conception of experience—is in this respect, then, to be considered a parallel to *sensualistic positivism*, which for a time had some influence on the development of the natural sciences; then, in the neopositivism of the Vienna Circle and similar movements, it evolved into a strongly logico-mathematical philosophy which, due to political developments, at first did not have any effect upon Continental thought.[6] Both philosophical movements emphasized the importance of pretheoretical experience as a means of acquiring knowledge; but in one case it was more the "outer," in the other more the "inner," experience. To put it another way, while the one wished above all to have recourse to *sense experience*, the other placed great value on the *experience of*

---

[5] See Johann Gustav Droysen, *Historik. Vorlesungen über Enzyklopädie und Methodologie der Geschichte*, 4th ed. (Munich, 1960), pp. 22 and 328, as well as my article, "Geschichte und Gesetz," in *Sozialphilosophie als Aufklärung. Festschrift für Topitsch*, ed. Kurt Salamun (Tübingen, 1979).

[6] The irrationalism associated with hermeneutic thinking has assured that the epistemologically interesting results of this philosophical position have not been perceived in German thought.

*meaning*, which seemed to play an analogous role in the understanding of sociocultural situations.

In both cases, at any rate, the foundation of knowledge is attained with the help of experience—that is, the unmediated "given," in the one case presenting itself as sensible, and in the other as meaningful, but in either case occurring as the *factum brutum* which purportedly was given before all interpretations.[7] We do not need to refer here again to the "myth of the 'given,' " which has already been adequately criticized. Whether contexts of meaning or causal relationships are under question, the idea of a theory-free and immediate experiential access to reality has been so sufficiently discredited that one need not dwell upon it further. Whether experience is interior or exterior, of the senses or of meanings, it is inadequate to understand it as a passive incorporation of a "given." In the one case as much as in the other, the character of that experience is codetermined by the activity of interpretation as informed by social influences and the norms and theories they incorporate. It is nonetheless interesting that this idea still has some aftereffects within hermeneutic philosophy, and indeed throughout the realm of influence of the so-called method of understanding; but they are effects that do not contribute to the clarification of the problems.

## 22. HERMENEUTICAL THOUGHT: PHILOSOPHY AS THE CONTINUATION OF THEOLOGY

The methodological conception of hermeneutic thought has an initially very plausible ontological basis in the distinction

---

[7] See, for instance, Rudolf Carnap, *The Logical Structure of the World*, trans. R. George, 2d ed. (London, 1969), which develops a system of the constitution of concepts on a foundation of sense perceptions, an approach that Carnap certainly abandoned soon; and Martin Heidegger, *Being and Time* (1927). The analogy is naturally not adequate in every respect. While Carnap wishes to achieve a structure on the basis of the "given" through deliberately constructive thought, Heidegger wishes his undertaking to be understood as pure interpretation, denying any notion of construction—a view of his own project which involves a considerable misunderstanding.

between the external world of nature, which can only be comprehended *from the outside in*—that is, by recourse to external experience and the application of laws, and thus by explanation—and the world of human life, of actions, orders, and interpretations, in which man himself participates, and which, therefore, can only be comprehended *from the inside out*— that is, on the basis of internal experience and by utilizing meaningful relationships and, thus, by understanding. This distinction found its most extreme expression in the dichotomy that dominates Spenglerian metaphysics between "world as nature" and "world as history."[8] It seems deceptively obvious that knowers ought to have a better access from the beginning to the objects of the cultural realm, an access that allows a deeper kind of insight into relations within this realm than one could ever gain into natural relations. Understanding, as Droysen says, is "the most complete knowledge that is humanly possible" for us. Thus, it is said to occur "like an immediate intuition."[9]

Droysen, as also later defenders of hermeneutical thinking, again and again offers understanding as an *alternative to explanation* for the human realm—and indeed, usually as a better alternative, a procedure through which a sort of insight

[8] This bifurcation, as is well known, can already be found in Giambattista Vico (see *The New Science of Giambattista Vico*, trans. T. Bergin and M. Fisch [New York, 1968]) and again later in Hegel and his successors— for example, Benedetto Croce, who refers back to Vico; cf. Croce, *The Philosophy of Giambattista Vico*, trans. R. Collingwood (New York, 1964), where the connection of this epistemological idea with the ontological bifurcation of the world into nature and mankind is clearly expressed, with agnosticism characteristically restricted to the first realm. Croce himself, in his *Logica come Scienza del Concetto puro*, ascribes practical uses to natural science, but no true cognitive value. See also Karl Löwith, *Meaning and History* (Chicago, 1949), pp. 109 ff.

[9] See Droysen, *Historik*, p. 26: "To understand is the most human act of the human being, and all true human action is based on understanding, seeks understanding, finds understanding. Understanding is the innermost bond between humans and the basis of all moral existence." The understanding, he says earlier, is exactly that with which we understand those who speak to us (p. 25), and only men understand other men (p. 23).

can be achieved that is unobtainable in any other way. Related to the excision of the human realm from the natural world is almost always the idea of a higher, deeper, or more certain knowledge, a knowledge for which the normal methods of natural science are irrelevant. Theory building and nomological knowledge, it is suggested, are hardly possible here; but they would in any case be superfluous, for in this realm an autonomous method is available which functions quite nicely without them, and indeed accomplishes more. This does not exclude the fact that one sometimes values "generality" or even "necessity," but these terms are not used to refer to regularities, as is usual in natural science. Instead, they are applied to institutional facts, relative invariants of a socio-cultural character, often of the sort concerned with the nor-mative regulation of social life:[10] law, customs, language— "givens," in other words, which we believe ourselves to be able to "understand" without further ado. It is thus precisely the universals in the cultural realm, in contrast to the laws of the natural sciences, which also seem "understandable." It is in its reference to such states of affairs that the meaning-laden character of sociocultural reality and the necessity for an "in-ner," meaning-saturated experience for its knowledge is made most plausible. "Objective spirit" seems as accessible to un-derstanding as do the actions of individual persons; language and its grammar are as accessible as particular sentences in specific situations. In each case, contexts of meaning must be grasped, and the universal aspect of language, its regularity, is rendered concrete in each particular speech act.

There is little doubt that something like "understanding" occurs in everyday life and in special—or indeed, in all— realms of knowledge. This thesis is not debatable, but the particular ways of characterizing this procedure are as is the claim of defenders of the methodological autonomy of the

[10] Droysen points to such facts already; see pp. 27 and 202 ff.: they are, as we will soon see, basically the same facts that, under the influence of the later philosophy of Ludwig Wittgenstein, are emphasized and elevated to the status of ultimate "givens."

humanistic sciences to have exhibited a particular method of knowledge that is in some respects superior to that of the natural sciences. This claim is particularly controversial since until recently little attempt has been made to reconstruct the logic of this procedure, which in various ways has been set apart and described—as re-living, re-enactment, living-into, empathizing, interpretation, and so forth—as being in a position to be considered as an acceptable alternative to explanation. In this situation, for critics of this claim of methodological autonomy, it was a possible route of escape, to locate this procedure in heuristic—from which, indeed, anything is seldom excluded, particularly when a method whose function is cloaked in considerable obscurity is at stake. But methodologists of the humanistic sciences certainly never declared themselves satisfied with this; they held to the completely correct opinion that to allow such a move would be de facto to give up their claims, particularly the claim that runs counter to the consequences of Darwinism for the modern world view: that of epistemologically honoring the idea, rooted in sociocosmic thought, of the unique status of man in nature—an idea of predominantly theological significance.

The problem of an autonomous methodology in the humanistic sciences has been discussed extensively within these disciplines since the turn of the century, as one would expect, considering the dominant philosophical tendencies of that period. Martin Heidegger's book, *Sein und Zeit*, became a focal point of this controversy, not because an explication of this method—a logic of understanding—might be found there, nor because it provides anything like a theoretical basis for such a method. But it was important for another reason, namely, because through an analysis that is in a deep sense hermeneutic, an "analytic of the existentiality of existence"[11] in which the "historicity of existence" is ontologically worked out as the "ontical condition for the possibility of history,"

[11] Cf. Martin Heidegger, *Being and Time*, pp. 37, 38. [Author's translation here and following.]

this work claims to provide a transcendental knowledge, and simultaneously to lay bare the roots of "the methodology of the historical sciences," which, of course, could also be termed "hermeneutic" but "only in derivative sense." However interesting the Heideggerian investigations might be from various points of view, the following must be said from the methodological viewpoint: it represents a paradigm of problematic essentialism, and of an orientation to concepts which has long lingered in the humanistic sciences as a relic of pre-Galilean thought, to which precisely that impulse of phenomenological thinking, which Heidegger quite consciously indulges to the hilt, contributes a great deal. What this book offers is a purely conceptual analysis in which a conceptual apparatus is constructed and illustrated to dramatize certain aspects of human life and experience. Its ontological meaning, however, remains unexplicated, unless one concedes such a meaning a priori to every descriptively usable conceptual apparatus. Despite Heidegger's preference for unusual terminology, constructed by him expressly for his own purposes, his analyses consistently remain in the realm of everyday thought. He describes quite ordinary and well-known phenomena with this novel terminology. A definite way of seeing is generated through such analyses, which might seem plausible to some people; but its value cannot be determined until it can be shown which problems can be solved better with its help.

Heidegger's rejection of construction, his emphasis on the "receptive" reason and on the phenomenon as "that which reveals itself in itself" (das "sich-so-an-ihm-selbst-Zeigende"),[12] are expressions in hermeneutical form of that revelation model of knowledge that we have already criticized in its classical versions. But while the classical version also purports to offer an interpretation of scientific method, this new version rather offers a stylization of prescientific everyday thinking, and proposes it as the superior, or even as the only, appropriate way of thinking in the humanistic sciences. The

[12] Cf. ibid., pp. 16 and 50, and pp. 33 ff.

ontological bifurcation of the world that we found in the earlier versions of the hermeneutical position is already revealed in Heidegger by the fact that he finds it necessary to term the characters of being of Dasein "existentialia," while dubbing as "categories" the forms of being that do not attain the status of Dasein,[13] thus imposing a terminological obstacle to the incorporation of the knowledge of humanity into the knowledge of nature. But despite all broader claims by Heidegger, what is attempted within the human realm, so demarcated, is in fact little more than a salvage operation on qualitative Aristotelian thought, which is displaced and excluded from other realms by post-Galilean methodology. The success of these efforts would not further the humanistic sciences, but would only serve to solidify them as that which they have until now essentially remained—as a preserve for Aristotelian thought. It is thus no misuse of Heideggerian thought that it should be the recourse of those in the social sciences who wish to ward off the incursion of modern methods, but perfectly consistent. It is in accordance with its basic tendencies that it serve the legitimization of such attempts of protection and demarcation.[14]

Understanding from this perspective becomes a "fundamental existential," a "basic mode of the *Being* of beings," so that the particular form of understanding that until now was the subject of the methodological discussion must be interpreted "as an existential derivative of that primary understanding which is one of the constituents of the Being of the there (*das Da*) in general."[15] If one takes into consideration the Heideggerian passages about the character of the original understanding as project, it seems possible to have an inter-

[13] Cf. ibid, p. 44.

[14] But Heidegger himself has seen the new kind of thinking in mathematical physics; cf. *Being and Time*, p. 362, and Alexandre Koyré, *Galilean Studies*. However, a theoretical social science in the style of mathematical economics, which worked according to Galilean methods, would not fit into the perspective he suggests. His basic ontological dogma precludes this possibility.

[15] *Being and Time*, p. 143.

pretation that comes close to the problem of the relationship between conceptual apparatus and world perspective, which has also been discussed in the analytic tradition.[16] But Heidegger's approach to these questions is not designed to shed much light. Rather, it obscures the interesting nucleus of these problems, submerging it in an esoteric jargon that cloaks even the most trivial claims in an atmosphere of mystery and makes them appear like deep insights.[17] Incidentally, the crafting of this concept of understanding, which is supposed to disclose the nature of reality with the help of linguistic interpretations, is terminologically very skillfully done and apparently creates a prejudice in favor of a universal hermeneutics; from this point of view, the knowledge of the natural sciences might seem derivative and superficial. But this is a trick which, upon closer examination, shows itself unable to contribute to a conclusive solution to the problems of method that we have been discussing. For, in the first place, according to Heidegger's own words, understanding as a special kind of knowledge, which is at issue here, has as derivative a character as explanation. Second, explanatory theories in the fundamental sense fixed by Heideggerian terminology are by definition exactly as hermeneutical in nature as the results of the way of knowing that is "understanding in a derivative sense." To be precise, whatever else one might make of them, Heidegger's investigations remain irrelevant to the treatment and solution of the problem of method.

If one then turns to the hermeneutical conception of Gadamer which is often viewed as methodically relevant by rep-

[16] See, for instance, Kasimir Ajdukiewicz, *Sprache und Sinn*, and his "Das Weltbild und die Begriffsapparatur," *Erkenntnis*, vol. 4 (1934); "Die wissenschaftliche Weltperspektive," *Erkenntnis*, vol. 5 (1935); and "Sinnregeln, Weltperspektive, Welt" in the same volume—which is a response to the discussion note by Carl G. Hempel, "Zur Frage der wissenschaftlichen Weltperspektive"—or later works by Carnap and Quine.

[17] Cf., for instance, Heinrich Gomperz, *Über Sinn und Sinngebilde. Verstehen und Erklären* (Tübingen, 1929). Gomperz starts with a similarly broad notion of understanding, but he analyzes the problem clearly and does not create any ontological illusions such as those in *Being and Time*.

resentatives of the humanistic sciences, in order to see what it has to contribute to the solution of problems of method, one will do well not to lose sight of three things: the fact that he, too, argues for the universality of the hermeneutical point of view and thus, to a large extent, orients himself upon Heidegger; that in the process, however, he turns explicitly against the concept of method of modern science, and wishes his enterprise to be understood as arising out of the tradition of the concept of education (*Bildungsbegriff*); and finally, that he rejects, largely in passing, the instrumentalist theory of signs without any critical appraisal of the relevant views, although in view of the fact that linguistic phenomena are of great importance for his own theory, it does at least seem worth considering it as an alternative.[18] His investigations clearly display the consequences of a hermeneutics that can no longer become aware of the questionability of its own presuppositions because it refuses to take rival theories into serious consideration. This might be related to the fact that the political developments of the last thirty years have virtually excluded any rivalry from other philosophical movements in German-speaking culture,[19] so that for some time one has been able to convince oneself, however mistakenly, that through Heidegger the other philosophical conceptions have been overcome and one need no longer be concerned with them.[20]

However that may be, one consequence of this approach is antinaturalism, and the associated disqualification of the methods of the natural sciences, which, furthermore, are so

[18] See Hans Georg Gadamer, *Truth and Method*. Regarding the last point, it is interesting that he does not even mention some significant contributions to the problematic of meaning, such as Gomperz's book or Karl Bühler's *Die Krise der Psychologie* (1927), 3d ed. (Stuttgart, 1965), which already applies cybernetic ideas to these problems. He also obviously considers Max Weber's contributions irrelevant.

[19] Except for East Germany, where an equally one-sided but a rather differently oriented selection took place.

[20] See the interesting remarks of Walter Kaufmann about this philosophical ethnocentrism of German thought in his "Deutscher Geist heute," *Texte und Zeichen*, III (1957), no. 6.

represented as to embody the Baconian myth of inductivism. As Gadamer explicitly states, he has no intention of renewing the old methodological battle between the natural and humanistic sciences.[21] Rather, his concern is "to seek out the experience of truth, which transcends the domain of scientific methodology, wherever it is to be found, and to demand of it its own legitimation." This legitimation of the truth claims of ways of knowledge that stand "outside science" is to be achieved by "immersion in the phenomenon of the understanding." The rather premature claim that nothing can come of the method of modern science within the realm being considered by Gadamer because other goals of knowledge stand in question, is not, as one might expect, supported by appropriate argument nor even rendered plausible. Rather, he conveys the impression that in the face of the fact that the knower is "drawn into a truth event," questions of method become either secondary or completely irrelevant. In understanding, according to his view, the knower seems to be the recipient of an "event of being" in which the truth reveals itself to him, without being able to contribute anything of significance himself, either through his own activity, or through methodological procedures.

It is quite clear that Gadamer identifies the character of the scientific method against which he normally polemicizes in a way characteristic of his own intentions; as when he claims, for instance, that "the certainty which the application of scientific methods provides does not suffice to guarantee truth," while the "discipline of research and query" considered appropriate for the humanistic sciences is so constructed as to "guarantee the truth."[22] Now, as we have seen, there is no such thing as a guarantee of truth; but the scientific method aims at an approximation of the truth through the exposure of errors[23]—an intention which certainly should not be con-

[21] See his foreword to *Truth and Method*.
[22] Cf. Gadamer, *Truth and Method*, part 3.
[23] On this point, see the relevant part of Karl R. Popper's work.

sidered foreign to the humanistic sciences as well, insofar as they have not given themselves completely over to quasi-theological thinking. Their statements, too, are to be considered hypotheses, which can be submitted to certain tests and are subject to revision under some circumstances. In this respect the cognitive aim of the humanistic sciences can hardly be distinguished from that of other sciences. If under the influence of the turn brought about by Heidegger one wishes to renounce the method of critical examination, it amounts to a subjective decision to opt voluntarily out of the science game and that means out of the humanistic sciences as well. An ontology that is in the position to legitimize such decisions, and thereby de facto to open the possibility of exempting some components of our convictions from criticism, does so only at the cost of revealing its own dubiousness.

In this connection, it is interesting to note, incidentally, that Gadamer explicitly has his eye on reorientating humanistic thinking toward juridical and theological hermeneutics,[24] aiming for a solution of hermeneutical problems modeled upon the exegetical practices of dogmatic sciences, which support rather than expose the illusions of some practitioners of these sciences. The dogmatic restriction, given here as one component of the task of interpretation, would be an obstacle to critical thought; for Gadamer it presents no difficulty. Rather, he wishes to elevate the dogmatically restricted form of hermeneutical thought to a model for hermeneutics in general. This suggestion is consonant with his peculiar attitude toward tradition. In contrast to the naiveté of the belief in a method that does not hesitate to make tradition an object of investigation, which is constantly criticized in his book, Gadamer places a great value on the idea that the understander has to hand himself over to tradition; for whoever reflects himself out of his lived attitude to his tradition destroys its true meaning.[25] Representatives of hermeneutical philosophy are argu-

[24] Cf. Gadamer, *Truth and Method*, part 2, pp. 2, 3, and esp. p. 289.
[25] Cf. ibid., p. 341.

ing again and again that one can and ought to refrain from "making" various relationships—chiefly those most precious and valuable to whomever is speaking—"into objects," from "objectifying" them—an admonition generally associated with attempts to overcome the so-called "subject-object cleavage." But this is a naive recommendation, insofar as these theoreticians, when they wish to utter statements of any kind, are themselves constantly forced to speak "about" things, and thus perform such "objectivizations." The claim to convey truth without any such objectification taking place presumably rests on a misunderstanding of the activity of human language, which is distinguished from the means of communication of animals by exactly this capacity to represent facts, and, beyond that, to allow argumentation.[26] Even hermeneuticists use language to talk about things and to argue, thus utilizing the subject-object split, the dramatization of which has unfortunately caused a great deal of confusion about methodological issues as well. It is hard to see just what is supposed to be so problematic about it, so long as one does not fall into a misunderstanding of this straightforward state of affairs. It is just the methodology of modern science that explicitly takes account of the peculiarities of languages and the accomplishments they make possible; one seldom finds comparable analyses in the sphere of hermeneutic thought. That one cannot have a positive attitude in regard to traditions, which, with methodological distance, one has made an object of critical analysis, is a peculiar thesis, which, in the face of available counterexamples, deserves no credit.

Certainly, two things are very clear: first, the fact that a

[26] This result is, of course, contained in the work of a representative of the instrumentalist theory of signs, which is rejected by Gadamer; cf. Karl Bühler, *Sprachtheorie. Die Darstellungsfunktion der Sprache* (1934), 2d ed. (Stuttgart, 1965), passim, as well as Karl R. Popper, "Towards a Rational Theory of Tradition" (1949) or "Language and the Body-Mind Problem," both in *Conjectures and Refutations*, where the argumentation function of language is emphasized. Compare also Popper's *Of Clouds and Clocks* (St. Louis, 1966), pp. 18 ff.

philosophical hermeneutics with such tendencies will receive a positive echo from representatives of modern Protestant theology, who would encounter great difficulties with a more adequate treatment of language and objectification problems; and second, that Gadamer himself is able to find positive aspects to the products of this theology.[27] In the course of an ontological turn of hermeneutics guided by language, he finally arrives at a comprehensive exploitation of his textual model of analysis, together with polemical attacks against the ideal of the objectivity of science—which one can well, and with some justification, call a continuation of theology through other means. These are the consequences of a conception that is prepared unhesitatingly not only to sacrifice the ideal of the objectivity of science, but also to sacrifice the critical impulse expressed in scientific method and in philosophical rationalism, in favor of intuitive reason in the service of dogmatic modes of thought.

## 23. ANALYTIC THOUGHT: PHILOSOPHY AS ANALYSIS OF LANGUAGE

In analytic thought one finds a parallel in the Anglo-Saxon world to what hermeneutic thought, descended from historism and similar intellectual movements, means to the German-speaking world. Analytic thought arose out of the changes undergone by positivism in this milieu, and above all out of the late philosophy of Ludwig Wittgenstein. Here as well, the problematic of meaning has occupied the center of interest for a long time, even though thinkers have not been ready to take as decisive a position against the scientific quest for ob-

[27] Cf. Gadamer's remarks about incarnation, the mystery of the trinity, and so forth, in *Truth and Method*, as well as his thesis in part 3, mentioned above, where he speaks of interests that transcend science, namely, interests of faith and of correct preaching, which raise questions on which the "layman" can adopt no position. In the sixteenth century, philosophers, as "laymen," no doubt would also have been forbidden to adopt positions on demonology.

jectivity as is common in hermeneutic philosophy. This may be connected with the fact that the analytic concern for the problem of meaning initially arose from investigations into the logic of science and from researches into the foundations of logic and mathematics.

It has been correctly observed that the development of analytic philosophy out of positivism led to a treatment of understanding similar in some ways to its treatment in hermeneutic thought.[28] The focus on language as a means of communication in both cases especially involves a critical attitude toward the psychological empathy theory of the sort characteristic of the earlier phases of hermeneutics. It could be said, with some justification, that grammar has now taken the place of psychology;[29] but we will see that one might just as well speak of the sociologizing of the problem in analytic thought, for the "language games" that come into consideration were in fact understood as social forms of life. The difference between the analytic and the hermeneutic movements of philosophy lies, among other things, in the fact that the latter has developed from a problematic that refers to concrete historical texts into a direction that leads to a universal ontology oriented on the text model, while the former, beginning with an analysis of the logic of scientific discourse, switched to an investigation of the grammar of various "language games," with the emphasis less on particular texts than on specific types of statements. On the whole, in the sphere of influence of positivism, the language problematic is of no less importance than in the realm of hermeneutics, and when the two movements are compared, the frequently minute investigations of the analysts may favorably contrast to the pre-

[28] See Karl-Otto Apel, "Die Entfaltung der 'Sprachanalytischen' Philosophie und das Problem der 'Geisteswissenschaften,' " *Philosophisches Jahrbuch* 72 (1965), pp. 239 ff., as well as his "Wittgenstein und das Problem des hermeneutischen Verstehens," *Zeitschrift für Theologie und Kirche* 63 (1966), pp. 48 ff.

[29] In analytic philosophy, of course, grammar means the set of all rules of whatever "language game" is being analyzed.

tentious but often foggy language games of the hermeneuti-cists.[30]

While the typical follower of hermeneutical thought usually deals unabashedly with concepts of meaning without sub-mitting them to logical analysis, the analyst attempted early on to clarify his concepts through just such a procedure. The reduction to rules, which appeared in the later philosophy of Wittgenstein and which became familiar to German readers through his work, is already apparent in the thought of the earlier followers of this philosophical movement. What dis-tinguishes the later philosophy of Wittgenstein from the work of Heidegger and his followers is Wittgenstein's criticism of essentialism, which even today is still partially characteristic of humanistic disciplines,[31] and which tends to ontologize the grammar of certain statements and—as was the case to some extent in Heidegger's thought—to leap from plausible de-scriptions of everyday forms of language to conclusions about the constitution of the world. As is well known, he presented this criticism in aphoristic form, through the analysis of one new example after another, each postulated to show that the grammar of our language lies behind particularly deep-rooted and apparently self-evident statements—that is, that their strong appeal and self-evidence stem from the fact that they are part of the forms constituted by the rules of the language game in question.

Now, Wittgenstein—and, for that matter, Heidegger too—adopted a purely descriptive standpoint while strongly repu-diating explanations of any kind. He had no wish either to theoretically illuminate or to criticize certain states of affairs.[32]

[30] Only relatively recently have there been attempts to bridge this gap; see, for instance, Georg Jánoska, *Die sprachlichen Grundlagen der Philosophie* (Graz, 1962); Ernst Tugendhat, "Die sprachanalytische Kritik der Ontolo-gie," in *Das Problem der Sprache*, ed. Gadamer (Munich, 1967), as well as the works by Apel cited above.

[31] Cf. Ludwig Wittgenstein, *Philosophical Investigations* (Oxford, 1953). Karl Popper has subjected this position to thorough and systematic criticism.

[32] Cf. Wittgenstein: "124. Philosophy may in no way interfere with the

De facto, to be sure, the matter is somewhat more complicated than Wittgenstein's self-interpretation would lead one to believe. One might well defend the thesis that a theory of language is implicit in his investigations, and indeed even a theory precisely of the sort explicitly rejected by Gadamer.[33] But he does not wish to have his theory taken seriously[34]—as an alternative to earlier theories of meaning, for instance—because he has no interest at all in theories of that sort. Obviously, in his later philosophy the idea is still apparent that one here actually can say *nothing* but can *only show something*—an idea which, as is well known, is dominant in the *Tractatus*. His means to this end are his fragmentary analyses, his "sketches of a landscape," to use his term. Now, on this point, there is without doubt a kinship with Heidegger's phenomenological analyses; they, too, are not designed for the theoretical penetration of certain phenomena, but only wish to exhibit them. Linguistic analysis and phenomenology meet here in their positivistic tendency, their inclination to make manifest the "given." The disadvantage of this strategy is that it does not allow theoretical conceptions that lie in the background to be clearly visible as such, and thus they are allowed to escape criticism.[35]

In view of this situation, it is easy to understand that the late philosophy of Wittgenstein has had extremely conserva-

---

actual use of language; it can in the end only describe it. For it cannot give it any foundation, either. It leaves everything as it is." *Philosophical Investigations*, trans. Anscombe (Oxford, 1953), p. 49.

[33] It is an "instrumentalistic theory of signs," or better, a combination of instrumentalism and institutionalism. Language is viewed as a tool of communication, a tool grounded in certain social game rules.

[34] Paul Feyerabend has pointed this out; see his criticism in "Wittgenstein's *Philosophical Investigations*," *Philosophical Review* 64 (1955), pp. 449 ff., esp. p. 479.

[35] In some of the more pretentious German books the reader is occasionally given to understand that the author is not considering mere opinions, but that it is "the thing itself" that is moving when he propounds his thoughts—the "thing" being, of course, in special cases, the "language" as well.

tive consequences in the hands of his followers.[36] Here, too, we can find a parallel to German hermeneutics. When it is only a question of allowing all language games and forms of life to exist, because they must be taken as a "given," then the critical impulse of philosophical thought, which was at work in the original positivism and can still be recognized in some of Wittgenstein's analyses, must vanish. A philosophical critique of religion, like that of Feuerbach or of Nietzsche, cannot be expected from thinking of this kind. Theology is, in the last analysis, also just another language game, which must thus be left alone, and which cannot, for instance, be critically scrutinized, because it has proved impossible to bring it into harmony with certain cognitions, which are themselves, after all, only moves in other language games. Just as German hermeneuticists lend support to theology, even in its most peculiar shifts and evasions, so one might expect the same from the analyst, who has completely adopted the above-mentioned conservative principle.[37]

The Oxford manner of carrying out such investigations sometimes creates the impression that logical analyses, which are immune to empirical objections and involve no statements having the status of hypotheses, are at stake. But insofar as such investigations refer, however impressionistically to actual linguistic usage in certain fields, this is not the case. The results of investigations into the logical grammar of specific expressions and statements of an existing language are in principle not exempt from empirical testing, unless such a protection is artificially introduced through specific immunization strategies. This is of interest insofar as a new apriorism has de-

[36] On this point, see Ernest Gellner's radical criticism in *Words and Things* (London, 1959).

[37] On this point, consider Van Austin Harvey, "Die Gottesfrage in der amerikanischen Theologie der Gegenwart," *Zeitschrift für Theologie und Kirche* 64 (1967), pp. 325 ff.; whoever reads this article will see that many analytic philosophers have retained the critical impulse and create considerable difficulties for theological thinking. Similar things happen in hermeneutic circles; consider Wilhelm Weischedel's part in Gollwitzer und Weischedel, *Denken und Glauben*.

veloped out of Wittgenstein's later philosophy, which seeks to reveal the hidden sociological implications of his conception.

That this philosophy contains such implications, or at least something like a sociological perspective, is blatantly obvious to anyone who is familiar with sociological thought. A critical observer has even gone so far as to claim that in this philosophy we are presented with only a watered-down version of Durkheimian sociology—without claiming, of course, that its author need have read Durkheim.[38] However that may be, it would not be the first time that an interesting theory with considerable content has petrified into a metaphysics that is hard to attack because it is immunized. Let us shelve that issue. In any case, Peter Winch has explicitly taken the step that ought to be taken if one wishes to protect a theory against empirical objections. Out of the aphoristic investigations of Wittgenstein, he has produced the outline of a sociology that purports to be a priori.[39] Beginning with the merger of language and forms of life, as found in Wittgenstein, Winch believes the task of philosophy is to elucidate the respective forms of life, such as art, science, or religion; and to epistemology falls the task of "clarifying the implications of the concept of a form of life as such."[40] According to Winch, this means that "the central problem of sociology—to give an account of the nature of social phenomena in general," itself belongs to philosophy, for it is only a matter of clarifying the concept of the "form of life." This part of sociology is for him "actually neglected epistemology"—neglected, because the respective problems have been treated as special kinds of scientific problems, and thus, until now, "for the most part falsely posed and therefore wrongly treated."

Winch's treatment of his problem makes it clear that a new

---

[38] See Ernest Gellner, "The Crisis in the Humanities and the Mainstream of Philosophy," in *Crisis in the Humanities*, ed. J. H. Plumb (Harmondsworth, 1964), pp. 64 ff.

[39] Cf. Peter Winch, *The Idea of a Social Science and its Relation to Philosophy* (London, 1958).

[40] Ibid., p. 56.

essentialism has emerged within analytic philosophy, which from the Wittgensteinian idea that essences are expressed in grammar draws the consequence that conceptual analyses of this sort are, without further ado, able to convey a priori insights into essence. This has immediate methodological consequences, for it turns out "that the idea of a human society implies a conceptual scheme that is logically incompatible with the types of explanation offered by the natural sciences."[41] Against attempts to apply the methodology of explanation to social contexts, Winch engages the possibility of using everyday speech to describe the events in question in order to make them understandable; and he insists thereby that the possibility of understanding presupposes a different type of regularity than that which comes into play in explanation within natural science—a regularity characterized by the following of rules. No arguments can be found in Winch's work for his thesis that describing human behavior with the help of concepts that involve this type of intelligible regularity not only saves us from further explanations of the usual sort, but is even incompatible with them.[42] The fact that "understandable" behavior could also be explained by recourse to general theories is found "implausible" by him through purely conceptual considerations, in which the central methodological questions are not even once considered.

Incidentally, Winch quite clearly articulates in his conception that the linguistically packaged essentialism of Oxford analysis can completely eliminate the critical impulse that is still felt in Wittgenstein. The idea that philosophy leaves everything as it is actually leads, in the analysis of forms of life, as one might expect, to the consequence that the use of scientific results and methods in the critique of religion is precluded from the outset.[43] It is only important to grasp through the analysis of concepts the essence of various forms of life and

[41] Ibid., p. 94.
[42] Ibid., p. 121.
[43] Ibid., p. 132.

to reenact their linguistically formulated practices of disclosing the word by understanding. Criticism is not the task of philosophy. If one compares Gadamer with Winch, a striking parallel emerges between hermeneutic and analytic thought. Whether one emphasizes the historical dimension, as is the case in hermeneutic thought, or whether one gives priority to the coexistence of different forms of life, as is done in analytic thought—in either case, the overemphasis on the problem of meaning overwhelms not only the drive for theoretical penetration of reality, including sociocultural reality, but also the concern to promote its critical illumination, which has traditionally been considered a possible, indeed a useful, task of philosophy. Theory and criticism, explanation and enlightenment vanish together and give way to a conservative descriptivism that is suited only to accept without explanation, and to take over without criticism, whatever exists at any given time, as embodied in the traditional forms of life. Of course, the difficulty then appears that, in fact, traditions and ways of life compete with one another and contradict one another in their claims, so that nothing is gained by this sanctification of the "given."

Moreover, at least one important tradition is also incompatible with this attitude, namely, the tradition of critical thought, which is embodied above all in the critical form of life of science and in the method of rational discussion and critical examination practiced therein.[44] Anyone who wishes to preserve this tradition can neither acknowledge the tendency to obediently adopt the traditional, which is cultivated by hermeneutic thought, nor accept the neutrality-thesis of the analysts that contradicts not only a critical theory of knowledge, but also a critical moral philosophy.[45]

---

[44] Cf. Karl R. Popper, "Science: Conjectures and Refutations," in his collection, *Conjectures and Refutations*, and other works by the same author, as well as my article, "Tradition und Kritik," in *Club Voltaire*, II, ed. Gerhard Szczesny (Munich, 1955).

[45] See my criticism of this position in my article, "Ethik und Meta-Ethik."

## 24. The Problem of Meaning in Criticist Perspective

We have seen that in the analytic tradition of philosophy, as in the hermeneutic, conceptions have developed which not only strive for a solution to the problem of meaning from an *anti-naturalist* point of view—and thus represent an ontologically based methodological separatism that sharply distinguishes the human realm from the rest of nature—but which also go so far as to adopt an *anti-rationalistic* stance, in that they wish to preclude any possible criticism of the meanings presented to the understanding. A critical philosophy must find this view objectionable. By accepting as "givens" contexts of meaning, and the rules, maxims, and criteria on which they are based such positions favor a solution of the problem by resignation. They are ready to forgo possible explanation and criticism, and thereby to inhibit the development of sociocultural life. Insofar as it is a question of the theoretical penetration of sociocultural reality, of its nomological interpretation, this renunciation is based on the fact that from the outset to investigate its structure through uncovering corresponding regularities is held to be impossible or uninteresting—a result that rests completely on intuitive and conceptual analyses of a highly problematic character. This is also true for the critical examination of this part of reality. In this respect the above-mentioned renunciation is rooted in the tendency to treat the actually developed and traditional standards for the evaluation of sociocultural conditions themselves as "givens" that can only be described, understood, and then taken over as they stand—a tendency which, like the anti-theoretical tendency springs from a "positivistic" attitude.[46] Instead of construction and criticism, we find here the passivity of the receptive reason, which does not aspire to a higher or

---

[46] "Positivistic," that is, not in a sense that applies to those philosophers who are usually so anathematized by the German-speaking world, but rather that applies to the historists who, content with the rejection of natural laws and natural rights, do not try to transcend the "given," but only try to understand it.

deeper form of knowledge, but satisfies itself with that which appears to be given, that is, with the way the "given" appears. This understanding can pretend to be a more perfect kind of insight only because it deals with relations of meaning, relations that do not seem to be accessible to brute sensation. So we have in analytic thought, as in hermeneutic, a more or less veiled "positivism," although both feel they are superior to the vulgar positivism that declared the "given" of sense experience sacrosanct. The sanctification of sense seems to be superior to the sanctification of the senses.

We now can inquire whether the philosophy of critical examination allows the construction of a conception of sociohistorical reality which is an alternative to that provided by the above-mentioned ways of thinking—a conception, that is, in which the problem of meaning can be solved, and in which the meaning relations do not appear as final "givens" that are exempt from the causal relationships of the natural world. Concerning the relation of the natural world to the sociocultural realm, it is first necessary to recognize that the arbitrary break between nature and history as developed in the modern cult of historicity, a product of the dramatization of relative differences, can in no way be justified on the basis of an a priori contemplation of essences. The dualistic ontology displayed here is similar to the ontologically inspired dualism of the world in Aristotelian thought—its division into the sublunary and the supralunary sphere—which was overcome during the scientific revolution of the seventeenth century. Anyone who expects to prevent the incursion of the methods of theory building and testing developed in the natural sciences into the sociocultural realm by artificially imposing an ontological barrier that is more or less camouflaged as a linguistic one, suffers from some illusion about the methodological value of such demarcations, even relatively plausible ones. For historical research, the analysis of the history of science, has revealed the questionability of such boundaries. Even inductivistic misinterpretation, which is still dominant today in the humanistic sciences, and instrumentalistic devaluation of the natural sciences, which is often employed just for the purpose of stressing the higher quality of humanistic knowledge and which is endemic in the realm of influence of Hegelian thought—these are protectionistic strategies that will not be successful in the long run. Though such attempts at demarcation might temporarily discourage the application of scientific method to the human realm, progress in research usually pays no regard at all to efforts of this sort.

In contrast to such efforts, the first three decades of this century witnessed several attempts at sober discussion of the problem of meaning. In many cases they are suppressed in the German hermeneutical literature, or are rejected after superficial consideration in favor of more ambitious solutions, simply because they seem too infected with scientific thinking.[47] However one views the details of the solution to this problem suggested by Max Weber, one in any case finds in him three accomplishments, the conjunction of which still deserves attention: an analysis of the *significance of rules*—of normative regulations—for human behavior; an attempt to understand the *causal embedding* of normatively regulated ways of behaving; and finally, the acknowledgment that despite their "intuitiveness," propositions relating to this realm have the *status of hypotheses in need of examination*. All this was developed in the framework of a theory of the cultural sciences that presumes that these sciences have to provide understandable explanations by the use of nomological knowledge. The fact that causal relationships in social life originate in meaningful action is no impediment, in this view, to the attempt to interpret them nomologically. Weberian theory of science was, in its time, an attempt to exhibit the importance of the-

---

[47] I am thinking here, above all, of the works of Max Weber, Heinrich Gomperz, and Karl Bühler; see Weber's *Gesammelte Aufsätze zur Wissenschaftslehre*; Gomperz, *Über Sinn und Sinngebilde*; Bühler, *Die Krise der Psychologie* and *Sprachtheorie*. See, too, the work of George H. Mead, who attempts the solution of such problems by the methods of the natural sciences; e.g., see his *Mind, Self and Society* (Chicago, 1934).

oretical thinking in an area which historicism wished to oc-
cupy for antitheoretical historical investigation.

The work of Heinrich Gomperz contains an analysis of the
problem of meaning which tries to show that the basis of
understanding lies in the *habitual disposition to comprehend,*
thereby stressing the importance of dispositional characteristics of the individuals in question, and which highlights the
importance of *regularity* and *familiarity* for this capacity. Insofar as nomological knowledge involves regularities, the explanatory function of such knowledge also belongs to the
realm of the fundamentally understandable, in this broad sense
of the word. Certainly, there can be a methodologically very
interesting conflict between a drive to deepen and widen our
knowledge and this need for familiarity and understandability.
Recognizing that, in my view, puts certain characteristics of
the hermeneutical program for knowledge in the right light.
In contrast the conception of science in the natural sciences,
which prizes the *invention of new and more efficient patterns
of comprehension*—theories, explanations, or means of description—this program typically emphasizes the *classification
in old familiar patterns of comprehension.* So it is not at all
surprising that this program predominantly occurs in frameworks that also display a conservative way of thinking in their
other traits. On the other hand, newly developed ways of
explanation can, of course, subsequently acquire the patina
of familiarity one tends to expect of the understandable. Viewed
from this aspect of the problematic of understanding, the depth
of the insight that is purportedly attained through this procedure of interpretive understanding is revealed as an illusory
quality, the real basis of which is to be found in the deep roots
of the respective habits of comprehension.[48]

In the studies of Karl Bühler the problem of language plays
a prominent role in the solution of the problem of meaning.
His works articulate the continuity with biological research
through the emphasis on the *importance of reciprocal control*

[48] See my criticism of intuitionism in chapter 2.

for social cause and effect relationships in human as well as in animal spheres. He developed a conception of understanding which, in anticipation of modern cybernetic concepts, emphasizes this regulatory character, and finally, within his semantic approach, he explicated the *representational function* as characteristic of human, as contrasted with animal, languages—thus emphasizing exactly that aspect of interpretive behavior which allows *objectivization*. In this, and especially in the fact that *understanding* is explicitly characterized as an *interpretive activity*—not as a passive state of subjection to an occurrence of being—one can see its essential difference from the hermeneutical view discussed above, which takes no account of conceptions that are methodologically bound to scientific thinking.[49]

These contributions show that a solution to the problem of meaning appears indeed to be possible within the framework of a conception aiming at the theoretical illumination of sociocultural reality, which is oriented toward the method of critical examination, if one is prepared to bridge the artificial gap between nature and history left behind by idealistic philosophy—if one is prepared, that is, to refuse to tolerate dogmatic shielding principles. A solution to the problematic of meaning within the framework of the criticist view, as an alternative to the solutions suggested by hermeneutic and analytic thinking, seems to me basically to require the following considerations:

1. Recognition of a *problem of explanation* which transcends the problem of understanding as treated by hermeneutic and analytic thought, and which includes the *nomological* interpretation of behavior that can be understood as *meaningful actions*, without thereby having to contest the possibility and usefulness of this demarcation;

2. The quest for a usable *theory of behavior* that is ex-

[49] Beginning where Bühler ends, Karl R. Popper, as mentioned earlier, emphasized the *argumentation function* of language; see the references in note 26 of this chapter. He saw this as a function that makes a new level in *problem-solving* behavior possible.

planatory in character and can serve as a basis for a *technology of understanding* because it makes possible an *explanation of human interpretive activities*; and finally,

3. Recognition of the task of subjecting to *criticism*, in conjunction with our knowledge, goals, and ideals, given socioculturally anchored or suggested *rules, standards,* or *criteria*—that is, norms of behavior and standards for their evaluation and for the evaluation of their products and consequences; in other words, analyzing them in a critical context in which dogmatizations of all kinds are suspended.

That only meaningful action is removed from nomological interpretation—a thesis disputed in the first point—may appear plausible to theoreticians who have accustomed themselves in their thought to extract man and his activities from the causal relationships of nature and to transpose them into a realm in which there are no general restrictions of a structural character. But the statements on the problem of understanding by the representatives of hermeneutics make this thesis extremely implausible; for what is manifest in these utterances is precisely a striving, however vague and trivial, to characterize a general human activity according to its structure, a striving that goes wholly in the direction of a theory of nomological character *about* this activity, although the theoreticians in question certainly are not inclined to so understand the import of their own efforts; this is an interesting paradox of a hermeneutical practice that believes it has the problem of understanding under control. That there is such a thing as everyday understanding need not be controversial. That this phenomenon displays any sort of lawlike regularities should be difficult to contest by those who again and again take the trouble to clarify the peculiar character of this activity, even though without much success. When in the humanistic sciences one attempts to convert understanding into a special method that is generally applicable to problem situations of a particular sort, one is bound to arouse the suspicion that if such a procedure can function, it is only because there are universal structures that make it possible.

Should one wish to develop this procedure, favored by humanistic thinking, from a tradesman's everyday procedure to a scientific method, then it may be advantageous, as suggested in our second point, to seek a technological basis for it. Anyone who starts from the normal methodology of scientific thought will be inclined to extract this technology of understanding out of a theory that has explanatory character, for we are sufficiently informed by the theory of science about the relationship between such theories and technological systems. The representatives of hermeneutic and analytic thought have not yet shown which other solutions they envisage for this problem. The solution suggested here arises out of the usual methodology of theory formation and theory application. An alternative based on either hermeneutical or analytical foundations may be difficult to find, all the more so as the general character of the problem of understanding is usually not denied. It seems to me that the defenders of such ways of thinking are often not clear about what they require, according to their own more or less implicit presuppositions, for the solution of their problems. They frequently insist that one must also *understand explanatory arguments*, and conclude from them that understanding is complementary to explanation, or even takes precedence over it.[50] That one can still further seek an *explanation of understanding*, and that a theory of nomological character that would make such an achievement possible would be required even for the grounding of the so-called method of understanding—this condition seems to escape their notice. How they can conceive of a hermeneutic doctrine for the guidance of understanding that would not have a technological character, and so could not be traced back to an explanatory theory of understanding—

[50] On this view, see Karl-Otto Apel, "Szientistik, Hermeneutik, Ideologie-Kritik," in Apel, *Transformation der Philosophie*, II (Frankfurt, 1973), pp. 96-127, and other essays in this volume and in volume I. For my criticisms of Apel's position, see my *Transzendentale Träumereien* (Hamburg, 1975), and the chaper, "Münchhausen und der Zauber der Reflexion," in my book, *Die Wissenschaft und die Fehlbarkeit der Vernunft* (Tübingen, 1982).

which means, a theory of human interpretative activity—is not clear. In any case, on this basis *"understanding"* in the narrower sense could be further developed into a true *research technique* or a set of research techniques *within the framework of normal methodology.*[51]

From the perspective of this methodology, one can undoubtedly suggest to the representatives of hermeneutical thought, as an alternative to their own conception of these problems, the conception of a nomological theory of the normal sort for the explanation of meaningful behavior, and thereby for the explanation of human interpretative activities out of which a technology of understanding can arise. One could offer them this conception even as an interpretation of their own intentions, from a perspective that seems foreign to them only because they themselves stand on a tradition that habitually dramatizes the contrast of nature and mind and tends to draw premature methodological conclusions out of ontological demarcations of this sort. If the "understanding," as is repeatedly suggested, refers to a general, structurally determined phenomenon of the sociohistorical reality, then one can at least view this phenomenon as in need of explanation, and it is pure dogma that explanations are not needed or not attainable in this area. A methodology of the human sciences that denies such possibilities or refuses to discuss them, simply because of an aversion to the method of natural science, which properly understood has little to do with the special objects of the natural sciences, would contribute little to the progress of knowledge in those sciences because it obscures the structural basis for the researches carried out within it. The question, *"How is understanding possible?"* which today is often categorized as a "transcendental" question,[52] can be ade-

[51] Doubtless this thesis would sound odd to the defenders of humanistic anti-naturalism; but that is because they tend to give a special status to the mind and to see "understanding" as an alternative for "explaining" for the realm where spirit is at home. Why should we honor such habits?

[52] "We have an inflation of so-called transcendental questions now, and in most cases the special character of such questions remains largely unclear,

quately conceived of as a normal problem. It is especially important that very interesting scientific contributions to the solution of this problem already exist.

A theory of behavior that includes human activities of interpretation can begin with the assumption that theoretical elements already play an important role in normal human perception and in human problem-solving behavior.[53] The horizon of expectation at any time is partially constituted by the theoretical convictions of the agent, which can be understood as hypotheses. Where a range of objects is in question in which meaning relationships play a role—as, for example, norm-regulated human behavior, or human speech, or even texts, as they are made into objects of analysis in philology, jurisprudence, and theology, or as they are treated as sources in historiography or incorporated into social causal relations— in any of these cases *hypotheses of interpretation* arise that are developed on the basis of more or less implicit theoretical views about such actions and their results, and are subject to examination and eventually to revision. That such ranges of objects should in principle not be subjected to analysis of the sort practiced in the natural sciences can be made plausible only by one who has a very narrow notion of this method— one who identifies it with research techniques that have a limited range or with the application of special models. From the point of view of this method, the understanding itself, under some circumstances, appears to be a special research technique—or range of such techniques—for sciences which,

---

so that there is no clue for possible kinds of answers. It is as if one need only present a question of the form, "how is . . . possible?" to evoke the response that we are confronted with a transcendental question. The net result of elevating questions to the status of transcendental problems is to postpone their resolution, for this philosophical classification absolves us from the effort of applying scientific knowledge and methods to their solution.

[53] Cf. Karl R. Popper, "Naturgesetz und theoretische Systeme," in *Theorie und Realität*; idem, "Clouds and Clocks"; Dember's *The Psychology of Perception*; Bohnen's *Ratio* article; and the often-cited work of Gombrich, as well as my article "Hermeneutik und Realwissenschaft," in *Plädoyer für kritischen Rationalismus* (Munich, 1971).

judging from the objectives they set for themselves, have often only descriptive and historical character,[54] however important and interesting their results might be. The formulation of singular hypotheses of interpretation found in many human sciences—and the identification of the meaning of particular texts, for example, amounts to the formulation of such hypotheses—is in itself a descriptive activity, but one which can draw considerable benefit out of nomological knowledge about man and his predominantly linguistic activity of interpretation.[55]

Thus it is not the case that the representatives of the hermeneutical movement in philosophy have discovered a problem complex—the problematic of meaning and understanding—that cannot be treated from the point of view of the normal scientific method. Rather, today they usually reject such a treatment from the beginning without even attempting to achieve clarity about the possible form a solution of such problems might take within the framework of this method, about the consequences of the refusal which they insist upon, and about the logical structure of the alternative which they envisage.[56] Reference to the naiveté of faith in method cannot replace such analysis, especially when one then proceeds to demonstrate, through a relapse into quasi-theological think-

[54] Philology is probably the prime example; it is also the paradigm for hermeneutic philosophers, who are inclined to prefer it to the theological or juridical model because they are uncomfortable with the latters' dogmatic associations.

[55] Modern linguists often strive for theories that have the character of nomological systems; see, for instance, Noam Chomsky, "Current Issues in Linguistic Theory," in The Structure of Language, ed. Fodor and Katz (Englewood Cliffs, N.J., 1964), pp. 50, 105 ff., as well as Manfred Bierwisch, "Strukturalismus, Geschichte, Probleme und Methoden," in Kursbuch, 5 (1966), ed. Hans Magnus Enzensberger, pp. 77 ff., 147; and, above all, Geoffrey Sampson, The Form of Language (London, 1975). This does not mean, of course, that they fall into crude behaviorism.

[56] One might well ask how the propositions sought by the hermeneutic philosopher might look—what is their logical structure and content, how can they be tested, and how are they differentiated from the statements of other sciences—questions to which one never really receives a clear answer.

ing, where inadequate reflection about methodological questions can lead.

This brings us to the third point in our sketch of a solution to the problem of meaning. In hermeneutical as in analytical thought, the cult of understanding is associated not only with a rejection of theoretically based explanation, but beyond that, with an attitude that is designed to insulate certain facts of a meaningful character, such as traditions and forms of life, from criticism by considering them ultimate "givens." So this style of thought can be readily utilized within the realm of dogmatic-apologetic thinking, while at the same time it is practically impossible for these philosophical movements to distance themselves from such use. The anti-Enlightenment tendencies inherent in this thought, particularly noticeable in Heidegger and Gadamer, seem very sympathetic to such an attitude. It is not accidental that especially the conservative aspects of the Bultmannian demythologization conception are oriented on Heidegger's existential analytic of Dasein. The possibility of a political hermeneutic also emerges here which supports all kinds of political theologies, in explicit contrast to criticism of ideology from the viewpoint of enlightenment. The receptive reason of the hermeneuticist then shifts very easily into the justificational thought of the political ideologues, who use the revelations of the interpreters of being to expound their own intentions and partialities as the objective meaning of history. From the critical point of view, for which traditions, to be sure, can indeed serve as "springboards," but not as legitimating authorities, such a philosophy of history with practical intention on a hermeneutic basis is nothing else but a continuation of theology by other means.[57]

[57] Cf. the analysis of Ernst Topitsch in his book, *Die Sozialphilosophie Hegels als Heilslehre und Herrschaftsideologie* (Neuwied und Berlin, 1967), and compare it to the products of those philosophers to whom the meaning of history seems to have been revealed.

# SEVEN

# The Problem of a Rational Politics

## 25. The Cult of Revelation: Political Theology and Sacramental Politics

IT DOES not normally occur to those who read the investigations of representatives of modern analytical or existential philosophy that there might be more than a mere psychological connection between philosophical positions and political beliefs. That Marxism openly tries to establish such a connection makes it rather suspicious in the eyes of the proponents of "pure" philosophical thought. Yet such a connection can almost always be found,[1] although the "purer" the philosophy—that is, the more it has degenerated into esoteric exercises for academic specialists—the more this connection fades and recedes into the background, it becomes a *pudendum*. Insofar as the critique of ideology has rendered any such connection suspicious, it has certainly supported a philosophical purism that is contrary to its own intentions, intentions which above all aimed at destroying the old political theology and its derivatives and substitutes, up to and including utopian philosophy of history.

This *political theology*, whose repercussions are still felt today in many areas, was developed within a world view that attempted to grasp the whole cosmos as one coherent *context of meaning*—and which therefore had to interpret it in analogy to familiar phenomena of the human social sphere—a *sociomorphic cosmology*,[2] in which the problem of the justifi-

[1] Cf. Karl R. Popper, "On the Sources of Knowledge and Ignorance"; J.W.N. Watkins, "Epistemology and Politics," *Proceedings of the Aristotelian Society* (1957); and my book, *Traktat über rationale Praxis* (Tübingen, 1978).

[2] Cf. Hans Kelsen, "Gott und Staat," *Logos*, vol. XI (1923), also reprinted in his *Aufsätzen zur Ideologiekritik*, ed. Ernst Topitsch (Neuwied/Berlin,

cation of social order and political decisions could be solved by recourse to revelations of a divine authority. Divine powers of some kind, a multitude of gods or a single god, were, as sources of unchanging norms or of varying commands, the final authorities for this procedure, the ultimate reference points for the attribution of whatever factual consequences resulted. Political theology was therefore an intergral component of a metaphysics of the cosmos which attempted to offer an interpretation of the whole of reality, which tried to give it a meaning, and which, through a firm anchorage in this meaning, served also to legitimize political orders and measures. The Archimedean point to which one could resort was of a cosmic-religious nature and therefore in general exempt from critical analysis. By having recourse to it political authorities and institutions of such societies could also be sanctified. Politics was, to a certain degree, intertwined with religious ritual and attained by means of this sacramental character.[3]

It is easy to see that within such a sociomorphic view *hermeneutic strategies* could acquire considerable significance. When it comes to ascertaining the will of divine powers, it is necessary to interpret signs in which this will manifests itself. On the basis of such needs, interpretative doctrines with scientific pretensions developed. Babylonian astrology, in contrast to present day astrology, did not originally satisfy private needs; rather, it fulfilled a political function,[4] and it can be

---

1964), as well as other articles in this volume; Carl Schmitt, *Politische Theologie* (Munich, 1922); Ernst Topitsch, "Kosmos und Herrschaft. Ursprünge der 'politischen Theologie,' " in *Wort und Wahrheit* (1955 ), pp. 19 ff.; and his book, *Vom Ursprung und Ende der Metaphysik*.

[3] Cf. Henri Frankfort, *Kingship and the Gods: A Study of Ancient Near Eastern Religion as the Integration of Society and Nature* (Chicago, 1948), where, among other things, the essential differences between the Egyptian and the Mesopotamian world view and social order are pointed out, pp. 215 ff., 231 ff. In Mesopotamia, the monarchy was apparently less firmly established and its theological aspect less pronounced; cf. also Henri and H. A. Frankfort, John A. Wilson, and Thorkild Jakobsen, *Before Philosophy: The Intellectual Adventure of Ancient Man* (Chicago, 1946).

[4] Cf. Ernst Topitsch, "Kosmos und Herrschaft," pp. 26 ff.

considered one of the earliest hermeneutic sciences. It was believed that the interpretation of stars, dreams, and other phenomena that were considered relevant—i.e., those facts that were believed to mediate meaning—made it possible to come to an understanding of those cosmic manifestations of the divine will that were relevant for the justification of decisions. Such was the function of hermeneutics in the framework of a political-theological cosmology. It began its career as the servant of political theology and has not fully freed itself from this bond in its later versions, in which the interpretation of texts was emphasized. Revelation, interpretation of meaning, and justification are the three components that determine the style of thinking of political theology and in part the related political praxis as well. Christianity not only salvaged essential components of the sociocosmic interpretation of reality, it has also carried over the political theology of ancient oriental thought into the Middle Ages, and partially—especially in Catholic thought—even into modern times.[5] In those social areas in which this intellectual heritage is still influential, we can still find the tendency to have recourse to the interpretation of allegedly revealed truths to buttress correct rules and measures; politics is thus propped up by the authority of theologically sanctioned texts, the origin of which is attributed to the co-authorship of divine powers—a practice that is diametrically opposed to the scientific way of thinking developed in the womb of Greek antiquity and of modern Western civilization.[6]

[5] Cf. especially Rudolf Hernegger, *Macht ohne Auftrag. Die Enstehung der Staats- und Volkskirche* (Olten and Freiburg, 1963), where, among other things, the role of the Constantinian turning point in the transmission of these ideas is analyzed in detail.

[6] For a relatively modern formulation of the typical way of thinking of political theology, see, for example, Juan Donoso Cortés, *Über die Irrtümer unserer Zeit* (1852), and his "Über Mittelalter und Parlamentarismus" (1852), in *Donoso Cortés, Kulturpolitik* (Basel, 1845), where the anti-liberal and anti-rational characteristics of this type of thought are expressed very clearly. Carl Schmitt, in his anti-liberal polemics, had recourse to Donoso Cortés; cf. his book, *Politische Theologie*, pp. 72 ff.

Naturally, a society that had to resort to such a process of legitimation would require mediation between the human and the divine spheres, a connecting link in the form of a hierarchy of mediators who monopolized the interpretation of revelation. Divine or quasi-divine qualities were often ascribed to the social representatives who fulfilled these mediating functions, so that the boundary between these two spheres was within society.[7] Within such a sociomorphic view of the world, the authority of such mediator hierarchies can be, in an apparently very natural way, theologically rooted and thereby made legitimate. Because of the interpretative functions conceded to them, a *fiction of representation* can always be construed, according to which the mediators can, even though not themselves included within the divine sphere, act as the representatives of divine powers. A *theory of the vicarious function* of the rulers can be set up fairly easily on the basis of their interpretative and mediational function. Moreover, on the basis of such a theory, infallibility can be ascribed to their pronouncements to a certain extent. By means of this theory, the existing social order, together with its relations of authority, is normatively distinguished and interpreted in the light of a sociomorphic cosmology. Society is embedded in a cosmos in which by means of a suitable interpretation, directives, guarantees, and sanctions important for society's stability and functioning are incorporated. The authority of the ruling cosmic-religious powers radiates, as it were, over the whole social order;[8] it glorifies the established power structure

---

[7] As is well known, the Pharaoh was considered a god in ancient Egypt; cf. the citations in note 3 of this chapter. But the custom of deifying role bearers is also found elsewhere, from the Roman caesar cults (cf. Ethelbert Stauffer, *Jerusalem und Rom im Zeitalter Jesu Christi* [Berne, 1957], pp. 20 ff.) to the cult of the pope in the Catholic church (cf. Paul Blanshard's "The Devices of Deification," in his *Communism, Democracy, and Catholic Power*, pp. 65 ff.) and analogous cults in totalitarian societies with secular ideologies. Such qualities are carried over even to members who are lower in the hierarchy.

[8] Erich Vögelin has pointed out in his book, *Die politischen Religionen* (Stockholm, 1939), that the Symbol of Radiance from a divine source, which

and thereby largely immunizes it to a great extent against potential criticism from its subjects. This is a typical pattern of the interpretation of social events in advanced preindustrial cultures, a pattern that seems extremely well suited for the justification of the existing order.

## 26. HOPING FOR A CATASTROPHE: POLITICAL ESCHATOLOGY AND UTOPIAN POLITICS

As was already pointed out above, quite often there are elements in ideologies justifying social orders that can be used in quite a different manner:[9] to legitimize social mass movements whose goal is to revolutionize existing conditions. As is well known, there is an apocalyptic-eschatological component in political-theological thought that the official hierarchy—the proponents of the ruling orthodoxy—tries to repress, decontaminate, or suppress, or, in any case, to *sterilize*, as far as possible, for without this treatment it is likely to make the existing social situation appear provisional, unstable, and doubtful. The embedding of political and social events in a sociomorphic cosmos can be found in the apocalyptical-eschatological conceptions as well. There, however, it concerns an imminent cosmic catastrophe that supposedly leads to a complete transformation of human society and to the overthrow of the political system.[10] It is hardly necessary to dwell upon the fact that this kind of sociocosmic fantasy, which is connected with the needs of oppressed social classes dissatisfied with the existing social order, cannot attain any

---

can already be found in Echnaton's myth of the sun and later in the Plotinian philosophy of emanation, is a basic pattern for legitimizing authority. It is also of significance for the European course of development (ibid., pp. 29 ff.).

[9] Cf. section 16 above, "Dogmatization as Social Practice and the Problem of Critique."

[10] Concerning the development of the notion of "God's Kingdom," which is central for this sphere of ideas, see Albert Schweitzer, *The Kingdom of God and Primitive Christianity*, trans. Garrard (New York, 1968).

real importance within systems that serve to legitimize that order. If they are to be found at all in these systems, which can happen, for historical reasons—one need only call to mind the emergence of subsequently scholasticized ideologies out of the utopian conceptions of acute mass movements—it is in the direct interest of the ruling powers to render them politically sterile.[11] In contrast to this, social mass movements that arise in times of crisis tend to *revitalize* these components of the ideological tradition. They tend to base their interpretation of social events mainly on these components and to utilize them to mobilize all social forces available against the existing order.[12]

Thus, there are static and dynamic varieties of political theology that differ in the way they treat such wish-fulfilling fantasies: the *scholastic* versions sterilize such components; the *utopian* versions, in direct contrast, reactivate and accentuate them. The latter are often associated with a *radical negation* of the existing order, and characterized by a historico-theological *catastrophe theory*, which sees radical ovethrow as the only way to remedy an unsatisfactory social situation.[13] Insofar as ideologies, which serve to legitimize radical and revolutionary trends on a utopian basis, reduce, under the influence of secularization, the original cosmic context of meaning to the meaning of history, they are no less authoritarian and dogmatic in structure than the old political theology. They are but secularized forms of the same modes of thought, in which justification and revelation are connected.

[11] This point of view might play an important role in some other cases of the "postponement of parusia," e.g., in the communist one of the last fifty years.

[12] Cf. the above-mentioned (chapter 4, note 38) works of Norman Cohn, Emanuel Sarkisyanz, and Wilhelm E. Mühlmann, in which such processes are analyzed and partially explained; cf. also Karl Löwith, *Weltgeschichte und Heilsgeschehen*.

[13] In this connection, Mühlmann has pointed out the "mythological scheme of the inverted world," which is as influential in modern nativistic movements as it was in the early Christian movement; "the first will be the last . . ."; cf. Mühlmann, *Chiliasmus und Nativismus* (Berlin, 1961), pp. 307 ff.

The justification, however, is not intended for the existing order but for its overthrow, and thus has a negative character. The dominance of the utopian element and the related thought of catastrophe corresponds to a *total criticism*, which condemns radically and universally the existing conditions in the name of a necessarily rather vague utopia, and makes no attempt to analyze alternatives rationally.[14] Revolutionary practice, which is justified in this way, aims first and foremost at establishing a *tabula rasa*, in order to make possible the complete reconstruction of society—a vacuum idea analogous to the one we found in the classical theory of knowledge.[15]

Since the defenders of such positions tend to be absolutely certain that they represent the fulfillment of the meaning of history, and that their opponents are absolutely wrong, they tend to think quite freely in terms of ends and means, in such a way that the admissibility of any means whatever to realize the desired state does not pose any problems. Every sacrifice and all available means, even those of terror and violence, seem to be vindicated in the service of a goal legitimized by the meaning of history itself. It is true enough that the violence of the long-established powers is condemned by such interpretations, but that of the new revolutionary forces is glori-

[14] Such utopian critiques can be found on the extreme right and left of the political spectrum. They fail to analyze the possibilities realistically, and they openly defame positions arguing in favor of such a type of rationality and the methods it requires. For an analysis of the views of some advocates of a nationalistic ideology—Lagarde, Langbehn, and Möller van den Bruck—who thought along these lines, cf. Fritz Stern, *Kulturpessimismus als politische Gefahr. Eine Analyse nationaler Ideologie in Deutschland* (Berne/Stuttgart/ Vienna, 1963). It is hardly worth mentioning that the above-mentioned catastrophe thinking and the related total criticism are operative in Marx's early analysis as well. But even his work in later years can hardly be understood without this background. Concerning the theological-utopian motives in Marxism, cf. Ernst Topitsch, "Entfremdung und Ideologie. Zur Entmythologisierung des Marxismus" (1964), and his "Marxismus und Gnosis" (1961), in his above-mentioned volume of essays, *Sozialphilosophie zwischen Ideologie und Wissenschaft*.

[15] For a criticism of this idea of a radical practice, cf. Karl Popper, *The Poverty of Historicism* (New York, 1960), part 3.

fied.[16] As a result, however, this legitimation of violence leads to the custom of deciding by violent methods all important questions in which agreement cannot be reached. These methods are, of course, not reserved to only one side. The anti-liberal mode of thought of a friend-or-foe kind propounded by Carl Schmitt is by no means a specific feature of his decisionism. Rather, it is common to all those who purport to have the certain possession of politically relevant truth, and therefore believe themselves justified in their choice of such a radical praxis, regardless of whether they practice the dynamic version of sacramental politics before their victory, or the static version afterwards.

The revelations of meaning that serve the objectives of the proclaimers and proponents of secular-eschatological doctrines, of course, deserve as little credit as political theology of the older variety. Strictly speaking, they deserve even less credit, for in a sociomorphically interpreted universe it was at least to some degree plausible to speak of purposes for the whole universe. After all, there were concrete entities within the sociomorphic framework to whom it was, in principle, possible to ascribe such purposes. But it is difficult to see how one can attribute authority and the capacity to legitimize goals and tendencies at all to the abstract and fictional agency of history. To root political aims in a sociomorphic cosmology has become obsolete; and to root them in history is a relic of the sociocosmic way of thinking, meaningless without the original framework.

## 27. THE RECOURSE TO INTERESTS: POLITICAL ARITHMETIC AND CALCULATORY POLITICS

The anthropological turn in social philosophy, which took place when the old metaphysics of the cosmos was undermined

---

[16] Cf. the interesting critical analysis of Bolshevik ideology and practice by Bertrand Russell (1920) in his book, *The Practice and Theory of Bolshevism*, 2d ed. (London, 1949); cf. also Karl R. Popper's essay, "Utopia and Violence" (1948), in *Conjectures and Refutations*.

by the emergence of modern science,[17] has had the consequence of gradually rendering obsolete the legitimation of social orders and political decisions by referring to divine powers and their revealed purposes. New methods arose that appealed to authorities of a nonsacred type—to the common weal, to the interest of the collective, to the needs and the welfare of all members of society. But neither the idea of justification nor the model of revelation was sacrificed. Even in the democratic ideology that replaced classical political theology, it was important to legitimize social orders and political measures, existing or envisioned, by referring to an authority to verify its justification; therefore, even the classical theory of democracy aims at justification, and requires methods of interpretation for this purpose. However, the object of the interpretation is not the divine will; it is the will of the people.[18] Thus, it makes the causal connections of social events appear to be a supra-subjective context of meaning.

The democratically organized society, however, can no more do without authority than could earlier societies—in other words, it cannot manage without institutional arrangements to make decisions for the collective and to transform them into effective political measures. Even this kind of society requires mediation of the will that is considered authoritative; and, in order to legitimize the authority of those to whom this mediational function is ascribed, it can avail itself of a *fiction of representation*: the idea of the vicarious function of representatives elected by the people, representatives chosen to interpret the general interest, and to take or to consent to the pertinent decisions. The machinery of election is supposed to provide for this transfer of will. In contrast, however, to the divine choosing or calling of the representatives singled out in political theology, the elections, whatever else one thinks

---

[17] Cf. the introduction to my volume of essays, *Marktsoziologie und Entscheidungslogik*, pp. 14 ff.

[18] Occasionally, as with the slogan "vox populi, vox dei," a clear connection between the two was established so that one can speak of a democratic political theology.

of them, are an institutionally regulated procedure that can be subjected to a detailed analysis of conditions and effects, because it takes place within good reach of our knowledge. Thus, even the conception of a transfer of will is, on account of such knowledge, subject to criticism.

The political theology of the ancient metaphysics of the cosmos sought to achieve the justification of political facts, which from its point of view were considered relevant in a *quasi-deductive* manner, by inferring them from revealed proclamations of the will of a divine authority. The appeal to interests brought a *quasi-inductive* element into the context of legitimization, insofar as one attempted to trace back the people's will, which aimed at the common welfare, to the actual interests of the members of society, or at least to establish a plausible connection between the two. This attempt has led to that peculiar mixture of a *communist* and an *inductivist* fiction, which is characteristic for this ideology—not just in its political but also in its economic variant.[19] On the one hand, a common will is postulated which aims at the general welfare, and which, under certain institutional conditions—i.e., under those of a parliamentarian system of government or under those of a free market economy—regulates the actual social activities. On the other hand, there is an attempt to reduce this general and common interest to the interests of the individuals within the society, by constructing a quasi-logical context of imputations which connects them with the collective interest. The general will of the respective social system is constituted by the merging of the individual

[19] Cf. my essay, "Rationalität und Wirtschaftsordnung" (1963), chapter 4 in *Marktsoziologie und Entscheidungslogik*; cf. also my *Ökonomische Ideologie und politische Theorie* (Göttingen, 1954), pp. 116 ff. Josef Schumpeter criticized the theory of classical democracy in his work, *Kapitalismus, Sozialismus und Demokratie* (1942; 2d German ed., Munich, 1950); he especially criticized the "communist fiction" of the relationship between a united will of the people and the common weal. Gunnar Myrdal, who coined this term, criticizes the application of this fiction to economic problems; cf. his book, *The Political Element in the Development of Economic Theory.*

wills of all those who participate in its formation, by participations in elections or in the market. The institutional arrangements of democracy and of the market guarantee the establishment of a unified total will that expresses the true interests of all who partake and is oriented to their common truth: the common weal, the maximum welfare of the community. The democratic as well as the commercial process reveals a fundamental consensus concerning the goals to be attained, and its justification ultimately has recourse to the will of all members of society—all voters or all consumers.

This democratic ideology is orientated on the principle of sufficient justification, as was classical political theology before it. It, too, applies classical methodology to political thought, except that the legitimizing authority is no longer a being which transcends society, but the will of the community constituted by individual interests. The decisions of the ruling powers are no longer justified by recourse to divine authority, but rather by referring to the sovereignty of the voters or of the consumer, which—if all processes take their ideal course, assuming due process—guarantees their correctness from the viewpoint of the common weal. The decision-making powers no longer present a transcendent will, but the empirical will of the voters or consumers. However, the fiction of representation itself remains, and the whole approach involves the *interpretation* of this will in *terms of the factual decisions*, which is at least afflicted with the very same problems that afflict the interpretation of any other empirical relationship.

This conception was originally developed under the influence of utilitarianism for the economic sphere into a discipline that, because of its mathematical elaboration, fully deserves the name of *political arithmetic*, especially since, as a matter of fact, it is mainly of interest because of its political consequences.[20] This is the only discipline that actually approached

[20] The development of neoclassical economics—especially of its political branch, the so-called welfare economics—can be seen as an attempt to carry out *Bentham's program*—to reduce all social processes to the striving of those participating in them and those affected by them in order to satisfy their

with the available means the problem, contained in the classical theory of democracy, of establishing a controllable relationship between the common weal and the individual interests of the members of the society in question, thereby transforming the quasi-inductive relationship implicitly assumed in this framework into a calculable context of imputations. The attempt to solve this problem—originally for the commercially regulated sphere of society—by the application of available mathematical instruments was, despite the weaknesses that gradually appeared, important for social philosophy, for it aimed at treating politics in a way that seemed compatible with the results and methods of the modern sciences. This cannot be said for the residues of the sociocosmic conception in political thought—for example, the idea of natural rights. The transition from political theology to political arithmetic follows quite understandably, if one refrains from resorting to authorities that have no place within the scientific world view. It opens the possibility of criticizing social orders and institutions, norms and ideals, political decisions and measures by recourse to the individual needs of the participating people, a critique which can, in principle, avail itself of the results of scientific thought.

As is well known, the earlier attempts to solve the problem of imputation—the Maximum Theorem of neoclassical economics, the Pigovian version of welfare economics, and finally also its Paretian variant—ran into difficulties that could not be mastered within the original approach.[21] In order to over-

---

needs; cf. my above-mentioned essay, "Zur Theorie der Konsumnachfrage," pp. 140 ff. On the philosophical radicalism of Jeremy Bentham, cf. Elie Halévy, *The Growth of Philosophical Radicalism* (London, 1928). The label "political arithmetic" is an old one, and has long since fallen out of use; but it is a good term for this particular development in social scientific thought.

[21] Since I cannot deal with these difficulties in detail here, let me refer the reader to my contribution to the Popper Festschrift, "Social Science and Moral Philosophy," which also appears as the third chapter in *Marktsoziologie und Entscheidungslogik*; my essay, "Politische Ökonomie und rationale Politik. Vom wohlfahrts-ökonomischen Formalismus zur politischen Soziologie," in *Theoretische Grundlagen der Wirtschaftspolitik. Theodor Wessels zum 65.*

come these difficulties, the more general idea of a social welfare function was utilized. With this idea political arithmetic was once more extended to the whole sphere of politics. Its role was no longer restricted to the evaluation of results of behavior controlled by the market, but directed toward evaluating states of the entire social system on an individualistic basis. Therefore it encompasses the whole realm of decisions covered by the democratic ideology.[22] The political problem of democracy—a constitution of society in which, ideally, the ruling forces are bound in their decisions to the will of the members of this society—is transformed in this conception into the question of the possibility of constructing a social welfare function that has individualistic character and satisfies certain conditions of adequacy. This function should enable all possible social states of affairs to be evaluated in terms of the attitudes of the affected individuals—a mathematization of politics that carries over the above-mentioned Leibnizian ideal of knowledge into the sphere of decision making. Concerning the possibility of constructing an adequate function of this kind, there exists an extensive discussion which we cannot deal with here.

What is interesting in this context is the implicit assumption, probably common to all those participating in this discussion, that with the solution of this formal problem something essential is gained for the solution of political problems. In my opinion, this assumption demonstrates a considerable overestimation of the importance of formal problems in general, and in particular of the importance of a formal logic of decision for finding answers to questions that can actually only be answered through advances in our knowledge of factual relationships. This approach has conceptualized the problems

---

Geburtstag, ed. Hans Besters (Berlin, 1967), also reprinted in my collection of essays, Aufklärung und Steuerung; and the fifth chapter of my Traktat über rationale Praxis.

[22] Cf. Kenneth J. Arrow, Social Choice and Individual Values (New York/London, 1951; 2d ed., 1963); cf. also Jerome Rothenberg, The Measurement of Social Welfare (Englewood Cliffs, N.J., 1961).

from the start in such a way that the issue of actualizability fades completely into the background. It sounds as if one could solve political problems without even taking into consideration the nature of social reality; therefore, it appears as if one would need to approach the question of the institutionalization of the ideal decision mechanisms appropriate for an "adequate" function of this kind only when these formal solutions are already on hand. The theory of social welfare functions is a mathematical calculus whose transformation into suitable institutional arrangements requires a social vacuum. In this theory it becomes evident that the communist fiction of a common scale of social values for all political decisions, which makes it possible to transform problems of social order and of the optimal arrangement of social relationships into problems of economic efficiency, is, in the final analysis, incompatible with the individualistic assumptions of utilitarianism. For even this social scale of values itself cannot escape individual evaluation if the individualistic point of view is applied consistently. If one wanted to nominate the designer of such a function for the fictitious dictator, one would have abandoned the individualistic approach de facto.[23] Therefore, one may say that the *program of a political arithmetic*, which was intended to replace the old political theology, though interesting from a social-philosophical point of view, has *failed* in spite of all efforts. In fact, it has failed for reasons similar to those we considered decisive for the failure of classical epistemology.

Like classical epistemology, this conception resorts to some-

[23] This is taken into consideration in the conception developed by Buchanan and Tullock, in which the transition from the problem of economic efficiency to the problem of political constitution becomes evident; cf. James M. Buchanan and Gordon Tullock, *The Calculus of Consent: Logical Foundations of Constitutional Democracy* (Ann Arbor, Mich., 1962). On this problem and the idea of the social welfare function, cf. my contribution mentioned in the preceding footnote, "Politische Ökonomie und rationale Politik," pp. 71 ff. Even this conception, in the final analysis, is based on a social vacuum fiction, with respect to the situation in which the fundamental choice of a constitution takes place; cf. ibid., pp. 254 f., 272 ff. and passim.

thing that is ultimately given and beyond criticism. However, the final authority is no longer a transcendent factor as in political theology; rather, it consists of the empirical individual needs and interests revealed in acts of buying or voting. It requires as well the quasi-inductive construction of a larger context of meaning, by reference to which the major orderings and decisions of social life can be legitimized. Thus, the adequate evaluation of the entire life of the society and its control to accord with the wishes of its members seems to be placed on a secure empirical foundation analogous to the way in which knowledge is based on pure experience in empiricist epistemology. However, the needs and interests of the individuals, considered in this view an ultimate "given," the final reference point for political imputations and therefore sacrosanct and exempt from all critical objections, are in fact just as problematic as the sense experiences of epistemological empiricism. Both are dependent on context, formed by the sociocultural environment and therefore variable.[24] The needs and interests claimed as data by democratic ideology and its mathematicized variant, political arithmetic, are actually themselves the result of social processes and the interpretations connected with them. The proclamations of will of the individuals to which this ideology chooses to resort are furthermore dependent on their factual beliefs—all of which are, in principle, open to critique and revision. Thus, the ideal of certainty turns out to be questionable, not only with regard to knowledge claims but also with regard to the will of the participants in social processes. Whoever immunizes his will against possible cognitive and other objections acts just as irrationally as the dogmaticist in the sphere of knowledge, and this—among other reasons—because of the close ties between

[24] There currently exists a plethora of investigations that should not be ignored in the search for a solution to such problems; cf. Allison Davis, "The Motivation of the Underprivileged Worker," in *Industry and Society*, ed. William F. Whyte (New York, 1946), as well as the essays in parts 4 and 5 of *Motives in Fantasy, Action, and Society*, ed. John W. Atkinson (Princeton/Toronto/London/New York, 1958).

knowledge and decision mentioned above. If this holds true for all individuals, then there is no reason why a critical social philosophy should consider the proclamations of will and the decisions of individuals sacrosanct and exempt them from critical examination. This does not mean, of course, that such preferences and decisions should be ignored when one constructs institutional arrangements for the regulation of social life or putting political decisions into effect. It only means that the dogmatic break-off at this point of the regress of justification is just as problematic as the analogous break-off in classical epistemology. Hence it follows that the principle of sufficient justification, on which democratic ideology, including its mathematical version, is oriented as its epistemological conception, is here exposed to the very same objection as it has been in the other frameworks that incorporate classical methodology. Recourse to ultimate uncriticizable authorities produces the same dubious type of solution in all versions of this doctrine.

But even if we concede, for argument's sake, that needs, interests, or proclamations of will can serve as ultimate and certain sources for the justification of the social order and of political decisions, the method of inference constructed for this purpose—the quasi-inductive procedure of imputation[25]—would still be exposed to objections similar to those that apply to any inductive procedure proposed for theoretical knowledge.[26] If such an inference serves as a justification, then it is necessary to justify its basic principle of justification, its *imputation principle*—as, for example, some social welfare function—a demand that leads to the Münchhausen trilemma, which we characterized in our critical analysis of epistemology.[27] Furthermore, as already mentioned, the problem of

[25] This expression, which comes from the Austrian school of marginal utility, is applied here to every method developed in political arithmetic that attempts to transform individual needs into collective values.

[26] Cf. the criticism of inductivism in the first chapter.

[27] Kenneth J. Arrow postulates ad hoc certain conditions of adequacy for the social welfare function he demands. These conditions seem intuitively

institutional realization must be considered as an additional burden in this case, for the formal way in which the logical calculus of decision is set up abstracts completely from this problem so that a subsequent consideration is virtually excluded. Instead, economic analysis again and again attempted to project into the actual course of events an ideal decision mechanism that corresponds to the ad hoc constructed principle of imputation. This projection was accompanied by the formulation of ideal conditions which—so it was said—could only be approximated in social reality. In this way, the more or less obvious imperfections in the functioning of existing institutional arrangements could be interpreted as anomalous deviations that had to be tolerated in view of their other merits.

This interpretation of the social apparatus—the institutional systems of representative democracy or of the free market economy—as an inductive machine for the transformation of individual interests into political or economic decisions aimed at realizing general welfare tended to glorify the actual functioning of the institutions in question and to conceal the social phenomena of power and conflict associated with these institutions. Such attempts at justification would only have the consequence that the criticism of those who took the concrete social disadvantages connected with such systems more seriously than did those who defended the attempts to harmonize the deviations hit not only the ideology used to interpret the institutions, but also the institutions themselves, because they seemed to be necessarily connected with such defects. This was at least in part because the critics often tended toward that kind of total criticism that springs naturally from utopian thinking. The program of political arithmetic has failed intellectually not only because of the unrealizable postulate of justification taken as its point of departure.

---

plausible to him but have turned out to be quite questionable. Here it becomes evident again how dubious the postulate of sufficient reason is for this sphere as well.

Over and above that, the solutions resulting from it have become socially untenable, for they can stave off criticism only by pointing to how ideally the institutions would function in a social vacuum. But this condition cannot be realized, as critics are quick to point out.

In view of this criticism, it stands to reason, first of all, to admit that structures of authority, relations of power, and situations of conflict exist in modern as they did in earlier societies, and cannot be explained away.[28] It makes little sense to cover them up with constructions that serve to glorify and justify them. Society cannot, without further ado, be considered a cooperative unit with a common value scale and a natural convergence of interests, whose functioning only poses technical problems and the problem of economic efficiency for its members, as welfare economics makes it appear.[29] The scarcity emphasized in economic analysis is not limited to a narrow economic sphere but is a general social phenomenon involving not only the actual intra-subjective but also the inter-subjective incompatibility of many needs and interests. As a result, social decisions are necessary which see to it that needs and the possibilities of their satisfaction are put into accordance with each other. Furthermore, social authorities and mechanisms are needed to pass upon these decisions and transform them into action. It would be difficult to specify the minimal amount of government and social power to be ex-

[28] Cf. the pertinent studies by Ralf Dahrendorf in his volume of essays, *Pfade aus Utopia. Arbeiten zur Theorie und Methode der Soziologie* (Munich, 1967), as well as my above-mentioned volume, *Marktsoziologie und Entscheidungslogik*.

[29] Those who object that welfare economics has acknowledged a residual problem of distribution in addition to the problem of efficiency should know that economics de facto has always concentrated on this problem. The communist fiction has been instrumental in this endeavor, for it views society as essentially a cooperative unit of this kind, a "task oriented" group; for a criticism of this view, see Rutledge Vining, *Economics in the United States of America: A Review and Interpretation of Research* (UNESCO, Paris, 1956), pp. 34 ff. and passim; Myrdal's *The Political Element in the Development of Economic Theory* contains writings on this topic.

ercised, which these conditions require. This is all the more so as it demands considerable social-technological imagination to invent and elaborate institutional arrangements which will reduce this requisite amount to a minimum and which subject authorities to maximal control by the members of society.[30] Social philosophies that suggest that a modern industrial society could possibly be completely free of authority can be considered utopian as long as they have not shown how such a state of affairs can be institutionally realized.

Thus, there is in society neither a common will that could be transformed into action, nor a certain knowledge that could guarantee that by this means something like the common weal— a condition involving the optimum satisfaction of all concerned—could be effected. This is irrespective of the difficulty of constructing measurements that allow an appropriate evaluation of the results of social decisions. There can, therefore, be *no ideal social order* that would guarantee the transformation of individual wishes into a result acceptable to all and thus be legitimate in this sense. Any idea of such an order contains a utopian element. Views of the world from which political solutions of this kind follow contain an erroneous estimation of human possibilities as to knowledge and the formation of will, and they contain an incorrect picture of human problem-solving behavior, as can also be seen in the corresponding epistemological conceptions.

If there can be no ideal orders of this kind, then politics cannot fulfill the task of putting them into effect. Whoever would assign to social philosophy the tasks of constructing a priori such an ideal social order, and of legitimizing actual social structures and political decisions by reference to it, transforms it into a dogmatic-apologetic enterprise that deserves as little credit from the criticist point of view as the corresponding theories of knowledge. But it is just this kind of social philosophy that seems to be frequently expected,

[30] It should not be overlooked that conditions in addition to the above-mentioned ones contribute to the stabilization of power and authority.

even at a time when the constructions of political theology and of political arithmetic have become discredited. Perhaps this is due to the fact that one has grown accustomed to viewing the connection between philosophy and politics under the aspect of justification. But this same point of view will limit philosophy to hermeneutics or analytics once it concedes that this justificational link is a dubious one; it limits philosophy to a merely interpretative enterprise, which can at best serve to clarify but which does not allow normative consequences. As we shall see, this view is by no means convincing.

## 28. THE IDEA OF RATIONAL DISCUSSION: POLITICAL DIALECTIC AND EXPERIMENTAL POLITICS

Those who see the connection between epistemology and social philosophy[31] will not be able to deny that, besides the dogmatic-apologetic solution to political problems and besides the hermeneutic-analytical solution mentioned above, there is a further possibility of linking rationality and commitment. The point of view of critical philosophy provides a positive solution that goes beyond both unconditional and incorrigible commitment and skeptical neutrality. Neither the production nor the interpretation of ideologies, neither legitimation nor neutral analysis, need be considered the essential or the sole concern of philosophy with regard to society. It is not a question of uncovering the hidden meaning of social activities or of giving these activities a higher blessing; rather, it is important to contribute *critical* insights and *constructive* ideas to solve political problems. Philosophical thought can contribute in both respects, as has already been shown with regard to scientific problems.

From a criticist point of view, especially in regard to methodology, we can recommend that political solutions always be considered and treated as hypotheses, even if the dominant

[31] Cf. J.W.N. Watkins, *Epistemology and Politics*, in which the thesis of analytical neutrality is subjected to criticism.

ideology declares them sacrosanct and dogmatizes them. That does not mean that they are to be rejected because of their dogmatization. It only means that they are to be understood as, in principle, subject to criticism. The methodology of critical examination can also be applied to such problems if one considers that critical bridge principles of the above-mentioned kind can be constructed in order to criticize norms and values.[32] In this way, even institutions can be criticized, and for this purpose scientific knowledge can be drawn upon. Those in favor of a critical method in epistemology because they are of the opinion that one can learn from errors, and who, therefore, expose their ideas to criticism and confront them with potential alternatives compared with which their shortcomings show up more clearly, will prefer no other method for the solution of political problems. Since such alternatives are often presented most ably by those who really advocate them, it seems advisable to enter into discussion with proponents of divergent positions, and thus expedient to strive for *social and political pluralism*, in addition to theoretical pluralism. In order to bring about such a situation, it will be necessary to advocate freedom of thought, freedom of exchange of ideas, and everything else necessary to make this freedom effective. This also means adopting a position against obstructions such as censure, and quite generally against any intellectual control by authorities who prevent the diffusion of unwelcome views by coercion. Thus, the search for truth, the critical method, and political freedom are closely interwoven. The *critical method* must be *supported institutionally*, i.e., its functioning must be rendered possible by means of the institutional arrangements of society—even for its operation in the realm of science. For this reason alone, the criticist social philosophy cannot remain politically neutral.

In addition to the above, a certain attitude toward the problem of utopias results from the methodology of critical ex-

---

[32] Cf. section 9. Politics is methodologically analogous to ethics, as discussed above.

amination. Since the shortcomings of inveterate political solutions can best be pointed out by the construction of alternatives, even utopian conceptions can be utilized to criticize such solutions, for they normally indicate, at least roughly, other conceivable solutions. As mentioned in the analysis of the problem of knowledge,[33] *utopias* play a role in political thought analogous to that of *metaphysics* in scientific knowledge. Utopias formulate something that is considered *impossible* in the light of prevailing opinion. However, with changes in scientific knowledge or in social conditions, those things once considered impossible may prove to be possible after all. In addition, *desires* are often expressed in utopias which, under the given social circumstances, are not—and possibly cannot be—fulfilled. Thus, utopias are important, not so much because of the positive solutions they suggest, but because of the cues they offer concerning concrete existing abuses. The Marxist utopia of a classless society hardly contains any realizable suggestions for solving social problems; however, it critically points out the negative aspects of an extreme class society in which large sections of the population live under barely endurable conditions.

The total criticism of utopian thought infers from the negative evaluation of certain existing conditions the necessity of a purifying catastrophe, leaving a *tabula rasa* as a precondition for future reconstruction. However, while this mode of thought is ready to forgo a realistic analysis of alternatives and leaves the design of social reconstruction to the future, the method of critical examination makes it necessary to develop concrete and realizable alternatives that can be compared with the existing solutions. Although in the social vacuum of utopian thought all needs may seem compatible and therefore all wishes realizable, in social reality scarcity prevails. Therefore a realistic social critique must take into account the restrictions that exist on the satisfaction of needs. Those wanting to save social philosophy from irrationalism must see to it that uto-

[33] Cf. section 7 above.

pian thought in service of social criticism be adjusted realistically.[34] A rational evaluation of existing social conditions can only take into consideration real possibilities. It cannot be achieved on the basis of abstract possibilities that originate in the realm of wishful thinking. A rational social critique, therefore, cannot ignore the *problem of feasibility*. While it can throw light on existing conditions and thus identify abuses, it must not, of course, arouse the impression that all shortcomings can unrestrictedly and simultaneously be eliminated and that a perfect social order, a society without shortcomings, can be realized.

The question of feasibility touches upon an important function of social scientific knowledge. As we already saw in our analysis of the problem of value neutrality,[35] social scientific knowledge can contribute to the solution of practical problems to the extent that it is able to analyze real possibilities for action and therefore to answer the politically important question: What can we do? As we have already seen, the laws of the theoretical sciences—and thus the social sciences—must be considered from the practical point of view as furnishing restrictions that are to be imposed upon solutions offered by practical and political imagination. Here too, nomological knowledge can be transformed into technological considerations. In this manner, questions concerning the real compatibility of the formulated goals can be answered.[36] The foremost function of the nomological science, under practical aspects, is to point out limits of realizability,[37] including political feasibility. This makes them unpopular with the pro-

[34] In social criticism as well, the pleasure principle must be limited by the reality principle. Any social order whatsoever appears radically bad when seen in the light of total criticism guided by illusionary wishes.

[35] Cf. section 10 above.

[36] Cf. my essay, "Wissenschaft und Politik. Zum Problem der Anwendbarkeit einer wertfreien Sozialwissenschaft," in *Probleme der Wissenschaftstheorie. Festschrift für Viktor Kraft*, ed. Ernst Topitsch (Vienna, 1960), pp. 223 ff.

[37] Cf. also Karl R. Popper, *The Poverty of Historicism*.

ponents of utopian beliefs,[38] since they naturally dislike taking into account the social costs of the radical changes they contemplate.[39] While utopian thought may furnish critical points of view for the evaluation of existing social conditions, nomological sciences make it possible to subject utopian ideas to a realistic critique. In this way it is also possible to expose the total criticism that is easily produced in the light of such conceptions to a critical analysis. The search for relevant contradictions, which in the methodology of critical examination replaces the search for certain foundations, does not halt in the face of the schemes of utopian, catastrophe-oriented thinkers.

It is not the case that alternatives play absolutely no role in the radical thought of political utopians. They do consider alternatives—surprisingly enough, however, alternatives quite similiar to those propounded by extremely conservative political thinkers. Both kinds of political thought tend toward an *alternative radicalism*, in which only abstract alternatives figure: on the one hand the existing system with all its shortcomings, and on the other hand a completely changed system, the formation of which—abstracting from the question of its realizability—would demand an overthrow of all conditions. Naturally, radicals and conservatives *evaluate* the alternatives differently. The former see only the shortcomings of the existing system. Since they do not care much about the problem of feasibility and are accustomed to ignoring the costs, they advocate radical upheaval. The latter see the utopian character of the radical alternative and the costs of an attempt to realize it. They therefore prefer to accept the existing system. Thus, the former are misled by their alternative radicalism into en-

[38] Occasionally, it is expressed in the claim that a new kind of philosophy of science has been developed in which the search for nomological knowledge about social phenomena can be considered passé.

[39] In contrast to this, Max Weber, who was very sensitive to the moral aspects of rationality, pointed out in his time that one of the most important tasks is to promulgate acknowledgment of inconvenient evidence; cf. Weber, "Wissenschaft als Beruf," in his *Gesammelte Aufsätze zur Wissenschaftslehre*, p. 587.

dorsing total criticism, and the latter on the basis of the same kind of thinking, into totally accepting the present state of affairs. Of course, it should not be forgotten that political alternative radicalism can also be found in some philosophers who do not harbor a predilection for the utopian ideas of radical leftists,[40] but who nevertheless apply total criticism to the existing system and strive for its radical change.

Thus, from a critical point of view, it cannot be advisable to defame utopian radical thought only because it criticizes existing conditions—for there are, in every society, aspects well deserving of criticism. The main objection to this mode of thought is that it is *uncritical* regarding the problem of feasibility because it implicitly assumes that all good things must be compatible with one another and therefore capable of being realized simultaneously. It does not see that ideals must be transformed realistically into concrete alternatives if they are to be taken into serious consideration politically. Constructions in a social vacuum do not suffice. The main problem is, rather, the social-technological question: How can such projects be realized under the given conditions? Or else: How should one act under present social conditions in order to come close to such a realization? To answer such questions undoubtedly requires imagination, but it is the productive imagination of the inventor, not the unrestrained fantasy of the daydreamer.

On the other hand, it cannot be appropriate, from a critical point of view, to reproach conservative thought for the fact that it joins traditions and wants to preserve traditional social and political solutions. For it is a radical prejudice that we can do without traditions—a point we need not dwell upon. At best, one can object that conservative thought underesti-

[40] For example, Carl Schmitt's radical criticism of parliamentary democracy and his preference for the authoritarian state were based on a kind of alternative radicalism. In its structure, his critique is quite similar to the mode of thought of the radical left in its anti-liberal emphasis, but it differs in the political direction. Cf. the interesting analysis by Jürgen Fijalkowski in his book, *Die Wendung zum Führerstaat. Ideologische Komponenten in der politischen Philosophie Carl Schmitts* (Cologne and Opladen, 1958).

223

mates the extent to which traditions can be criticized, and as a consequence, often treats solutions that have been handed down as sacrosanct. Here again, objections are raised against a credulous, uncritical attitude—in this case toward the existing state of affairs—where the possibility to criticize and thus improve upon the existing conditions exists. In order to improve upon the present, it is necessary to search for critical points of view and for constructive ideas that are suitable for overcoming traditional solutions to problems.

Those who want to avoid the alternative radicalism described above and wish to make the results and methods of scientific thought fruitful for the solution of political problems will have to start from the fact that society is not a *tabula rasa*. It cannot be informed by political means with whatever arbitrary pattern is desired. On the contrary, each and every political action represents an intervention into a more or less strongly structured social situation. It would therefore be advisable to take into account the *institutional a priori* that characterizes these situations, not because the social phenomena are unalterable, but because of the unavoidable restrictions set by prior conditions on possible changes. Realistic politics must take account of these restrictions. The analysis of alternatives that precedes political decisions must take the structure of the respective initial situation into consideration if realizable alternatives are to be determined. Insofar as nomological knowledge is required for the construction of such alternatives, its application, as is well known from the philosophy of science of the theoretical sciences, requires the delineation, by means of theoretical instruments, of the relevant characteristics of the situation being considered[41]—including delineation of the relevant institutional quasi-invariances. In this concretization of nomological restrictions, about which in a general form our theoretical knowledge informs us, it becomes evident that the political utilization of scientific knowledge gains a historical dimension. This can only be neg-

[41] Cf. my introduction, "Probleme der Theoriebildung," in *Theorie und Realität*, 1st ed. (Tübingen, 1964).

lected at the cost of a realistic orientation of political thought and action.

If one accepts the method of critical examination sketched here, one will in political thought—as in scientific knowledge—have to analyze traditions critically, which means in this case: transmitted social structures. These structures can be considered as handed down and in part institutionally stabilized attempts at solving social and political problems. Concerning these problems, one can ask to what extent the traditional solutions have stood the test of time and what their shortcomings and disadvantages are. Such an approach requires the construction of realistic alternatives and the bringing into play of relevant nomological knowledge, for a comparative analysis is necessary for the improvement of political solutions. If durable solutions are to be found for the long-run, *institutional alternatives* must be compared with one another and available social-technological knowledge must be drawn upon to construct and work out these alternatives. It is comparatively easy to show that here neither logic alone, nor imagination or historical knowledge alone, nor a combination of these three most important instruments for the analysis of situations suffice. In order to effect any such analysis, answers to questions of the following kind are necessary: What *would* happen, *if* this or that measure *were* taken? Under what circumstances *could* this or that effect be produced? What side effects would be *inevitable*, *if* one wanted to reach this or that goal or combination of goals? The answer to all these questions requires technological deliberations based on nomological knowledge. Propositions, which can be taken as answers to questions of this kind, are derivable from applied nomological knowledge. For those wanting to give answers in accord with the ideal of critical rationality—thus answers that can best be put to the test—this type of answer is preferred to all others.[42]

[42] It is worth pointing out the importance of the social-technological components of political thought. For in the social sciences, there is a strong tendency to underestimate these components; cf. my above-mentioned essay,

Thinking in terms of justification is characteristic of political theology and democratic ideology. Our examination of the prevailing views on political problems has led us to reject this type of thought. Thinking in terms of alternatives, a mode of thought cultivated in the economic tradition of social scientific knowledge can be considered a useful model of rational problem-solving behavior, namely, for the analysis of situations through the construction of alternative proposals that utilize available sociotechnological knowledge. This seems to be an adequate method of political thought, a method in which theoretically founded social criticism can be combined with theoretically based social technology. This method does not place emphasis upon stabilizing and legitimizing traditional solutions, but instead encourages the discovery of new ones, as well as critical confrontation with those to which we have become accustomed and which we far too easily take for granted. With regard to the tranformation of this method into the practice of social life, we must especially take two facts into account: the first is the fact that the transition from an analysis of alternatives to their realization bestows upon politics the character of *rational social experimentation*. However, one should not overlook—in this case and generally— that uncertainty and risk play an important role in experiments, the significance of which is here dramatized because of the social importance of the respective decisions. The second aspect to be taken into account is the fact that the analysis of alternatives is itself embedded in social practice, and to a certain extent, can assume the form of a *rational discussion between proponents of different conceptions*. Here, as in the realm of science, the methodological principle of critical examination has a social dimension and is politically significant

"Rationalität und Wirtschaftsordnung." It critically examines attempts at solving the problem of political order which do not take social-technological aspects into account. On the other hand, this very component seems to be underdeveloped in Marxist thought as well. In both cases this is related to highly problematical methodological conceptions.

226

insofar as different political forces back these divergent conceptions, forces in whose interest it is to examine closely various aspects of the proposed alternative solutions, in the light of their predominant values, and to accentuate the advantages and disadvantages of these solutions on the basis of these values. Something like *real dialectics*, if we properly understand that term, results from the actual representation of incompatible conceptions in the field of social forces. The expression "real dialectics" need not arouse the suspicion that here, as is often the case, logical contradiction and factual opposition are confounded. Nor does it mean that the suspension of the principle of noncontradiction, frequently recommended by dialecticians, is to be interpreted as a fundamental characteristic of reality and thus endowed with ontological dignity.[43]

In the light of the critical point of view, it is not necessarily a fault that contradictory conceptions are socially anchored in the actual constellation of power and interests of a society. For it cannot be assumed that truth—or the common weal—is manifest, so that controversies are unnecessary, or that any privileged authority would be in the position to proclaim perfect solutions. The proposal of different solutions from diverse points of view may be advantageous if the solutions are subject to debate, if they are elucidated in different manners according to the various points of view. Of course, discussion may fail to lead to agreement, as is often the case in science. Thus, when a political decision cannot be postponed, a solution to the problems must be found and implemented in spite of di-

[43] The fact that logically incompatible conceptions cannot be simultaneously true naturally does not hinder their being believed or accepted at the same time. This is especially the case when one is dealing with different individuals or social groups. The advocacy of logically incompatible conceptions and factual antitheses, however, may be factually connected with social conflicts: *incompatible* conceptions are represented socially by individuals and groups, who for this reason come to *oppose* each other. One may describe these simple matters with the statement that in this way ideal dialectic becomes socially real dialectic. However, very little is gained by this, least of all something like a dialectical ontology.

verging views. This situation is to be expected all the more since in political controversies problems of value and problems of fact tend to occur jointly, and diverging values may lead to different solutions. What is at stake is not so much a question of truth, but a satisfactory solution to practical problems, although cognitive questions—and therefore also the question of truth—are extremely important as well. This does not mean that all participants need believe in the same "ultimate values" or must share the "final ends" to enable them to reach a practically effective consensus in political matters. Rather, it means that certain solutions to such problems are often judged suitable from different points of view and from diverging values and interest.[44] When such a consensus cannot be achieved, then, for practical reasons, decision mechanisms must often be put into effect in which the number of votes for or against specific solutions decides the issue. Further, it is often necessary in modern society to delegate, to a large extent, the right to make decisions to groups and individuals whose actions often cannot be controlled until after the fact by those who are affected. We have already seen that the interpretation of these facts by means of a democratic ideology, which assumes a transfer of will from lower to higher levels, amounts only to the justification and concealment of elements of the social order that unquestionably have the character of dominance. So long as it is not possible to do without institutional arrangements of this type—and at present it is hardly conceivable how that could be accomplished—a society without authorities is not possible. The idea of such a society therefore belongs to the realm of utopian thought.

We have no reason to accept an interpretation of democracy that misrepresents factual relationships in order to justify them. According to the critical point of view, it cannot be the concern of philosophy—not even of social philosophy—to justify just

[44] Cf. Charles L. Stevenson, *Ethics and Language* (New Haven, 1944), pp. 188 ff. Cf. also Gösta Carlsson, "Betrachtungen zum Funktionalismus," in *Logik der Sozialwissenschaften*, pp. 247 ff., and my above-mentioned essay, "Politische Ökonomie und rationale Politik."

any social orders, institutions, or social measures whatsoever. On the contrary, we have every reason to regard these as imperfect solutions that are, in any case, in need of improvement and revision. Here too, there is no Archimedean point that would allow one to distinguish a final solution. In this respect, the situation in social philosophy is exactly the same as in epistemology. In each case, we have the method of critical examination, which tries to expose all solutions to the possiblity of failure by subjecting them to rational argumentation in the light of alternatives and in the light of relevant experiments. Not even political orders are exempt from this procedure. But, as we have already seen, this does not mean that we must accept the type of radical criticism that stems from the irrational procedure we have analyzed above. Without taking account of any of the realistic restrictions on our possibilities that we know must exist, this type of criticism proceeds by directly counterposing unstructured utopian conceptions to the phenomena of social reality, in order to bring about the total rejection of these phenomena. Such criticism is closer to the doctrine of revelation and to the corresponding inquisitorial method than its proponents seem to suspect. It may be "dialectic" in the special sense of the word used by some modern Hegelian philosophers. But it is not dialectic in the sense of the tradition of critical thought, which can be traced back to Greek philosophy. In this tradition we have learned to solve our problems by subjecting speculative and logically constructed solutions to rational discussion. This method does not provide us with any kind of certainty, not even with the modest certainty that we are on the side of those forces whose operation is in accordance with the meaning of history. But it does give us the chance to learn from our mistakes, and thereby not to reject the help of our fellow human beings, the more so if they have other points of view, ideas, and experiences than our own.

# Subject Index

Alernatives, thinking in, patterns of, search for, 15, 44, 47, 49, 64ff., 95f., 96, 101, 112, 122, 129, 141, 149, 189, 192ff., 229; radicalism, 222f.

Analysis, of situations, 226

Analytic statements, 17; trend, thought, philosophy, 3ff., 5, 49, 88f., 101, 110, 180ff., 192, 194, 218

Anchoring, 118ff., 127, 182, 200, 227

Anomalies, 64, 68, 215

Anxiety. *See* Fear

Apologetic, 138f., 164, 198, 217f.

Apostasy, 126

A priori institutional, 224; apriorism, 43, 184f.; attitude, 36; validity, 63

Archimedean point, 12, 15ff., 19ff., 21f., 26, 30, 39, 46ff., 87, 200, 229

Argument, deductive, 16, 58

Argumentation, rational, 62, 90, 229; function, 179; rational calculation, 133

Assumptions, ultimate or first, or presuppositions, 45, 89ff., 97. *See also* Principle, highest

Astrology, 200f.

Atheism, 140, 152; atheist, 150, 158

Authority: authoritarianism, 32; sovereignty, structures of, 27, 32, 48, 112, 119, 122f., 146, 161,

200ff., 206ff., 219; structures of, 111, 202f., 207f., 216f., 228

Autonomy, claim, thesis, 6, 69, 72ff., 74, 97, 134, 157, 166f., 171

Axiomatic, 59f., 93; axiomatization, 60, 72, 87, 93; Euclidean, 58ff.; method, thinking, 49, 60, 93

Basis, firm, 12, 32, 74. *See also* Foundation

Behavior, interpretive, 192ff.

Belief: faith, 8, 18, 91f., 94, 101, 119, 122f., 132, 135f., 150, 155, 161f.; obligations to believe, obligatory belief, 24, 124; subjection of belief, 122f., 130, 135, 138ff.

Bridge-principle, 98ff., 134, 219

Calculation, 60, 85, 87, 206

Calvinism, 8, 27, 127

Cases, contrary, confirming, 67f.

Catastrophe thinking, 204ff., 221

Catholicism, 8, 26ff., 102, 123ff., 145, 156f., 201

Certainty, 12, 14, 19, 30ff., 39f., 61, 79, 94, 111, 128f., 155, 158, 163, 177, 205f., 213, 229; of faith, 155, 158

Certitude, 12, 33f., 40ff., 58, 86ff., 121f., 178

Christianity, Christian tradition, 8, 127f., 159

231

233

# INDEX

# Name Index

Acham, Karl, 100
Adorno, Theodore W., xi f.
Agassi, Joseph, 37, 49, 57, 63
Ajdukiewicz, Kasimierz, 14, 75
Apel, Karl-Otto, xi, xiv, xvi, 55, 181f., 194
Archimedes, 13
Aristotle, 31
Arrow, Kenneth J., 211, 214
Atkinson, John W., 68, 213

Bacon, Francis, 30f., 77
Barth, Karl, 144
Bartley, William Warren III, 20, 24, 39, 130, 138, 152
Bartsch, Hans-Werner, 138, 144, 151
Bastian, Hans-Dieter, 161
Baumgarten, Eduard, 90, 96, 139
Bellarmin, Robert, 135
Bentham, Jeremy, 209
Bergmann, Gerhard, 160f.
Besters, Hans, 112, 211
Bierwisch, Manfred, 197
Blanshard, Paul, 124f., 202
Bloch, Ernst, 153
Blumenberg, Hans, 135
Böckenförde, Ernst-Wolfgang, 125
Bohnen, Alfred, 37, 196
Brecht, Bertolt, 115
Broszat, Martin, 126
Bruno, Giorano, 65
Bubner, Rüdiger, xxii
Buchanan, James, 212
Bühler, Karl, xix, 176, 179, 190

Bultmann, Rudolf, 139ff., 147, 153ff., 198
Bunge, Mario, 34
Buri, Fritz, 144, 150
Burke, Kenneth, 129
Burtt, Edwin Arthur, 62

Carlsson, Gösta, 228
Carnap, Rudolf, 16f., 169, 175
Chomsky, Noam, 197
Cohen, Morris R., 145
Cohen, Robert S., 27, 57
Cohn, Norman, 128, 204
Colodny, Robert G., 37
Conzelmann, Hans, 150, 159
Copernicus, 114, 134
Croce, Benedetto, 135, 170

Dahrendorf, Ralf, xii, 76, 216
Darwin, Charles, 114
Davis, Allison, 213
Delius, Harald, 110
Dember, William N., 37, 196
Descartes, René, 13, 28ff., 55
Deschner, Karl-Heinz, 125f.
Dingler, Hugo, xiii f., xvii, 13, 19, 41ff., 54, 66
Donoso Cortes, Juan, 201
Droysen, Johann Gustav, 168, 170f.
Dublislav, Walter, 20, 78
Duhem, Pierre, 33, 134
Durkheim, Emile, 185

Ebeling, Gerhard, xix
Euclid, 58

237

LIBRARY OF CONGRESS IN PUBLICATION DATA

Albert, Hans, 1921-
Treatise on critical reason.

Translation of: Traktat über kritische Vernunft.
Includes index.
1. Criticism (Philosophy) 2. Knowledge, Theory of.
3. Philosophy and religion. 4. Political science. I. Title.

B809.3.A413 1984    142    84-15095
ISBN 0-691-07295-7